T0351500

BOOK M

The Other Voice in Early Modern Europe:
The Toronto Series, 26

The Other Voice in
Early Modern Europe:
The Toronto Series

SERIES EDITORS Margaret L. King *and* Albert Rabil, Jr.
SERIES EDITOR, ENGLISH TEXTS Elizabeth H. Hageman

Previous Publications in the Series

MADRE MARÍA ROSA
Journey of Five Capuchin Nuns
Edited and translated by Sarah E.
Owens
2009

GIOVAN BATTISTA ANDREINI
Love in the Mirror: A Bilingual Edition
Edited and translated by Jon R. Snyder
2009

RAYMOND DE SABANAC AND SIMONE
ZANACCHI
Two Women of the Great Schism: The
Revelations *of Constance de Rabastens
by Raymond de Sabanac and* Life of
the Blessed Ursulina of Parma *by
Simone Zanacchi*
Edited and translated by Renate
Blumenfeld-Kosinski and Bruce L.
Venarde
2010

OLIVA SABUCO DE NANTES BARRERA
The True Medicine
Edited and translated by Gianna
Pomata
2010

LOUISE-GENEVIÈVE GILLOT DE
SAINCTONGE
Dramatizing Dido, Circe, and Griselda
Edited and translated by Janet Levarie
Smarr
2010

PERNETTE DU GUILLET
Complete Poems: A Bilingual Edition
Edited by Karen Simroth James
Translated by Marta Rijn Finch
2010

ANTONIA PULCI
*Saints' Lives and Bible Stories for the
Stage: A Bilingual Edition*
Edited by Elissa B. Weaver
Translated by James Wyatt Cook
2010

VALERIA MIANI
*Celinda, A Tragedy: A Bilingual
Edition*
Edited by Valeria Finucci
Translated by Julia Kisacky
Annotated by Valeria Finucci and
Julia Kisacky
2010

The Other Voice in
Early Modern Europe:
The Toronto Series

SERIES EDITORS Margaret L. King *and* Albert Rabil, Jr.
SERIES EDITOR, ENGLISH TEXTS Elizabeth H. Hageman

Previous Publications in the Series

Enchanted Eloquence: Fairy Tales by Seventeenth-Century French Women Writers
Edited and translated by Lewis C. Seifert and Domna C. Stanton
2010

Gottfried Wilhelm Leibniz, Sophie, Electress of Hanover and Queen Sophie Charlotte of Prussia
Leibniz and the Two Sophies: The Philosophical Correspondence
Edited and translated by Lloyd Strickland
2011

In Dialogue with the Other Voice in Sixteenth-Century Italy: Literary and Social Contexts for Women's Writing
Edited by Julie D. Campbell and Maria Galli Stampino
2011

Sister Giustina Niccolini
The Chronicle of Le Murate
Edited and translated by Saundra Weddle
2011

Liubov Krichevskaya
No Good without Reward: Selected Writings: A Bilingual Edition
Edited and translated by Brian James Baer
2011

Elizabeth Cooke Hoby Russell
The Writings of an English Sappho
Edited by Patricia Phillippy
With translations by Jaime Goodrich
2011

Lucrezia Marinella
Exhortations to Women and to Others if They Please
Edited and translated by Laura Benedetti
2012

Margherita Datini
Letters to Francesco Datini
Translated by Carolyn James and Antonio Pagliaro
2012

Delarivier Manley and Mary Pix
English Women Staging Islam, 1696–1707
Edited and introduced by Bernadette Andrea
2012

The Other Voice in Early Modern Europe: The Toronto Series

SERIES EDITORS Margaret L. King *and* Albert Rabil, Jr.
SERIES EDITOR, ENGLISH TEXTS Elizabeth H. Hageman

Previous Publications in the Series

CECILIA DEL NACIMIENTO
Journeys of a Mystic Soul in Poetry and Prose
Introduction and prose translations by Kevin Donnelly
Poetry translations by Sandra Sider
2012

LADY MARGARET DOUGLAS AND OTHERS
The Devonshire Manuscript: A Women's Book of Courtly Poetry
Edited and introduced by Elizabeth Heale
2012

ARCANGELA TARABOTTI
Letters Familiar and Formal
Edited and translated by Meredith K. Ray and Lynn Lara Westwater
2012

PERE TORRELLAS AND JUAN DE FLORES
Three Spanish Querelle *Texts: Grisel and Mirabella, The Slander against Women, and The Defense of Ladies against Slanderers: A Bilingual Edition and Study*
Edited and translated by Emily C. Francomano
2013

BARBARA TORELLI BENEDETTI
Partenia, a Pastoral Play: A Bilingual Edition
Edited and translated by Lisa Sampson and Barbara Burgess-Van Aken
2013

FRANÇOIS ROUSSET, JEAN LIEBAULT, JACQUES GUILLEMEAU, JACQUES DUVAL AND LOUIS DE SERRES
Pregnancy and Birth in Early Modern France: Treatises by Caring Physicians and Surgeons (1581–1625)
Edited and translated by Valerie Worth-Stylianou
2013

MARY ASTELL
The Christian Religion, as Professed by a Daughter of the Church of England
Edited by Jacqueline Broad
2013

SOPHIA OF HANOVER
Memoirs (1630–1680)
Edited and translated by Sean Ward
2013

Book M:
A London Widow's Life Writings

KATHERINE AUSTEN

Edited by

PAMELA S. HAMMONS

ITER

Iter Inc.
Centre for Reformation and Renaissance Studies
Toronto
2013

Iter: Gateway to the Middle Ages and Renaissance
Tel: 416/978–7074   Email: iter@utoronto.ca
Fax: 416/978–1668   Web: www.itergateway.org

Centre for Reformation and Renaissance Studies
Victoria University in the University of Toronto
Tel: 416/585–4465   Email: crrs.publications@utoronto.ca
Fax: 416/585–4430   Web: www.crrs.ca

Iter and the Centre for Reformation and Renaissance Studies gratefully acknowledge the generous support of James E. Rabil, in memory of Scottie W. Rabil, toward the publication of this book.

Library and Archives Canada Cataloguing in Publication
Austen, Katherine, 1628–1683, author
Book M : a London widow's life writings / Katherine Austen ; edited by Pamela S. Hammons.
(Other voice in early modern Europe. Toronto series ; 26)
Modernized version of: Katherine Austen's Book M : British Library, Additional Manuscript 4454.
Includes bibliographical references and index.
Contents: Illustrations—Acknowledgments—Introduction—Book M—Bibliography—Index.
Issued in print and electronic formats.
Co-published by: Iter Inc.

ISBN 978-0-7727-2150-1 (pbk.).
ISBN 978-0-7727-2151-8 (pdf)

1. Austen, Katherine, 1628–1683—Early works to 1800. 2. Widows—England—London—Early works to 1800. I. Hammons, Pamela S., writer of introduction, editor II. Victoria University (Toronto, Ont.). Centre for Reformation and Renaissance Studies, issuing body III. Iter Inc, issuing body IV. British Library. Manuscript. Additional 4454 V. Title. VI. Series: Other voice in early modern Europe. Toronto series ; 26

PR3316.A685B66 2013   828'.403   C2013-906458-3
C2013-906459-1

Cover illustration: *Penelope Undoing Her Tapestry* (oil on canvas), Bassano, Leandro da Ponte (1557–1622) / Musée des Beaux-Arts, Rennes, France / Giraudon / The Bridgeman Art Library XIR 223259.

Cover design:
Maureen Morin, Information Technology Services, University of Toronto Libraries.

Typesetting and production:
Iter Inc.

Contents

Illustrations

Cover illustration: *Penelope Undoing Her Tapestry* (oil on canvas), Bassano, Leandro da Ponte (1557–1622) / Musée des Beaux-Arts, Rennes, France / Giraudon / The Bridgeman Art Library XIR 223259.

All figures in the text are © The British Library Board and are from BL, MS Additional 4454.

Acknowledgments

I first encountered Katherine Austen's fascinating book of life writings, *Book M*, two decades ago when I was a graduate student at Cornell University enrolled in Andrew Galloway's paleography seminar. Every year since then, I have developed an increasing appreciation for and understanding of Austen's book, and I have greatly benefited from the support of many mentors, colleagues, institutions, friends, and relatives along the way. I am especially grateful to Andy for his enthusiastic interest in Austen from the start and his firm belief in the importance of *Book M*. In addition to Andy, the first readers of my scholarship on Austen were the members of my dissertation committee: Barbara Correll, William Kennedy, Dorothy Mermin, and Rachel Weil. Special thanks go to Dorothy for having struggled valiantly through my first rough transcriptions of Austen's verse. Among my graduate peers at Cornell, Bernadette Andrea and Teresa Feroli were particularly supportive of my early work on Austen's engagement with prophetic discourse. Margaret J. M. Ezell, Nigel Smith, Diane Purkiss, and Ursula Appelt kindly provided me with valuable feedback on some of my first interpretations of *Book M*.

At the University of Miami, my friend, colleague, and mentor, Mihoko Suzuki, has been especially supportive of several different stages of my work on Austen. I have also profited from and greatly enjoyed comparing textual editing projects with Patrick McCarthy, who has been an important friend, colleague, and mentor to me since my arrival at the University of Miami and whose sustained engagement with my work on Austen has helped me to see it from a new perspective. Pat, thanks for sharing my obsessive interest in tiny details. My colleagues at the University of Miami who participate in our Center for the Humanities Early Modern Studies Research Group have provided valuable interdisciplinary perspectives on *Book M* that have made this volume much richer; special thanks, in particular, go to Anne Cruz, Viviana Díaz Balsera, Richard Godbeer, Karl Gunther, Tassie Gwilliam, Mary Lindemann, Jeffrey Shoulson, Maria Galli Stampino, and Barbara Woshinsky. I am also grateful to the University of Miami for the crucial support of a Max Orovitz Summer Award in the Arts and

Humanities and a General Research Support Award, which made it possible for me to complete this book. I thank Leonidas Bachas, Angel Kaifer, Michael Halleran, Perri Lee Roberts, and the University of Miami's College of Arts and Sciences for providing a generous book subvention for this project.

I am deeply grateful to Elizabeth H. Hageman for her scrupulous attention to detail and tireless labor in helping to make this edition the best that it could be, and I am very thankful, too, to Albert Rabil for his guidance and support. My sincere thanks also go to the Centre for Reformation and Renaissance Studies and Iter's excellent team—especially Linda Gail Stone, Margaret English-Haskin, Anabela Piersol, and Sharon Brinkman—for their patience and professionalism. Of course, any errors in the volume are my own. Many thanks to the British Library Board for their kind permission to publish images of *Book M* and to the Bridgeman Art Library for the use of *Penelope Undoing Her Tapestry* (oil on canvas, XIR 223259) by Leandro da Ponte Bassano (1557–1622) on the book cover. This volume is all the better because of the keen and helpful insights of an anonymous reader, whose advice has strengthened the introduction, in particular. In addition, I am profoundly grateful to Sarah Ross, who most generously shared with me the galleys for her excellent scholarly diplomatic edition of *Book M* for the series Medieval and Renaissance Texts and Studies in time for me to incorporate references to her book into this one.

I thank all of my friends—too many to name here—without whose steady moral support over the last two decades I would never have finished this project. You know who you are, and I am, as always, deeply grateful to you. I owe my greatest debt to my family: Mom, Curtis, Tim, Laura, Sarah, Lucas, Duncan, Lynn, Bruce, Sally, Roger, Jan, Jon, Ben, Martha, and David, thank you so very much for your love; sense of humor; shared joy in good conversation, good music, and good food; and rock-solid support in life. I am also grateful to my extended family in Spain, especially Mercedes, Clara, Ricardo, Juan Pablo, Beatriz, Pablo, and Maricarmen. I cannot thank my mother, Anna Suttle, and my stepfather, Curtis Olsen, enough for showing so much interest in and unflagging support for every academic project I have, for asking questions about my work and actually listening to my long-winded answers about topics that often seem odd to most folks outside the field of early modern studies. My mother, a biologist, deserves an honorary degree in the humanities for her patient, serious engagement with my research: thank you, Mom, for your love and for going far beyond the call of duty. My partner, Gema Pérez-Sánchez, has supported my work on Austen every single step of the way—from Ithaca, to New York City, to Orlando, to Coral Gables, to London, and back again and has encouraged me never to give up: *mil gracias por todo, mi amor,* and especially for being so incredibly brave in 2012, when so many of our beloved family members died. I dedicate this book in loving memory to my father-in-law, Adolfo Pérez Luiña (1927–2012), nuclear chemist; Aunt Maribel Sánchez Buendía (1930–2012), educator and creative writer; and my father, Charles Edwin Hammons (1941–2012), mathematician and computer scientist: thank you for sharing your beautiful lives with us; we miss y'all more than words can say.

Introduction

The Other Voice

Katherine Austen (1628–1683) is one of the many early modern women once thought to have left no written record of their voices and thus, for the purposes of literary history, to have been completely silent. It is only recently that the writings of some women have gained significant, sustained attention from literary scholars, but for the most part, Austen's life writings have remained overlooked. She is well worth reading, however, for her fascinating multigeneric manuscript compilation of texts, *Book M*, which provides us with an astonishingly lively and revealing firsthand account of how an especially clever, self-aware, upwardly mobile seventeenth-century woman successfully navigated her way through the perilous patriarchal world in which she lived.[1] Widowed at a young age, she fiercely protected her children and astutely managed the family resources without the assistance of a husband. During her lifetime, there were many potentially damaging, negative stereotypes of widows, and *Book M* reveals Austen's skillful use of rhetorical strategies to counter those stereotypes.[2]

1. Austen was from a wealthy family, and she had strong ambitions to be recognized fully as a member of the gentry. As Barbara J. Todd explains, Austen was "liminal as head of a family moving from mercantile to gentry status." "Property and a Woman's Place in Restoration London," *Women's History Review* 19.2 (2010): 182. During Austen's era, the social category of "gentry" was somewhat amorphous. Felicity Heal and Clive Holmes explain that "land, lordship … local acknowledgement," and wealth are among the most important partial criteria for determining who was a member of the gentry; however, "blood lineage and the ability to exercise martial skills" could also be considered key attributes. *The Gentry in England and Wales, 1500–1700* (Stanford, CA: Stanford University Press, 1994), 7, 9. For a thorough discussion of the complexities of defining the social rank of gentry to which Austen aspired, see Heal and Holmes, *The Gentry in England and Wales*, 6–19.

2. Groundbreaking early studies of the complexity of women's social location based upon gender, class, life stage, and so on (and their strategies for negotiating that complexity) include, for example, Linda Woodbridge, *Women and the English Renaissance: Literature and the Nature of Women, 1540–1620* (Urbana, IL: University of Illinois Press, 1984); Susan Dwyer Amussen, *An Ordered Society: Gender and Class in Early Modern England* (New York: Blackwell, 1988); Elaine Hobby, *Virtue of Necessity: English Women's Writing, 1649–88* (Ann Arbor, MI: The University of Michigan Press, 1989); and Tina Krontiris, *Oppositional*

While Austen confronted personal challenges particular to her widowhood, she also lived through the dramatic upheavals of England's civil wars, its commonwealth and protectorate, the restoration of the monarchy in 1660, a deadly outbreak of plague in 1665, and the Fire of London in 1666, which left its indelible mark upon Austen's life by burning down buildings she owned.[3] She not only connects these important historical events to her own life and to family members in *Book M*, but she also vividly relates wide-ranging anecdotes and opinions—her own and other people's—about the rich and (in)famous, queens and emperors, poets and prophets, friends and foes.

Austen's *Book M* serves as a particularly rich resource not only for understanding the writer herself but also for understanding early modern English women's writing more broadly. It is a collection of texts in diverse genres, on many topics, woven together by Austen as a means through which to understand, to negotiate, and to voice her view of her world—from her immediate family to the business of the nation. *Book M* includes Austen's spiritual meditations, sermon notes, financial records, letters, personal essays, and more than thirty occasional and religious lyric poems, including elegies and country house verse. She wrote and compiled her book primarily between 1664 and 1666, but it has entries dated as late as 1682, which suggests she returned to it periodically—reading, editing, and amending it.

Austen represents that "other voice" of early modern women who expressed their thoughts and feelings in manuscript rather than print; her voice has been here all along, waiting, and she has much to tell us.

Life and Writings

The daughter of a successful mercantile family, Katherine Austen was born to Robert Wilson, a draper, and Katherine Rudd in the parish of St. Mary Colechurch, London, in 1628, and she died in 1683, having

---

Voices: Women as Writers and Translators of Literature in the English Renaissance (New York: Routledge, 1992).

3. On Austen's Blackfriars properties, see Todd, "Property and a Woman's Place," 186–87.

spent much of her life in Hoxton, Middlesex, northeast of London.[4] She married Thomas Austen in 1645, when she was a teenager, but Thomas died in 1658, leaving her a young widow and single mother of three. The fact of her widowhood—a status she maintained for the rest of her life—is important because it gave her more independence than a wife would typically have and because it required her to protect herself and her children legally and economically. According to the common law doctrine of coverture, a married woman was eclipsed economically and legally by her husband. In the absence of marriage settlements specifying otherwise, whatever a woman owned before marriage theoretically became her husband's. According to coverture, a wife could not own property, and she could not sue or be sued.[5] However, when a woman became a widow, like Austen, she regained an independent economic and legal identity, which she could use to defend herself and her family. Austen's *Book M* thus provides us with vital, rare insights into how a young, urban early modern widow and

---

4. My sources for Austen's biographical information include Katherine Austen, *Book M* (British Library, Additional Manuscript 4454); Barbara J. Todd, "'I Do No Injury by Not Loving': Katherine Austen, a Young Widow of London," in *Women and History: Voices of Early Modern England*, ed. Valerie Firth (Toronto: Coach House Press, 1995), 207–11; Barbara J. Todd, "Property and a Woman's Place," 181–200; and Barbara J. Todd, "The Remarrying Widow: A Stereotype Reconsidered," in *Women in English Society, 1500–1800*, ed. Mary Prior (New York: Methuen, 1985), 76–77; Sarah Ross, "'And Trophes of His Praises Make': Providence and Poetry in Katherine Austen's *Book M*, 1664–1668," in *Early Modern Women's Manuscript Writing: Selected Papers from the Trinity/Trent Colloquium*, ed. Victoria E. Burke and Jonathan Gibson (Burlington, VT: Ashgate, 2004), 182–83; and in her introduction to *Katherine Austen's Book M*, Medieval and Renaissance Texts and Studies, vol. 409 (Tempe, AZ: Arizona Center for Medieval and Renaissance Studies, 2011), 6–15; and Jane Stevenson and Peter Davidson, eds., *Early Modern Women Poets: An Anthology* (New York: Oxford University Press, 2001), 313–14.

5. For more on coverture, see Amy Louise Erickson, *Women and Property in Early Modern England* (New York: Routledge, 2002), 24; Sara Mendelson and Patricia Crawford, *Women in Early Modern England, 1550–1720* (Oxford: Clarendon Press, 1998), 37–38; Lynne A. Greenberg's introductory note to *Legal Treatises*, vol. 1, *The Early Modern Englishwoman: A Facsimile Library of Essential Works*, Series III, *Essential Works for the Study of Early Modern Women: Part I*, ed. Betty S. Travitsky and Anne Lake Prescott (Aldershot, UK: Ashgate, 2005), xxiii–xxvii; and Tim Stretton, *Women Waging Law in Elizabethan England* (New York: Cambridge University Press, 1998), 129–35.

mother exercised her freedoms as a newly single woman by acting independently as the head of her family.

As a dedicated single mother, she managed the education of her children, sending Thomas to Oxford and Robert to school and teaching Anne herself at home. She seems to have kept Anne close at hand and encouraged her daughter's interest in learning how to manage the household. As she notes affectionately, "My Nancy is busy and inquisitive into all things of housewifery—to be informed and to learn—and every country affair delights in, which I am very well pleased to see" (186 below). She also wrote letters to all three children, individually and collectively, instructing them about life. Her maternal advice includes warning them not to take for granted a large inheritance and explaining how the maintenance of real estate can become a dangerous economic drain. In one letter addressed to all of them, for example, she first details a case of estate inheritance within their extended family and then concludes that "if he had not left him anything, it would been better" (98 below).

Austen certainly knew a great deal about finances, since she single-handedly oversaw the family's interests. She made loans within her local community and to family; she bought and developed real estate, including building rental houses; she invested in the East India Company; and she hired lawyers and personally attended hearings of a committee at parliament in an effort to secure possession of a large estate called Highbury.[6] As a relatively young widow, she struggled with the question of remarriage and found the suit of a Scottish physician, Alexander Callendar, tempting.[7] Ultimately, however, she decided against a second marriage in order to guard her children's inheritance; returning to the dependent status of a wife and introducing a new husband and stepfather into her small family would have

6. Taking possession of Highbury is a central concern of *Book M*; see Todd, "Property and a Woman's Place," 191–94; Ross, "And Trophes of His Praises Make," 183; and Ross's introduction to *Katherine Austen's Book M*, 9–11, for the legal details of the case. On early modern women's participation in legal and financial matters, see, for example, Erickson, *Women and Property*; Laura Gowing, *Domestic Dangers: Women, Words, and Sex in Early Modern London* (New York: Oxford University Press, 1996); Barbara J. Harris, *English Aristocratic Women, 1450–1550: Marriage and Family, Property and Careers* (New York: Oxford University Press, 2002); and Stretton, *Women Waging Law in Elizabethan England*.

7. Todd, "Property and a Woman's Place," 187.

jeopardized her ability to guarantee the economic security of her three children by Thomas Austen. Thus, she remained a widow until she died in her mid-50s.[8]

Although she desperately feared the plague of 1665 and personally witnessed its terrors, she was fortunate enough to escape it. She suffered through a number of respiratory illnesses, however, and once fell out of a tree and lost consciousness briefly as a result—an episode she relates with a sense of high drama and to which she ascribes great providential meaning. For the most part, however, she seems to have had a healthy life, despite the fact that she did not have the longevity of some of her relatives and acquaintances. In reflecting on what she considers her mother's premature death, she records her views on what it takes to live a long life:

> I observe what a long and healthy age my Grandmother Rudd lived, above 80, and Mr. Smith of Aldbury, 90, and Parson Wilson, about 80. All lived in the city and did not love the country. Their diet was temperate, their exercise little, a subtly pace ever went, not put Nature scarce ever in any violence by overstirring or heating, which makes a faintness oftentimes and a decay. Yet I attribute the chief part of this long life to the quiet of their minds, never engaged in anything disquieted or disordered that peace within them. How was my own mother's strong nature worn out by too much stirring and walking and the many cares and businesses which a great family gave occasions to her! That nature was spent which, in likelihood, by indulging to retirement would have prolonged. The distractions of the times wherein she lived gave her many discomposures and crosses by abuses. Dear Mother, thou hadst a great estate and a great burden, too. (96–97 below)

8. In contrast to Austen, her mother, Katherine Rudd, remarried after Austen's father, Robert Wilson, died in 1639. Her second husband—Austen's stepfather—was John Highlord, an alderman in the City of London. By 1641, Austen's mother was a widow again. See Todd, "Property and a Woman's Place," 183. For Highlord's significant financial influence on his stepdaughter, Katherine, see Ross, introduction to *Katherine Austen's Book M*, 7–8.

Before Katherine's death, she saw to it that her children Thomas and Anne made good marriages, but sadly, her daughter predeceased her. Her second son, Robert, did not marry or have children. As Barbara J. Todd notes, eventually, Thomas's son, John, "achieved most of the markers of full gentry status. Seated at the estate of Durhams (he sold Highbury), grandson John acquired a baronetcy, and became a Whig member of the House of Commons."[9] Grandmother Katherine Austen did everything within her power to make her grandson's social elevation possible.

Austen's writing is in a unique quarto volume, BL, Additional Manuscript 4454, which is held today by the British Library in London. Austen called this text *Book M*; it is entirely in her own handwriting and was not intended for print publication for a mass audience. She authored most of *Book M*, but she also copied, summarized, and adapted material from other sources, often without attribution. Until recently, scholars of the early modern period have tended to overlook the vital importance of the manuscript circulation of texts during the sixteenth and seventeenth centuries in England. The printing press with moveable type was introduced into England in 1476, a century and a half before Austen's birth.[10] However, the advent of print did not mean that people simply abandoned the long-standing practice of manuscript publication. Instead, a new print culture developed alongside and intermingled with a preexisting manuscript culture.[11]

Manuscript and print were socially marked forms of textual transmission that influenced how people read the contents of a work.

9. Todd, "Property and a Woman's Place," 194; Austen's grandson John died without an heir (also see 198n63 on Robert's death in 1699 and his companion, Ursula Gardner, "to whom Robert had proposed marriage and with whom he lived").

10. For a landmark study of the forms of social, economic, religious, and cultural change associated with the printing press, see Elizabeth Eisenstein, *The Printing Press as an Agent of Change: Communications and Cultural Transformations in Early-Modern Europe* (Cambridge, UK: Cambridge University Press, 1979).

11. On the continued importance of the manuscript circulation and publication of texts throughout the seventeenth century, see, for example, Harold Love, *Scribal Publication in Seventeenth-Century England* (Oxford: Clarendon Press, 1993); Arthur Marotti, *Manuscript, Print, and the English Renaissance Lyric* (Ithaca, NY: Cornell University Press, 1995); and Margaret J. M. Ezell, *Social Authorship and the Advent of Print* (Baltimore, MD: The Johns Hopkins University Press, 1999).

Printing one's writing for a broad readership was thought by some to be demeaning or vulgar because it meant exposing one's ideas to the common masses; from the elite perspective, printed texts could thus carry negative connotations. Given how hierarchical early modern English society was and how much power was in the hands of the few, writers often sought to connect with the highest ranking or most powerful readers, rather than with the greatest number. In this view, better that one king or queen read and approve of one's writing than thousands of commoners. The notion that printing one's words was a form of intimate, personal exposure to a mass population also linked it to the idea that it signaled a lack of chastity in women. Since chastity was pervasively represented as the single most important female virtue—indeed, as the foundation of all other female virtues—it could jeopardize a woman's reputation for upstanding moral behavior for her to print her writing. By contrast, for her to share her ideas with friends and family members through manuscript transmission was seen as far more proper; in fact, some families encouraged this practice.[12]

To understand fully how these cultural attitudes relate to Katherine Austen's *Book M*, it is important not to conflate chastity with virginity. In the early modern English view, a virgin (or maiden) has never had sex and thus is also chaste, but a woman who is not a virgin is still considered chaste under the right circumstances. In particular, a married woman who is no longer virginal is chaste as long as she remains sexually faithful to her husband and conforms sufficiently to patriarchal expectations for properly feminine behavior (e.g., by submitting to male authority, refraining from excessive speech, etc.).

---

12. On women's coterie exchange of manuscript writing and for an especially helpful analysis of the limiting assumptions that have led scholars to overlook the importance of early modern women's manuscript writings, see Margaret J. M. Ezell's groundbreaking *Writing Women's Literary History* (Baltimore, MD: The Johns Hopkins University Press, 1993), 39–65. Also on women's participation in manuscript culture, see Marotti, *Manuscript, Print, and the English Renaissance Lyric*, 30–61; and Love, *Scribal Publication*, 54–58. On women's encouragement as writers in familial contexts, see especially Erica Longfellow, *Women and Religious Writing in Early Modern England* (New York: Cambridge University Press, 2004); Marion Wynne-Davis, *Women Writers and Familial Discourse in the English Renaissance: Relative Values* (New York: Palgrave Macmillan, 2007); and my own *Gender, Sexuality, and Material Objects in English Renaissance Verse* (Farnham, UK: Ashgate, 2010).

A woman who is innocent of any illicit sexual behavior but who transgresses openly against mainstream cultural beliefs concerning how "good" women should act—by talking too much or at the wrong times, by flagrantly disobeying her father, husband, or other figures of patriarchal authority, for instance—could *potentially* leave herself open to accusations or rumors of unchaste behavior because chastity was seen as the key virtue underpinning all other female virtues. Austen—a relatively young, marriageable widow—was thus not surprisingly concerned about portraying herself in *Book M* as a proper woman according to the dominant social expectations of her day in order to maintain her reputation for chastity. Sharing her writings exclusively through limited networks of manuscript transmission, rather than seeking to disseminate them via print to a large, general readership, was one of several means by which she could protect her feminine virtue.

For women and men alike, in fact, circulating texts through manuscript transmission was more prestigious than printing them. It is also important to keep in mind that the capacity for mass distribution inherent in print publication did not lead directly to significant financial gain for writers. There was no authorial copyright, and writers sold their works to booksellers and printers outright for a low price. Writers in sixteenth- and seventeenth-century England did not make money primarily by printing and selling multiple copies of their books. High-ranking authors—such as Sir Philip Sidney—wrote not to make money but rather to strengthen social networks among like-minded elites, to display social graces appropriate to their rank, to entertain themselves and others, to demonstrate their learning and to teach their audiences, and to express their views. Lower ranking poets sought financial support—in addition to gifts and favors, such as lodging and food, secretarial and tutorial jobs, clothing, wine, and so on—from powerful social superiors or "patrons," and dramatists hoped for the support of patrons or for acting companies to purchase their work. As Margaret J. M. Ezell points out, while today we tend to think of success on the literary marketplace—measured in terms of the number of books sold and the amount of money made through sales—as one possible indicator of the value of a literary work, this

model does not work for sixteenth- and seventeenth-century England.[13]

Austen is not the only seventeenth-century author who did not
write to make money from her literary efforts or to publicize her ideas
to the greatest possible number of readers. Instead, as in the case of
many of her contemporaries, male and female, her writing practices
were, on one hand, contemplative activities that helped her to understand herself in relation to the mundane and spiritual worlds, and on
the other, forms of social engagement that reinforced her personal
connections to her family and local community. At times, her meditations even express and bolster her sense of national belonging. In her
entry, "Of English and Dutch Quarrel, 1665," for example, she angrily
figures the Dutch as an ungrateful serpent feeding cruelly on virtuous
mother England: "it is … unworthy that that nation should prove a
viper to eat out the bowels of the mother which has fed and nourished it, the English nation having been the instrument of the Dutch's
subsistence and greatness" (135 below). She reinforces the gendered
imagery she introduces into her personal meditation on England's
international conflicts by also focusing, with nostalgic admiration,
upon Queen Elizabeth's political role in assisting the Dutch in the late
sixteenth century; in Austen's account of history, "they made their
miserable laments known to Queen Elizabeth (who was the balance
to turn the scale of Europe). She adhered to their party and delivered
them from the Spanish insultment" (135 below). In this brief entry,
she figures England as a generous, self-sacrificing, victimized mother
whose internal organs are invaded and consumed by a phallic, poison-
ous snake, and she invokes the long-dead Elizabeth I as an idealized
heroic protector. By creating these charged images, Austen works out
her own gendered sense of national identity for her own benefit and
probably for an audience of like-minded family and friends.

Perhaps in the age of electronic social media, such as Facebook, MySpace, Twitter, and personal blogs, it is becoming easier for
us to recognize why someone would choose to write prolifically, stra-
tegically, and with deliberate craft and imagination without doing so
primarily to sell books. Perhaps our electronic writing practices today
can help us understand how writing as a member of a locally restricted

---

13. Ezell, *Writing Women's Literary History*, 4, 32.

community—or coterie—can support, in reassuring ways, one's sense of personal identity and how and where one fits into the world. In fact, one can draw an especially illustrative (although ultimately limited) analogy between a personal Facebook account and *Book M*. Like a Facebook account holder today, Austen portrays herself in *Book M* in a manner that is carefully tailored to how she would like her coterie audience to perceive her. *Book M*, like a Facebook page, does not give its reader transparent, unmediated access to its creator but instead allows her to display the personal attributes she wants others to see.

In addition to giving her readers a carefully controlled perspective on Austen herself, *Book M* reveals compelling glimpses of other texts that were especially important to her. Throughout *Book M*, for example, Austen includes cross-references to other books.[14] In some cases, those books were authored by other people, but she also refers to books designated by other letters of the alphabet that were probably her own. Thus, *Book M* was almost certainly one of many such books Austen wrote and compiled across her lifetime. According to what we currently know, those other books—*A* to *L* and after *M*—are now tragically lost. If Austen named *Book M* as she did to catalog it among her other writings, then she had probably been an active writer for many years before the day in 1664 when she opened a new book and began to pen *Book M* on its pristine, blank pages. Indeed, her inclusion of introductory pages giving her book a title and a table of contents indicates her experience with reading and writing and the deliberate care that went into her creation of *Book M*. In all likelihood, Austen was an even more prolific writer and an even more important chronicler of a remarkable century than *Book M* alone reveals her to be.[15] In opening this single, precious, surviving volume—humbly and simply designated by the thirteenth letter of the alphabet—we enter

14. Also on Austen's cross-referencing, see Sarah C. E. Ross, textual introduction to *Katherine Austen's Book M*, Medieval and Renaissance Texts and Studies, vol. 409 (Tempe, AZ: Arizona Center for Medieval and Renaissance Studies, 2011), 42–43.

15. Todd proposes that *Book M* was "focused on interpreting dreams and apparitions (earlier books may have examined other topics such as honour)." "Property and a Woman's Place," 190. Raymond A. Anselment speculates that "Austen intended to combine the surviving folios into a work that presumably included her earlier widowed years." "Katherine Austen and the Widow's Might," *Journal for Early Modern Cultural Studies* 5.1 (2005): 6.

Austen's fascinating life story *in medias res* and can only speculate about what we have most unfortunately lost before and after *M*.

Context, Contents, and Analysis

When Katherine Austen was born in 1628, Charles I was King of England.[16] He was the son of King James I, who reigned in England from the death of Queen Elizabeth I in 1603 until his own death in 1625. King James had advocated an especially authoritarian form of monarchy, and his son, Charles, also attempted to center absolute power in the crown. A complex combination of political, social, economic, and religious factors was already generating conflict when Charles I ascended to the throne in 1625. By the summer of 1642, the nation was divided in loyalties and erupted into civil war between the king's forces and the parliamentary army. By the end of January 1649, Charles I was defeated, tried for high treason, convicted, dethroned, and beheaded. Austen spent her teenage years living in a nation at war with itself. Whether she personally witnessed the king's death or not, she was certainly aware of this dramatic historical event—the public execution of an anointed monarch by his own subjects. During the next decade, England did not officially recognize a king or queen ruling over it: Charles Stuart, the son and heir of Charles I, fled England and lived abroad in exile. The national leader during much of this period was Oliver Cromwell, a military general who governed England under the title of Lord Protector. After Cromwell's death, parliament asked Charles to return to England as King Charles II; his return in 1660 represented the restoration of the monarchy that royalists—persons sympathetic to the perspective of the crown during the civil wars— like Austen had long awaited and saw as a proper return to the natural order of things.

Austen's royalism is discernible only indirectly, through, for example, her generally positive references to various monarchs. Todd provides telling material evidence of Austen's royalism through her discovery of the widow's role as a government creditor: she made small, short-term loans to the government, which meant economically

16. For a helpful introduction to seventeenth-century English history, see Christopher Hill, *The Century of Revolution, 1603–1714* (New York: Norton, 1980).

"supporting the Restoration government, playing the role of a citizen of London."[17] Austen's religious commentaries, which suggest she was Anglican,[18] also imply support for the monarchy, since royalism and Anglicanism were often (but not always) intertwined. In fact, the political, economic, and social upheavals of the 1640s and 1650s cannot be disentangled from religious conflict. When Austen was born, the national religion of England was Anglicanism, and there was an official state church. However, many other Protestant Christian groups or sects also existed in England. People who disagreed with those sects often referred to them disparagingly as "puritans," although we usually use the term today in a more neutral fashion. Those called "puritans" included Presbyterians, Baptists, Anabaptists, Congregationalists, Independents, Quakers, Seekers, Ranters, Muggletonians, and Fifth Monarchists, among others. Anglicans disagreed with the beliefs and practices of both puritans and Roman Catholics (Henry VIII had officially severed English ties with the Roman Catholic Church in the early 1530s). In *Book M*, Austen aligns herself with Anglicanism through her approving reflections on sermons and religious essays by Church of England divines such as John Donne, Daniel Featley, and Henry Hammond; her outraged disapproval of the Quaker rejection of the social courtesy known as "hat honor" (that is, removing one's hat in the presence of a superior to acknowledge and reinforce symbolically one's inferior place in the social hierarchy); and her negative opinions regarding Roman Catholics, to whom she refers scornfully as "papists" and whose views on saints she criticizes.[19]

---

17. Todd, "Property and a Woman's Place," 189.

18. An Anglican was a Protestant Christian who was a member of the Church of England, "the English branch of the Western Church, which at the Reformation repudiated the supremacy of the Pope, and asserted that of the Sovereign over all persons and in all causes, ecclesiastical as well as temporal, in his dominions" (*OED*).

19. Hill explains that "to say 'thou' to social superiors, to refuse to remove one's hat to constituted authority, was neither *merely* religious nor a harmless eccentricity in the explosive political atmosphere of the sixteen-fifties" (*The Century of Revolution*, 144). Austen sees the symbolism of "hat honor" as so rife with meaning that she writes a long, chastising letter to Thomas, her first son, on the importance of upholding the traditional custom (see 87–88 below). For a compelling argument about how mothers' advice to their children (including sons old enough to be away at college) regarding proper attire played a key role in shaping

While Austen thus associates herself with mainstream Anglican belief in many ways, she also reveals an ongoing fascination with prophetic discourses, which flourished during the 1640s and 1650s. Many people claimed to be prophets during the civil wars and interregnum; in fact, Christopher Hill has commented that the role of prophet during this period was "almost a new profession" for men and women alike.[20] However, most of those who claimed to be prophets aligned themselves with parliament against the king and his followers and with the more radical Protestant sects against the Anglican Church.[21] Prophetic discourse during this era was complex. Keith Thomas details the multiple traditions from which mid-seventeenth-century prophetic discourse borrowed:

> The real boost to ancient prophecy ... came with the Civil War, when Galfridian prophecies joined astrological prognostication and religious revelation to place an unprecedented amount of prophetic advice before the lay public. Although the three genres were distinct, their separate identity was not always preserved ... The literature of the Civil War period suggests a disposition to welcome any kind of prophetic utterance, regardless of the foundation upon which it purported to rest.[22]

A major feature of prophetic discourse during Austen's lifetime was the idea that the divine—in the form of God, the Holy Spirit, or the indwelling light—could use people's bodies as vessels through which to transmit important truths and urgent messages to humanity.

---

them as citizens and subjects, see Edith Snook, *Women, Beauty, and Power in Early Modern England: A Feminist Literary History* (New York: Palgrave, 2011), 86–111.

20. Christopher Hill, *The World Turned Upside Down: Radical Ideas during the English Revolution* (New York: Viking Press, 1972), 73

21. On the social status of the members of radical religious sects, see Hill, *The World Turned Upside Down*, 76, 80; Phyllis Mack, *Visionary Women: Ecstatic Prophecy in Seventeenth-Century England* (Berkeley, CA: University of California Press, 1992), 4; and B. S. Capp, *The Fifth Monarchy Men: A Study in Seventeenth-Century Millenarianism* (London: Faber and Faber, 1972), 82, 85, 93.

22. Keith Thomas, *Religion and the Decline of Magic* (New York: Scribner's, 1971), 409.

These supernatural communications could be very political and specific: for instance, *The Cry of a Stone* (1654), a printed religious pamphlet, relates how the Fifth Monarchist prophet Anna Trapnel had millenarian visions foretelling the doom of Oliver Cromwell for having strayed too far from a radical Protestant sectarian agenda in his role as Lord Protector.

Women were believed to be especially vulnerable to this kind of supernatural takeover because they were assumed to be physically and mentally weaker than men.[23] As Phyllis Mack explains,

> [t]he characterization of the female visionary as an empty vessel reflected an attitude that was far more complicated than simple misogyny, for the defects of rationality and the attuned intuition of visionary women were actually viewed with respect, even envy, by those philosophers who felt alienated from God by their compulsive, prideful reliance on the power of their own reason. Indeed, in this respect all women had a clear spiritual advantage over men, for the static resulting from their weak and intermittent surges of intellectual energy was less likely to interfere with their capacity to act as receptors for the divine, spiritual energy emanating from heaven.[24]

There were many women claiming to be prophets—and often sincerely believed to be prophets, even by powerful political leaders and by people who were not affiliated with their particular religious sects—when Austen was a teenager and young adult in London.[25] She must

23. On relevant assumptions regarding female biology and the prophetic body, see Phyllis Mack, 24–34; Diane Purkiss, "Producing the Voice, Consuming the Body: Women Prophets of the Seventeenth-Century," in *Women, Writing, History, 1640–1740*, ed. Isobel Grundy and Susan Wiseman (Athens, GA: University of Georgia Press, 1992), 139–58; and Sue Wiseman, "Unsilent Instruments and the Devil's Cushions: Authority in Seventeenth-Century Women's Prophetic Discourse," in *New Feminist Discourses: Critical Essays on Theories and Texts*, ed. Isobel Armstrong (New York: Routledge, 1992), 192.

24. Mack, *Visionary Women*, 33.

25. On the seriousness with which prophetic statements could be taken and the difficulties surrounding how to discern which prophetic claims were truly divine messages, see Mack,

have been aware of this cultural trend and the kinds of authority—paradoxical though they were, since they were predicated upon assumptions of female inferiority, weakness, and passivity—available to women prophets.[26]

Book M registers Austen's ambivalent fascination with prophecy.[27] As Diane Purkiss explains, "For the radical sects in the seventeenth-century, prophecy was any utterance produced by God through human agency. Hence, the prophecies of women ... include hymns, general moral exhortations, scriptural exegesis, prayers, spiritual autobiography and mystical revelations, as well as predictions."[28] Although Austen was not a member of a radical sect, she too participated in prophetic discourse in the sense Purkiss describes, and she too did so in multiple genres. Yet, because the prophets of the civil war era were so often associated with parliamentarians, puritans, and the urban rabble, Austen tries to distinguish herself from them.

Visionary Women, 79–83; Geoffrey Nuttall, *The Holy Spirit in Puritan Faith and Experience* (Oxford: Basil Blackwell, 1947), 34–47; and Esther Gilman Richey, *The Politics of Revolution in the English Renaissance* (Columbia, MO: University of Missouri Press, 1998), 1–3.

26. On the paradoxes of prophetic authority for women, see Wiseman, "Unsilent Instruments" and Purkiss, "Producing the Voice." Anne Laurence details religious behaviors considered acceptable for women: writing (but not printing) books of prayers, spiritual advice, and meditations; teaching religious ideas within the household; prophesying via dreams and visions; and modeling proper religious beliefs and practices. "A Priesthood of She-Believers: Women and Congregations in Mid-Seventeenth-Century England," in *Women in the Church*, ed. W. J. Sheils and Diana Wood (Cambridge, MA: Basil Blackwell, 1990), 346–47, 363. For references to Austen's dreams in the context of analyses of early modern dreams in general, see Mary Baine Campbell, "Dreaming, Motion, Meaning: Oneiric Transport in Seventeenth-century Europe," in *Reading the Early Modern Dream: The Terrors of the Night*, ed. Katherine Hodgkin, Michelle O'Callaghan, and S. J. Wiseman (New York: Routledge, 2008), 15–30; and Patricia Crawford, "Women's Dreams in Early Modern England," in *Dreams and History: The Interpretation of Dreams from Ancient Greece to Modern Psychoanalysis*, ed. Daniel Pick and Lyndal Roper (New York: Routledge, 2004), 96.

27. For a detailed analysis of Austen's ambivalence about prophecy, see my *Poetic Resistance: English Women Writers and the Early Modern Lyric* (Aldershot, UK: Ashgate, 2002), 129–49; and "Widow, Prophet, and Poet: Lyrical Self-Figurations in Katherine Austen's 'Book M' (1664)," in *Write or Be Written: Early Modern Women Poets and Cultural Constraints*, ed. Ursula Appelt and Barbara Smith, 3–27 (Aldershot, UK: Ashgate, 2001).

28. Purkiss, "Producing the Voice," 139.

She thus writes statements disparaging prophets and arguing against dream interpretation. For example, she entitles one essay, "How Ill to Desire to Know Our Fortune." She even includes this statement mocking diverse attempts at divination:

> If men do listen to whispers of fear and have not reason and observation enough to confute trifles, they shall be affrighted with the noise of birds and the night raven, and every old woman shall be a prophetess, and the events of our affairs—which should be managed by the conduct of counsel, of reason, and religion—shall by these vain observations succeed by chance, by ominous birds, by the falling of the salt, or the decay of reason, of wisdom, and the just religion of a man. (67 below)

However, she also records multiple views on the question of whether dreams can foretell the future and interprets her own dreams as prophecies.[29] She claims that she dreamed she saw her servant, William Chandeler, "fall down dead" four nights before he really did die (80 below), and she entitles her ninth numbered poem, "Upon My Dream the 20th October 1664, When I Dreamt I Saw 4 Moons in a Clear Sky: Meditation." She strongly implies that she has a vocation as a prophet when she asks herself, "Was not one of my dreams the presagement of blessing to the nation, as the dream of a poor stranger did confirm Gideon to go on with the more confidence to his victory?" (58 below). She relates legends of famous people who fail to interpret the signs around them and suffer for their mistakes. She speculates about whether certain numbers—such as six and seven—might have special meanings for her personally because they have been viewed in pagan and Christian traditions as supernatural signs.

While Austen thus flirts in a vacillating manner with prophetic discourse throughout much of *Book M*, she resists—with only partial success—her possible association with radical mid-seventeenth-century women prophets by looking instead to the distant historical past

---

29. Also on Austen's fascination with dreams, see Ross, introduction to *Katherine Austen's Book M*, 22–26.

for earlier models.[30] For example, she writes an essay, "Of the Sibyls, Their Transportations Not Heeded," about the famous female seers of classical antiquity, and she comments admiringly on the medieval Catholic prophet, Hildegard of Bingen: "She was of the pope's conclave and emperor's counsel, to whom they had recourse in difficulties. Yea, the greatest torches of the church lighted themselves at her candle, and patriarchs and bishops sent knots as passed their fingers for her to untie" (76 below). Yet, some times, almost despite herself, she sounds just like the radical women prophets of the previous decades:

> For this complaint of oppression, God hath punished
> the land formerly in the great calamities which fell
> upon the times, and surely if they pursue and commit
> the same crimes of injustice and injuries to poor men,
> and especially to act violence on widows and orphans,
> how will their cries and grievances pierce the ears of
> Heaven, who will hear and judge their cause against an
> unjust nation! (125 below)

She angrily asserts that the injustices done by parliament to her own family will bring down the wrath of God upon England. Like her radical prophetic sisters, she also identifies frequently, throughout *Book M*, with David the Psalmist.[31] While Austen probably thought

30. If Austen knew about the aristocratic female prophet, Lady Eleanor Davies, as a possible model, it is no wonder that she did not draw comparisons between Lady Eleanor and herself. Austen valued social propriety too highly to consider Lady Eleanor an acceptable predecessor, given that the aristocrat, despite her elite status, was notorious for being imprisoned and sent to Bedlam and for such acts as tarring the hangings behind the bishop's seat at Lichfield. On Lady Eleanor's exploits, see Thomas Spencer, "The History of an Unfortunate Lady," *Harvard Studies and Notes in Philology and Literature* 20 (1938): 43–59; and Esther Cope, *Handmaid of the Holy Spirit: Dame Eleanor Davies, Never Soe Mad a Ladie* (Ann Arbor, MI: University of Michigan Press, 1992). On gender and social transgression, see David Cressy, *Travesties and Transgressions in Tudor and Stuart England: Tales of Discord and Dissension* (New York: Oxford University Press, 2000).

31. As Ross notes, "Austen borrows widely from scripture and beyond as she slips freely in and out of differently gendered models of forbearance; she subscribes to the general wisdoms offered by the male, yet freely assumes the particular statuses offered to the female godly." Introduction to *Katherine Austen's Book M*, 21.

of herself as a devout, mainstream Anglican, her fascination with prophecy reminds us how very complex—even contradictory—a person's beliefs can be and how multifaceted an individual's relation to her historical moment can be.

Austen's engagement with the prophetic discourses of her era reveals only one intriguing aspect of her shaping of her sense of self in relation to her time and place. Another crucial part of this process was her great effort to police how she was perceived as a widow. This is important because widowhood was seen as a distinct life stage for women; the shift in status from wife to widow—as touched upon briefly above—brought with it many profound changes, including the potential for the newly single woman to experience, on the one hand, greater independence, and on the other, increased risk. When Austen started *Book M*, she had already lived as a young widow for several years. The contents of her book suggest that she was acutely aware of her widowed status and that she used her writing, in part, to counter negative stereotypes seventeenth-century literary and medical discourses created about widows. These discourses figured widows as lustful, power hungry, and uncontrollable because of their sexual experience as wives, their potential for economic independence, and their seeming freedom from the patriarchal surveillance of fathers and husbands.[32] *Book M* reveals that Austen's widowhood made her self-conscious about her female gender and how it affected her ability to protect her children and to manage the family finances, which included hiring lawyers and attending parliament to fight for possession of the Highbury estate and investing in the East India Company.[33]

She includes many meditations and poems explicitly commenting upon her widowhood. For example, in this brief lyric, she laments her past disregard for widows (which she aligns with the

32. On stereotypes and expectations of widows in early modern England, see Barbara J. Todd, "The Virtuous Widow in Protestant England," in *Widowhood in Medieval and Early Modern Europe*, ed. Sandra Cavallo and Lyndan Warner (New York: Pearson Education, 1999), 66–83; Todd, "The Remarrying Widow," 54–55; Erickson, *Women and Property*, 153; and Mendelson and Crawford, *Women in Early Modern England*, 68–69, 175.

33. On how Austen uses *Book M* to address her widowed status, see Todd, "The Virtuous Widow," 75n39, 80, 82; and my *Poetic Resistance*, 111–28; and "Widow, Prophet, and Poet," 3–27. On her self-figuration as a widow, see also Anselment, "Katherine Austen and the Widow's Might."

patriarchal perspective of thoughtless men in line 1); reveals the new knowledge she has gained as a result of her own widowed condition; asks for forgiveness for her sinful ignorance; and prays for pity, comfort, and relief on behalf of widows:

> Men never think their wives may be
> Necessitate by misery,
> Or their children be a prey
> When themselves are gone away.
> I not resented widow's tears   [5]
> Before I was distressed with fears.
> This retribution do I find:
> To meet with all the world unkind.
>
> My sin forgive, let pity flow,
> And comfort unto sad hearts show.   [10]
> Most gracious Heaven, relieve sad hearts;
> Be healing balsam in their smarts.
> O Heaven, send down thy full relief,
> Who art the help of all in chief. (113 below)

While she confronts the difficulties of her widowhood directly at times, as she does in this poem, she also resists identifying completely or consistently as a widow.

In fact, much like her contemporary Lucy Hutchinson, Austen figures herself occasionally as still effectively married to her dead husband, and thus, as a wife—not a widow at all.[34] She interprets her dreams of Thomas as giving her direct access to his advice, as if their marriage continued without interruption on a ghostly plane. She also compares herself with Penelope from *The Odyssey* when she resists

---

34. Todd notes that there was one "model" of early modern widowhood in which "the woman's responsibilities to her dead husband continued to be the central theme: a widow was merely perpetual wife." "The Virtuous Widow," 67. On Lucy Hutchinson's self-portrait as a wife operating under the common law doctrine of coverture, despite her actual status as a widow, see my *Gender, Sexuality, and Material Objects*, 178. As an interesting point of contrast to Austen and Hutchinson, Anne Clifford, according to Snook, used the reverse strategy and deliberately fashioned her appearance to "[look] like a widow before she was one." *Women, Beauty, and Power*, 169.

her Scottish suitor's efforts to woo her into a second marriage. "For my part," she relates, "I declined all things might give him a vain encouragement and told him I was like Penelope—always employed. 'Aye,' says he, 'her lovers could not abide her for it'" (169 below). In the classical epic, Penelope is the royal wife of the hero, Odysseus; she loyally waits twenty years for him to return home to Ithaca after the Trojan War. She has many persistent suitors, but she tells them she cannot marry again until she finishes weaving a shroud for Laertes, Odysseus's father. At night, as depicted on this book's cover in *Penelope Undoing Her Tapestry*, she unravels what she has woven during the day, thus delaying remarriage. By comparing herself with Penelope and asserting that she is "always employed" or busy, Austen uses an especially condensed, rich literary allusion to insist that she is really not a widow at all, but instead, an extraordinarily faithful, long-suffering—and clever—wife. Furthermore, her self-comparison to Penelope implies her view that suitors threaten a woman's economic resources and that their interests are primarily financial, rather than genuinely loving. She relates the following brief dialogue with her suitor, in which she deflates his professed romantic idealism—in a context where he flatters her by expressing how much he enjoys talking to her about learned matters—with pragmatic cynicism: "He then said to me and protested, if I was a very beggar woman, if I would have him, he would have me, and he would discourse with me all day, for he never talked with me but learned something of me. I told him he was mistaken, and if I was so indeed, he would not" (168 below). Fashioning herself as a seventeenth-century English Penelope suggests not only that Austen is a heroically loyal wife but also that she is a wealthy, powerful woman who has the good sense to protect her material resources.

Book M includes fascinating details about Austen's management of her family's money and property, and it thus provides especially valuable information about urban women's economic participation in early modern England. Although many women became impoverished when widowed, Austen was fortunate enough to have considerable wealth, and *Book M* demonstrates how active a wealthy widow could be in managing the family's money, real estate, and investments. Sara Mendelson and Patricia Crawford note that "[w]idows at all social levels appealed to the stereotype of the poor, distressed, and weak individual.... Some who were neither poor nor weak still deployed the same rhetoric to urge men to help them."[35] Austen is one of the many widows who used the tactic Mendelson and Crawford describe: throughout her book, she portrays herself as helpless and impoverished, even though she was actually wealthy, astute, and aggressive in managing her family's financial affairs.[36] For example, in one meditation, she prays, "O God, though my enemies seem to take advantage upon my weak and destitute and helpless condition—a woman without alliance of the family to help me—yet, O God, help me and make me overcome those bands that do environ me" (128 below). Austen thus frequently makes use of the stereotype of the weak widow to downplay her actual considerable material, familial, and personal resources.

Economic matters were foremost in Austen's mind much of the time; Todd argues that Austen was "a pioneer female financier" and uses her as a case study "to advance the project of imagining how tens of thousands of other women experienced the contradictions of a public economic presence."[37] Explaining how extensive Austen's investment activities were, Todd writes,

> she was involved in virtually every form of non-mercantile capital investment available to a woman of her time. I have yet to discover another woman with such wide-ranging interests. Her real-estate holdings extended from her home in Hoxton, a north-eastern London suburb, not just across London, but also from the western parts of Wales to the farthest eastern coast of Essex. Lending to government drew her to the Guildhall and Westminster, and investing in the East

35. Mendelson and Crawford, *Women in Early Modern England*, 175.

36. Austen's mother was skilled at advancing her children's economic interests; she served as a powerful model for Katherine. See Todd, "Property and a Woman's Place," 183–85; and Ross, "And Trophes of His Praises Make," 183.

37. Todd, "Property and a Woman's Place," 181, 182.

India Company led her into the wider world of nascent imperialism.[38]

Furthermore, Todd points out that "when Austen began buying and developing London real estate she was doing something distinctly uncommon" for a seventeenth-century woman.[39]

Many of her prayers to God and spiritual meditations expose her economic fears and ambitions for great material wealth. She makes financial lists detailing where her money has gone (in building efforts, loans to relatives, etc.). She sternly warns her children against the assumption that they will inherit enough land and money not to have to worry about their future financial well-being and instructs them to plan on making their own way in the world. "Suspend all craving and expectation," Austen tells Thomas, Robert, and Anne, "Go on in your own way of industry, and be the raiser of your fortune, and leave the rest to God, and he will do better than your own projects can" (98 below).

She pens multiple essays and poems about her efforts to secure the large estate of Highbury, which was also called Newington Barrow. For example, in the opening lines of her long poem, "Upon Courtiers at the Committee of Parliament Striving for Highbury, the 14th February That I Was There, 1664/5," she paraphrases biblical verses from Ecclesiastes so that they appear to address her own circumstances in order to dramatize her struggle over the estate:

> Wise Solomon, he tells me true,
> There is a time for all things due:
> A time to spare, a time to spend,
> A time to borrow, time to lend,
> A time of trouble, time of rest,   [5]

---

38. Todd, "Property and a Woman's Place," 182. Hill notes that "[m]erchants profited greatly by the trade boom. Between 1660 and 1688, apart from paying large dividends, the East India Company doubled, and the African Company quadrupled, its nominal capital." *The Century of Revolution*, 184.

39. Todd, "Property and a Woman's Place," 186.

A time there is to be oppressed.[40]
Such is this time, now men of power
Do seek our welfare to devour,
Confederated in a league
By an unjust and dire intrigue.   [10]
Envy, thou base encroaching weed,
Never did any noble deed;
We cannot be secure for thee
O thou most treacherous quality! (111–12 below)

In this poem, Austen vividly imagines a sinister conspiracy of envious men plotting intrigues against her; her personal economic and legal struggles take on the qualities of high drama. Furthermore, as mentioned above, her lively accounts of her suitor's efforts to court her frequently turn to money matters: she frets over the possibility that a second marriage could harm her children financially, and she hints to her suitor that his romantic pursuit of her hand disguises a self-interested pursuit of her riches.

While *Book M* thus gives us important insights into the historical events of Austen's era and a widow's strategic self-fashioning and property management, it also enables us to recognize the importance of creative or literary writing in a woman's everyday life. Austen wrote over thirty poems in her book, and she interspersed these lyrics with other genres of writing.[41] Most of her poems are spiritual meditations or biblical paraphrases—forms of religious reflection that were considered especially appropriate writing activities for women. She often uses verse to praise, to thank, or to express devotion to God; in several cases, her poems are inspired by or reflect upon specific psalms in the Bible.[42] For example, she entitles one poem, "Read Psalm 27: Of Sup-

---

40. In her metrical paraphrase, Austen revises the following lines from Ecclesiastes: "To everything there is a season, and a time to every purpose under the heaven" (3:1); "A time to get, and a time to lose; a time to keep, and a time to cast away" (3:6); and "A time to love, and a time to hate; a time of war, and a time of peace" (3:8).

41. As Marotti notes, "Typically, lyrics were inserted in books given over to other sorts of texts." *Manuscript, Print, and the English Renaissance Lyric*, 17.

42. See also Ross, "And Trophes of His Praises Make," 187–88; Ross, introduction to *Katherine Austen's Book M*, 28–32; and Anselment, "Katherine Austen and the Widow's

portation" (108 below). Although she did not systematically attempt to create her own version of the Book of Psalms, her strong general interest in psalms aligns her lyrical composition with a widespread poetic practice of her place and time; Hill notes that "[i]t is difficult to find a notable poet from Wyatt to Milton who did not try his [*sic*] hand at a version of the Psalms" and lists George Herbert, Henry Vaughn, Thomas Carew, Richard Crashawe, Henry King, Elizabeth I, James I, and Mary and Philip Sidney among the well-known poets who did so.[43] As Sarah Ross notes, "Interaction with and meditation through the Psalms permeate the life-writings of Lady Margaret Hoby, Alice Thornton, Lady Mary Rich, and Lady Anne Halkett, although none identifies herself as closely and explicitly with the Psalmist as does Katherine Austen."[44] It makes sense that Austen, like so many of her predecessors and contemporaries, would reflect both in prose and verse upon the Book of Psalms, given the great importance ascribed to it during her lifetime. Barbara Lewalski details the forms of knowledge and emotion associated with the Psalms: "On all sides the Book of Psalms is seen as a compendium of all theological, doctrinal, and moral knowledge; of all the modes of God's revelation—law, prophecy, history, proverbs; of all the emotions and passions of the human soul; and apparently, of all the lyric genres and styles appropriate to divine poetry."[45]

While some of Austen's poems are biblical meditations, others interpret the events of her life as guided by the protective hand of divine providence.[46] The first half of her poem, "On My Fall off the

---

Might," 15–16, on Austen's engagement with the Book of Psalms.

43. Christopher Hill, *The English Bible and the Seventeenth-Century Revolution* (New York: Penguin Press, 1993), 358, 359; on specifically Royalist translations of the Psalms, see 360–62.

44. Ross, introduction to *Katherine Austen's Book M*, 29.

45. Barbara Kiefer Lewalski, *Protestant Poetics and the Seventeenth-Century Religious Lyric* (Princeton, NJ: Princeton University Press, 1979), 50.

46. Austen displays an ongoing interest in how divine providence shapes her life. Sara Mendelson explains that "[t]he providential interpretation of life's accidents which moulded contemporary spiritual diaries offered a coherent and satisfying explanation of world-historical events. It could also transform an outwardly dull and unhappy life into scenes of high drama, punctuated by hairbreadth escapes from death or damnation." "Stuart Women's Diaries and Occasional Memoirs," in *Women in English Society, 1500–1800*, ed. Mary Prior

Tree," for instance, provides an especially vivid, dramatic rendering of an accident she has:

> It might have been a fatal tree
> And my last act's catastrophe,
> Yet all ways from that remote part
> My Genius ever did divert.
> An uncouth way, an if dark owls   [5]
> And dismal night birds had controls,
> At last was thwarted by my fate
> T'approach that most unhappy bait
> Laid to entrap. If Fame say right,
> A receptacle 'twas did fright: [10]
> Revolted spirits that place did haunt,
> Yet some are of opinion can't.
> Where were those foes? For what conspire?
> I have not logic to inquire.
> I can't determinate that thing,   [15]
> Only a supposition bring,
> Admit the crew of Beelzebub
> Weighted my rival with their club
> And that the regiment of hell
> Had there concentered out a spell   [20]
> (To make my traverse more replete
> And more than earthly foes to meet.)
> The plot was broke, and Heaven's bright eye
> Dissolved their black confederacy. (173 below)

A tumble from a tree she has climbed stirs Austen's richly imaginative mind to portray a confederacy of evil forces—from "dark owls/And dismal night birds" to ghostly "Revolted spirits" and the satanic "crew of Beelzebub"—as plotting to make her slip, while the supernatural forces of good—from her own spiritual "Genius" to the ever-watchful "bright eye" of Heaven—miraculously intervene to save her imperiled life.

(New York: Methuen, 1985), 186. On Austen's "providential world view," especially as it pertains to her verse composition, see Ross, "And Trophes of His Praises Make," 182.

All of Austen's poems include religious content, but a few simultaneously experiment with secular poetic conventions. This aspect of her verse composition strongly suggests that she avidly read the works of other poets.[47] For example, she is likely to have read poetry by Ben Jonson and John Donne. "On Valentine's Day, This 14 February 1665/6: My Jewel" borrows from and reshapes ideas typical of secular, male-authored Renaissance love poetry, such as Donne's "The Funeral" and "A Jet Ring Sent."[48] In the opening lines of what is effectively a love poem to herself, rather than from a lover, she writes,

> Welcome, thou best of Valentines,
> Firmer to me than lover's twines.
> Alas, they vanish, but this tie,
> A pledge, a surety annually,
> Grand omen of a bles't presage   [5]
> To wade me through a stormy age. (187 below)

In this unusual poem, she adapts to fit the context of her own life the competitive spirit of conventional Renaissance love poetry—in which the poetic speaker's lover is the best of all lovers and thus inspires the best poetry of praise—and the focus upon love tokens (here the jewel she feels divine providence led her to find near an old wall) typical of such secular verse.

47. She was an active reader of several genres of prose, drama, and verse. Todd notes that Austen was familiar with John Donne's sermons and refers to "Ralegh's *History of England* and Isaak Walton's *Lives*; she found inspiration in Thomas Fuller's account of the life and achievement of Hildegarde of Bingen." "A Young Widow," 212. Ross points out that "[s]he draws on the writings of Daniel Featley, Jeremy Taylor and other Church of England divines." "Katherine Austen," *Perdita Manuscripts*. http://www.perditamanuscripts.amdigital. co.uk/ (accessed August 12, 2009). Ross has also discovered that Austen borrows without attribution from William Shakespeare's *Henry IV, Part 2*; Richard Brome's *A Jovial Crew; or, the Merry Beggars*; Samuel Daniel's *The Complaint of Rosamond*; and Henry King's "The Legacy." Ross, introduction to *Katherine Austen's Book M*, 32. For a thorough discussion of the significance of Austen's reading practices, see Ross, "'Like Penelope, always employed': Reading, Life-Writing, and the Early Modern Female Self in Katherine Austen's *Book M*," *Literature Compass* 9, 4 (2012): 306–16. 10.1111/j.1741-4113.2012.00878.x.

48. For a detailed discussion of Austen's Valentine's Day poem, see my *Gender, Sexuality, and Material Objects*, 1–4 and 103–6.

Her country house poem, "On the Situation of Highbury," reveals her familiarity with the conventions of that widespread, popular genre, of which Jonson's "To Penshurst" and Aemilia Lanyer's "The Description of Cooke-ham" are particularly famous examples.[49] Like these other country house poems, Austen's "On the Situation of Highbury" celebrates a manorial estate—in this case, her own—by praising its seemingly supernatural Edenic pleasures and beauty and its limitless, labor-free, spontaneously occurring natural abundance

> So fairly mounted in a fertile soil,
> Affords the dweller pleasure, without toil.
> Th'adjacent prospects gives so rare a sight
> That Nature did resolve to frame delight
> On this fair hill, and with a bounteous load,   [5]
> Produce rich burdens, making the abode
> As full of joy, as where fat valleys smile,
> And greater far, here sickness doth exile.
> 'Tis an unhappy fate to paint that place
> By my unpolished lines, with so bad grace   [10]
> Amidst its beauty; if a stream did rise
> To clear my muddy brain and misty eyes
> And find a Helicon t'enlarge my Muse,
> Then I no better place than this would choose:
> In such a laver and on this bright hill,   [15]
> I wish Parnassus to adorn my quill. (181 below)

While Austen's poem borrows liberally from the conventions of country house verse, she also avoids employing certain characteristic features (extensive, direct praise of the landowner, in particular, which would be tantamount to praising herself). Regardless of what she leaves out, however, this poem engages so thoroughly with the typical tropes of the genre that she must have studied other poets' country house verse—Jonson's almost certainly, but possibly others, too.

---

49. For an analysis of how "On the Situation of Highbury" relates to the genre of country house poetry, see my *Poetic Resistance*, 149–63; and "Katherine Austen's Country House Innovations," *SEL: Studies in English Literature* 40.1 (Winter 2000): 123–37.

She must have also studied the elegy as a form—especially the subgenre of child loss verse. A striking number of seventeenth-century poets composed child loss elegies, including men such as Jonson, John Milton, Thomas Carew, and Robert Herrick and women such as Anne Bradstreet, Katherine Philips, Elizabeth Egerton, Gertrude Aston Thimelby, and Mary Carey. Austen's elegy, "On the Death of My Niece, Grace Ashe, 4 Years Old," contains the most metrically complex stanzas she composed in *Book M*:

> Sweet blooming bud
> Cropped from its stud
> When growing up
> Unto fair hope,
> Thy pretty sweetness time hath hid.   [5]
> As soon as shown, we are forbid
> To gaze upon that lovely hue
> On which Time's shady curtain drew.
>
> Yet, when we know
> The best mayn't grow   [10]
> In this dark vale,
> Where ills still ail,
> The great disposer sets them free,
> Whose better character doth see,
> And early in their nonage place,   [15]
> Where their chiefest part will grace. (99–100 below)

As is typical of seventeenth-century child loss poems written by nonparental consolers, Austen's lyric for her niece objectifies and aestheticizes the dead girl by figuring her as a beautiful, sweet budding flower cut prematurely from the stalk. Furthermore, as expected in an elegy, Austen attempts to help her audience—certainly family but also possibly members of a more extended coterie of readers—achieve emotional catharsis by working through their grief; she suggests that readers conceptualize her niece's death positively, as a welcome means of escape from the "dark vale" of earthly life where "ills still ail." Given that Austen clearly engages with the conventions particular to child loss verse in two of her lyrics, she must have encountered examples written by other poets that she used as models for her own.[50]

Because her poems are interspersed with other genres, reading them within the greater context of *Book M*—instead of treating them in isolation—allows us to see the interplay between her lyric composition and other facets of her life. Some of her poems have what today's reader might think are surprisingly long, detailed, specific titles. The title of her innovative poem reworking some of the conventions for children's elegies detailed in the previous paragraph is an especially good example of this tendency: "December 5th, 1664. Upon Robin Austen's Recovery of the Smallpox and Colonel Popham's Son, John, Dying of Them, a Youth of Very Forward Growth, Their Ages the Same, Popham 3 Years for Growth More" (90 below). As Arthur Marotti explains, it was typical for poets and scribes to "[attempt] to preserve the information that enabled [any given lyric] to be read in its social contexts."[51] Austen's manner of embedding her poems among other genres in her book and giving her lyrics titles highlighting their particular relation to her life is perfectly consistent with the manuscript lyric practices of her day; thus, she must have examined commonplace books, manuscript miscellanies, journals, diaries, and so forth authored and compiled by other people. Her Valentine's Day poem mentioned above, in which she writes a spiritual love lyric to herself celebrating God's gift to her of a jewel, takes on greater significance when one reads it alongside her essays meditating upon the day she found her providential gem near an old wall, communicating her worries about her financial affairs, and explaining why giving this particular jewel to her firstborn son as part of his inheritance means more to her than giving him a more expensive token of remembrance.

Austen weaves her poetic composition into the very fabric of her life, and *Book M* gives us a rare glimpse of the importance such creative writing had to an upwardly mobile, ambitious early modern woman whose daily practical concerns were typically managing her finances, educating her children and providing for their future, and

---

50. On elegies for children, including detailed analyses of Austen's, see my "Despised Creatures: The Illusion of Maternal Self-Effacement in Seventeenth-Century Child Loss Poetry," *ELH: English Literary History* 66 (1999): 25–49; and *Poetic Resistance*, 13–54.

51. Marotti, *Manuscript, Print, and the English Renaissance Lyric*, 15.

avoiding the considerable dangers of her time and place, such as smallpox, the plague, and the Great Fire of London. Not only did she attempt to shape her experiences, thoughts, and opinions into meter and verse, but she also must have spent a significant amount of time reading other people's writing. While it is unsurprising that a widow so dedicated to propriety and upward mobility read sermons in prose and wrote meditations on them, it is refreshing to realize that she must have also read a fairly wide variety of poems, including secular love lyrics, country house verse, psalms, and elegies. Reading and writing mattered immensely to Katherine Austen, and she seems to have wanted others to know about this aspect of her personality. It is telling that, whether she read a translation of *The Odyssey* or not, she certainly knew its main characters and plot, and she deliberately communicated that literary knowledge to her suitor—and to the readers of *Book M*. But other than Austen herself, who would have read *Book M*?

Afterlife of Book M

Austen includes a preface to *Book M* that might seem at first glance to today's reader to announce the absolutely private character of her writing: "Whosoever shall look in these papers and shall take notice of these personal occurrences will easily discern it concerned none but myself and was a private exercise directed to myself. The singularity of these conceptions doth not advantage any" (45 below). Upon examining the passage closely, however, one notices that it does not forbid others to read the book; on the contrary, it assumes a reader who "shall look in these papers" and signals to that person that the author and compiler, Austen, is a properly feminine early modern woman insofar as she renounces wishes for an audience and downplays her desire to share her "private" ideas.[52] From her first lines, Austen thus uses *Book M* to shape perceptions of herself.

As I mention above, the manuscript is a collection of texts in several genres, and those texts probably had different readerships. A limited analogy between a Facebook account today and the texts that

---

52. Ross, too, notes the "paradoxical" nature of Austen's disclaimer in assuming a reader while declaring *Book M* private. "And Trophes of His Praises Make," 181. On Austen's possible audiences, see also Ross, introduction to *Katherine Austen's Book M*, 35–39.

make up *Book M* might again prove illustrative here: different texts in Austen's book would appear to correspond to different levels of audience restriction and access. The letters she includes, for example, are likely copies of ones she sent to her children.[53] Certain poems—such as the elegy for her niece, Grace Ashe—must have been circulated at least within the extended family. Todd asserts that Austen's poems "were carefully transcribed from other notebooks [of Austen's]," while Ross proposes that the fact that "many but not all of the poems … are consecutively numbered" suggests "a process of selection, for poems perhaps to be extracted for presentation in another, more formal volume."[54] The meditations and letters she writes when she thinks she might be killed by the plague draw from the genre of maternal legacies that other seventeenth-century women typically wrote in recognition of the possibility of death in childbirth. The presence of these texts in *Book M* suggests that she wanted her children to inherit her book and to read all of it after her death, if not before.[55] Ross argues, in fact, that "Austen expected *Book M* to circulate to members of her extended family, who would read in its pages of God's 'acts of praise' in Austen's life" and proposes that "[i]t seems likely that Austen intended the manuscript for perusal—or at least assumed it may be perused—against the background of her very public defences of her family's fortunes."[56] Austen might not have assumed a mass audience, but she certainly assumed a coterie of readers. In perfect keeping with early modern manuscript culture, she expected a restricted readership consisting of people who knew her and who would value her writing for its intimate connection to her life.

More surprisingly, perhaps, in parts of *Book M*, she goes beyond these typical expectations for a limited audience and rather boldly flirts with the idea of pursuing a much larger one. One poem of religious meditation, for instance, concludes by implying her desire to disseminate widely her stories of God's providential interventions in her life:

53. See also Todd, "A Young Widow," 207.

54. Todd, "A Young Widow," 207; and Ross, "Katherine Austen," *Perdita Manuscripts*.

55. See also Stevenson and Davidson, *Early Modern Women Poets*, 314.

56. Ross, "And Trophes of His Praises Make," 197; and "Katherine Austen," *Perdita Manuscripts*.

My gracious Lord, wilt thou admit to me   [15]
Thy special favors, so much glory see?
O, that upon thy altar I may lay
A contrite heart and perfectly obey,
That every day and minute be confined
Thy bright memorials to bear in mind   [20]
And to the future generations tell
How high, how excellent thy glories swell! (179 below)

Not surprisingly, given her consistent, pervasive concerns about displaying properly feminine, devout behavior, she offers to sacrifice her "contrite heart" on God's "altar" and to "perfectly obey." In an interesting turn away from feminine submission and silence, however, she uses this scenario of profound religious self-sacrifice and obedience to justify telling "the future generations" of God's workings in her life. Similarly, in a prose meditation, she asks, "Has my God lengthened out my thread of life, and am I to tell his wonderful works that others may see them as well as I?" (139 below). Such comments about whether God wanted her to take a more active, public role in declaring his providential benefits imply that Austen may have desired an audience reaching well beyond the expected local, familial coterie. It has taken centuries for such an audience finally to find her.

The critical reception of *Book M* began in the last decades of the twentieth century. Feminist historians such as Todd, Mendelson, and Crawford first showed interest in Austen's manuscript because of its rich, detailed first-person account of a widow's daily life.[57] Todd and Mendelson have focused upon Austen's financial records and the crucial information her accounts provide about her management of her economic affairs. Raymond A. Anselment has examined how Austen shaped her widowhood in relation to her Christian beliefs.[58] Literary attention to *Book M* has centered primarily upon Austen's poetic practices in relation to manuscript culture. I have contextualized Austen's composition of elegies for children and country house verse

57. Todd, "The Remarrying Widow: A Stereotype Reconsidered," "I Do No Injury by Not Loving," "Property and a Woman's Place"; Mendelson, "Stuart Women's Diaries and Occasional Memoirs"; Mendelson and Crawford, *Women in Early Modern England*.

58. Anselment, "Katherine Austen and the Widow's Might."

in relation to male- and female-authored poetry in the same genres; analyzed how she used her composition of lyrics to shape her social roles as widow and prophet; and detailed how she uses her long Valentine's Day poem to rewrite the secular, masculinist Renaissance love lyric and to locate herself in relation to the material world.[59] Ross's work on *Book M* has examined Austen's rendering of her life's events into verse and the pervasive role of providential interpretation in her writing; in particular, Ross has argued that "Austen's defining poetic mode is in fact the providential occasional meditation as social occasional verse."[60]

The initial historical interest in Austen as a London widow was accompanied by the publication of brief transcribed fragments from *Book M*.[61] Her verse was first anthologized in 2001, in Jane Stevenson and Peter Davidson's *Early Modern Women Poets: An Anthology*; however, this volume includes only two of Austen's poems—one child loss poem and her country house poem, "On the Situation of Highbury."[62] The recent appearance of the *Perdita* online database of early modern women's manuscripts has allowed access to a complete digital image of *Book M*; this electronic copy is accompanied by a very helpful, detailed introduction and extensive glosses by Ross.[63] Ross has also recently published an excellent scholarly diplomatic edition of Austen's manuscript.[64] Her scholarly edition should be especially helpful to advanced students and Renaissance scholars who would like to work

---

59. Hammons, "Despised Creatures"; "Katherine Austen's Country House Innovations"; "Widow, Prophet, and Poet"; *Poetic Resistance*, 39–42, 100–63; *Gender, Sexuality, and Material Objects* 1–4, 103–6.

60. Ross, "And Trophes of His Praises Make," 194.

61. Early transcriptions of fragments from *Book M* include Todd, "A Young Widow," 215–37; Ralph Houlbrooke, ed., *English Family Life, 1576–1716: An Anthology from Diaries* (New York: Basil Blackwell, 1989), 79; and Patricia Crawford and Laura Gowing, eds., *Women's Worlds in Seventeenth-Century England* (New York: Routledge, 2000), 35–36, 184–85, 233, 279–81.

62. Stevenson and Davidson, *Early Modern Women Poets*, 313–16.

63. Katherine Austen, *Book M*, edited by Sarah C.E. Ross, *Perdita Manuscripts* (http://www.perditamanuscripts.amdigital.co.uk/): accessed August 12, 2009.

64. *Katherine Austen's Book M*, edited by Sarah C.E. Ross, Medieval and Renaissance Texts and Studies, vol. 409 (Tempe, AZ: Arizona Center for Medieval and Renaissance Studies, 2011).

with a printed version of *Book M* that scrupulously traces Austen's sources and retains the manuscript's original seventeenth-century spelling, capitalization, and punctuation, instead of modernizing these features to maximize accessibility for today's general reader, as does the present volume for The Other Voice series. Austen's writing is finally becoming widely accessible in several formats. She would be pleased to know that history has decided for her. Yes, she should "the future generations tell."

Note on the Text

In transcribing *Book M*, I have attempted to balance the preservation of the content, character, and style of Austen's writing against its modernization into standard twenty-first-century American English and its regularization according to the conventions of printed books. I have modernized Austen's spelling and regularized the letters "i"/"j," "u"/"v," the long "s," and "F" and "ff" for upper case "f." I have regularized her capitalization, including the capitalization of each new line of verse, but I have retained Austen's use of capital letters for personified, allegorized, or generalized figures (for instance, "Nature" or "Man").

Austen uses punctuation inconsistently and does not always write in complete sentences. I have altered or added punctuation (including commas, semicolons, colons, question marks, dashes, quotation marks, apostrophe marks, and periods) as needed to make her writing conform to twenty-first-century conventions as much as possible and to maximize clarity for a modern audience. For example, when Austen records oral conversations, I add quotation marks to signal that the words represent spoken dialogue; when the tone of a phrase indicates it is an interrogative, I add a question mark; and when a particular clause represents a specific example of the sentence preceding it, I separate them with a colon. When Austen ends a sentence with the symbol (:), I replace it with a period. When she uses what today's reader would perceive as a plural "s" (or "es") to indicate possession, I add an apostrophe before the "s" (and omit the extra "e"). When Austen uses the symbol (=) to hyphenate a word break at the right margin or bottom of her page, I omit the symbol and rejoin the word's syllables.

I have expanded contractions and abbreviations that are no longer used: for instance, I retain "etc." but expand "y^e" into "the" and "w^ch" into "which." When Austen uses an ampersand, I replace it with "and." I retain the contractions that Austen uses to make her words fit the meter of her verse: for example, I keep "'tis" and "th'eternal" instead of changing them to "it is" and "the eternal" because changing them would alter the meter of her poetic line. In cases in which I keep Austen's contractions or abbreviations because they are still current, I lower her superscriptions so that, for instance, "M^rs" becomes "Mrs."

I have silently corrected transposed letters (for example, "noen" becomes "none") and other obviously accidental misspellings (for instance, when Austen writes "in" but context indicates she meant "it"). When I have not been able to read a word with certainty, I have placed my best guess (based upon context and any partially visible letters) followed by a question mark in square brackets.

Austen uses old-style dates, which means that she understood each calendar year to begin officially on March 25, rather than on January 1. Thus, for dated entries in *Book M* that fall between January 1 and March 24, I indicate the year by first giving Austen's old-style date followed by a slash mark and the appropriate new-style date (for example, February 1665/6, where "1665" is Austen's old-style date and "/6" refers to "1666" according to the new-style calendar recognizing January 1 as the beginning of a new year).

I have not attempted to reproduce Austen's horizontal or vertical spacing between letters, words, or lines; the layout of her writing on the page; or her page breaks. I have regularized these features of her book, with just a few exceptions. Because she gives *Book M* front matter—a title page, author page, and table of contents—I follow her breaks for these first few folia to convey a sense of the way in which she formalized and organized her writings. The page numbers given in the table of contents are Austen's originals referring to the manuscript; they do not correspond to the pagination of this modernized volume. Keeping Austen's numbers helps to show the difference between how her handwritten text occupied the space of her book and how modern print does so. Also, a few irregularities in the pagination of the table of contents—which I explain in footnotes—give insight into her writing practices. Austen is inconsistent in her placement on the page of the titles she assigns to distinct parts of her manuscript: I have centered them all. While I have attempted to keep Austen's division of paragraphs (when those divisions are clear), which she indicates by left justifying new ones, I have formatted them by indenting their first words. When Austen repeats a word or phrase at the bottom of one page and the top of the next, I do not repeat it. Austen numbers some of her poems next to or above them in the left margin; I have consistently placed her numbers next to the title of each poem (or next to the first line, in the absence of a title). I have not added numbers to poems that she did not number. Austen does not give line numbers for her verse, so I have added them every five lines, in square brackets, to facilitate classroom discussion.

Austen's manuscript shows signs of revision: she often includes marks indicating that particular words or phrases should be inserted, replaced, or deleted. I have silently incorporated what appear to be her latest revisions into this transcription. However, I have also explained these revisions in detail in the footnotes so that anyone wishing to trace Austen's thinking process as a writer may easily do so. Austen not only revised her phrasing, but she also added material to *Book M* for several years after she started writing it. At the beginning of her book, in particular, she wrote mostly on the front or right-hand side of a given page (recto folio), typically leaving blank what we think of as the back or left-hand side of the page (verso). Thus, she would write on the front of a page (right side), turn the page, and continue writing the same passage—sometimes midword or midsentence—at the top of the next right-hand page. However, in some cases, she added new material to the pages she originally left blank. This material is usually related to whatever she first wrote on the right side of her book and serves as marginalia or side commentaries on her previous writing.[65]

---

65. Todd offers the following speculation on Austen's composition techniques:

> Judging from how she numbered her pages in this volume, Austen's practice was to use the first third of her working notebooks for study, abstracting her spiritual reading (mainly sermons) on the right-hand page, leaving the facing page blank and unnumbered for later comment and research.... Meanwhile, in the latter two-thirds of her notebook, Austen followed a different practice, numbering these pages con-

Figures 4 and 5 illustrate this practice (51–52 below). Sometimes she added cross-references to other books she owned or read. Because this print edition does not reproduce Austen's page breaks, it is not possible to represent perfectly the layout of this later material in relation to the earlier writing. Therefore, I have italicized the added passages, put them in brackets ("{...}"), and placed them as close as possible to the material upon which they comment. Each time this occurs, I have included explanatory footnotes that enable today's reader to understand Austen's writing practices.

Finally, in composing footnotes to illuminate Austen's personal history, her seventeenth-century vocabulary, and her biblical references, I have relied upon several important resources. Except in the cases of simple, obvious definitions (e.g., "glass" used to mean "mirror"), all definitions are from the 2012 online version of the *Oxford English Dictionary* (*OED*). All information about known people of historical importance is from the 2011 online version of the *Oxford Dictionary of National Biography* (*ODNB*). Biblical references are to the *Holy Bible: King James Version* (New York: Ballantine, 1991), unless otherwise noted. In rare instances, Austen used *The Book of Common Prayer* in citing Psalms; after the first reference in *Book M* below to *The Book of Common Prayer* (New York: Oxford University Press, 1969), I use the abbreviation "*BCP*" to signal when she uses it instead of the King James Bible.

---

tinuously, writing her meditations, poems and prayers on both sides of each sheet. "Property and a Woman's Place," 190–91.

See also Ross, textual introduction to *Katherine Austen's Book M*, 41–42, on Austen's use of space and numbering of pages.

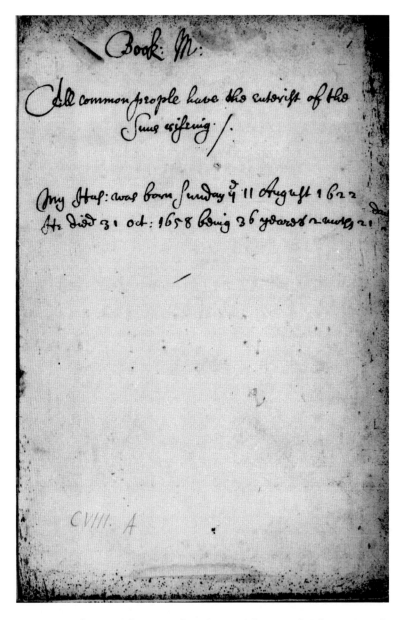

Figure 1. Folio 1r. Title page of *Book M*. © The British Library Board.
Add. MS 4454.

BOOK M

All common people have the interest of the sun's rising.

My husband was born Sunday, the 11 August 1622.[1] He died 31
October 1658, being 36 years, 2 months, 21 days.[2]

---

1. Katherine's husband was Thomas Austen, the son of a merchant; Thomas studied at
Lincoln College, Oxford University and Lincoln's Inn. Barbara J. Todd, "Property and a
Woman's Place in Restoration London," *Women's History Review* 19.2 (2010): 184.

2. Austen used a caret to insert "days" in the far right-hand margin of a recto page. As
mentioned in the introduction, Austen gave *Book M* front matter; this transcription
preserves her original page breaks after her title and author pages to highlight how she
formalized and organized her writings.

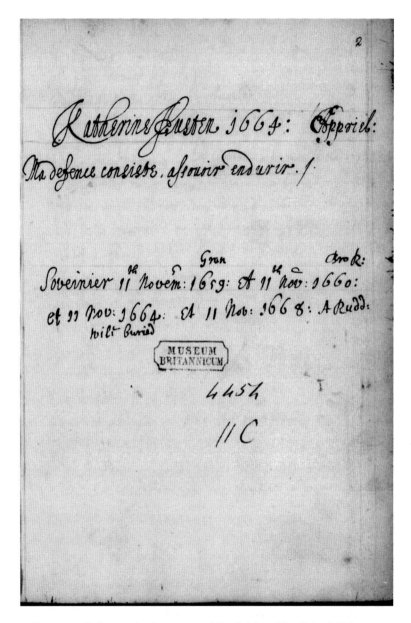

Figure 2. Folio 2r. Author page of *Book M*. © The British Library
Board. Add. MS 4454.

Katherine Austen 1664: April

Ma defense consiste assouoir endurir.[3]

Souvenir: 11th November, 1659, Gran, et 11th November, 1660, Brother R., et 11 November, 1664, William buried, et 11 November 1668, A Rudd.[4]

3. Although the letters in this French phrase are clear, what Austen means specifically by "assouoir" is not. It is possible that her statement is akin to "My defense consists of knowing how to endure/to suffer." Sarah C. E. Ross suggests, "My defence consists of/in suffering patiently" or "I defend myself, that is by suffering patiently." *Katherine Austen's Book M*, Medieval and Renaissance Texts and Studies, vol. 409 (Tempe, AZ: Arizona Center for Medieval and Renaissance Studies, 2011), 51n3. A less likely possibility is "My defense consists of surfeiting on suffering."

4. Austen reminds herself to remember dead relatives and members of her household. She detects a pattern among their deaths in relation to November 11. Throughout *Book M*, she demonstrates a fascination with the idea that certain numbers have special providential or predictive meanings for her. On Austen's extended family, see Todd, "Property and a Woman's Place," 183, Figure 1. Ross speculates that "Gran" refers to her maternal grandmother, Anne Rudd, and that "Brother R." refers to Richard Wilson. *Katherine Austen's Book M*, 51n5–6. "William" almost certainly refers to her servant, William Chandeler, whose death Austen discusses below.

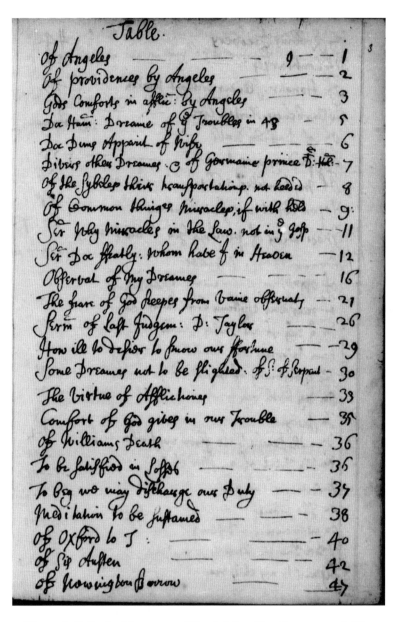

Figure 3. Folio 3r. First page of *Book M*'s table of contents. © The British Library Board. Add. MS 4454.

Table[5]

5. This table of contents reproduces Austen's original pagination in her manuscript.

6. Austen wrote "9" half-way between the title of her entry and "1." After composing her entry on page 9 (according to the original pagination of *Book M*), she must have decided that it, along with her entry on page 1, could fall under the title "Of Angels." Twice below in her table of contents, she again uses the same title for entries on different pages (i.e., "Meditations of Praising God and Dreams" on 65 and 73, and "On an Emergency, a Discourse" on 123 and 131).

7. Austen's page numbers are out of order. Since this entry is the last one on her page (this edition does not reflect her page breaks within her table of contents), perhaps she overlooked this item at first and then inserted it at the bottom of the page, out of order but as close as possible to where the entry should go.

8. Austen inserted "9" and then a line followed by "0" here; it is unclear why.

Whosoever shall look in these papers and shall take notice of these personal occurrences will easily discern it concerned none but myself and was a private exercise directed to myself. The singularity of these conceptions doth not advantage any.

Surely I [?] dark [?] nearest friends behold me in a cloud: those [?] know [?] superficially.[9]

On the Birds Singing in My Garden

Nature provides a harmony for me—
This airy choir, chanting out melody
So sweet, so pleasant by Zephyr's[10] pride;
I have a satisfaction here t'abide.
But, what's this Nature, which such order keeps?   [5]
That every plant, in its due season peeps?
'Tis from th'eternal order, which imprints
Their annual virtue and then gives their stints[11]
When they have flourished, then for to decline.

Such is the Nature God has made to mine;   [10]
I have my flourish, too, and I must fade.
I must return to an eternal shade
And leave these harmonies and pleasant things,
The end of which, much greater joys brings.

Yet as an antepast[12] of those to come,   [15]
By earthly joys, those future are begun;
By human joys, prepares us for divine.
The deity in outward things do shine.
The works of a great master does appear

9. Austen includes indecipherable shorthand marks in this line.

10. A personification of the west wind, typically considered a sweet, gentle wind; in classical mythology, the god of the west wind.

11. "Limitation, restriction" (*OED*).

12. "Something taken before a meal to whet the appetite; a foretaste" (*OED*).

Throughout the current of each day and year.　　　　　　[20]
Nature's a glass[13] of his supernal[14] hand;
In it, we comprehend and understand
His power, his love, which does all things create
And of his glory to participate.

O Lord, raise my soul from earth unto the sky[15]　　　　[25]
My great creator I may magnify
And see beyond the glass of finite things
A future state. Advance me with those wings
Of faith and hope I may fly up to thee,
Then shall be perfect, their perfection see.　　　　　　[30]

Of Angels[16]

That every man has a particular angel to assist him (enjoy your
Christian liberty): yet know you do all in the presence of God's angels.
And though to consider we do all in the presence of God, who sees
clearly into our hearts. Yet it is a bridle to refrain us from sin that the
angels behold us.

　　A thankful acknowledgement of the ministry and protection
of angels and of the prayers of the saints in heaven for us. All these
concur to our assistance, and we must bless God for, but not pray to,
them. See D. Featley.[17]

13. Mirror.

14. "That is above or on high; existing or dwelling in the heavens" (*OED*).

15. Austen revised line 25 by inserting "Lord" above the line. Her original line 25 is perfect
iambic pentameter. By inserting "Lord," she adds an extra syllable to the line, which makes
it irregular but also effectively breaks the rhythm and calls attention to it. Her alteration
of meter thus reinforces her shift in meaning at line 25, where she moves from describing
Nature's general role in reflecting the divine to praying to God on her own behalf.

16. Ross notes that Austen paraphrases sermons by John Donne throughout most of this
entry. *Katherine Austen's Book M*, 54n15–16.

17. Daniel Featley (1582–1645), Church of England clergyman (*ODNB*). Ross suggests
this note refers to Featley's sermon in *Clavis Mystica; A Key Opening Divers Texts of
Scriptures* (London, 1636). *Book M*, Ed. Sarah C.E. Ross, *Perdita Manuscripts*, http://www.
perditamanuscripts.amdigital.co.uk/ (accessed August 12, 2009): MS item no. 7.

Assistances by Angels

Good angels often give good assistances to men—invisibly and sometimes visibly—in such form as best befits the matter which is to be delivered and the capacity of the party.

It has been presented in the form of a wheel, beasts, a man with wings, a young man, a shepherd, etc.

How did God always refresh his church and servants with love and therefore taught them to look beyond the cloud and that there stood glories behind their curtain to which they could not come but by passing through the waters of affliction. And as the world grew more dark with mourning and sorrows, God did therefore send sometimes a light of fire and pillar of a cloud and the brightness of an angel and the luster of a star and the sacrament of a rainbow to guide his people through their portion of sorrows and to lead them through troubles to rest.

And sometimes God delivers his will by the voice of an angel without any visible sight, as to Hagar, to Abraham, to Samuel.[18]

Sometimes without voice as by dreams, for the souls being spirits and the angels being spirits also have no need of corporal organs to communicate what God has commanded.

And sometimes by visions, as to Abraham. And Paul[19] by a vision was assured that God had called him to the preaching of the Gospel. These visions are revealed only to the elect of God (plal:[20] it is thus). God in a vision hath spoken to his saints, and the ministry of the angels at last shall be to gather them together from all parts.

18. Old Testament figures who experience divine visitations. Hagar is the handmaid of Sarah, concubine of Abraham, and mother of Ishmael (Gen. 16:1–16). Abraham is a patriarch famous for passing God's test of faith; Abraham displays obedience through his readiness, when commanded by God, to sacrifice his son, Isaac (Gen. 22:1–18). Samuel is a leader and judge (1 and 2 Sam.).

19. Paul (also called Saul), a Roman citizen, has a vision of Jesus that converts him to Christianity and inspires him to join the disciples (Acts 9:1–30).

20. Although the letters in "plal" are clear, it is unclear what they mean. Ross assumes they refer to a source. *Katherine Austen's Book M*, 55n25.

Sometimes where there is not anything of Nature to be seen, God puts himself to the cost of a miracle for the comfort of his children in their troubles.

A special favor God gave to Gideon,[21] gave him a sign, and to Joshua.[22] When God does give signs, he gives also illustrations of the understanding that they may be discerned to be his signs and not esteemed natural accidents. God gives signs to illustrate the case and to confirm the person, which are high demonstrations of his mercy. And this is the sign of his love to me: that God has had such a care of all men is an expression and testification[23] to me he has likewise a care of me.

Truly,[24] Man is encompassed with a cloud of witnesses of his own infirmities and the manifold afflictions of this life in the departure of friends, of parents and wife and children out of this world. Every day makes him learneder than other in this sad knowledge. And surely Man, that has so many dark clouds to pass through, had need of some light to show him the right way and some strength to enable him to walk safely in it. One help to him is the assistance of an angel.

The angels are faithful and diligent attendants upon all our steps. They do attend the service and good of men.

Forevermore, it is best for everything to do that for which it was ordained and made. And they were made angels for the service and assistance of Man. They are messengers from God to Man, though they stand in the presence of God and enjoy the fullness of that contemplation.

Naturally, angels do not understand thoughts. "Curse not the king" for "that which hath wings shall tell the matter" is understood of

---

21. Gideon, an Old Testament warrior and judge, asks for and receives signs from God to prove that he will successfully save Israel from its enemies (Judg. 6:11–40).

22. Joshua, an Old Testament hero, leads the Israelites into the promised land of Canaan after the death of Moses. When Joshua commands the sun and moon to stand still so that he can finish a battle in daylight, God grants him this miracle (Josh. 10:12–14).

23. "A fact or object (as a document, etc.) serving as evidence or proof" (*OED*).

24. Austen paraphrases sermons by Donne for the remainder of this entry. Ross, *Katherine Austen's Book M*, 56n27–29.

angels.[25] Yet they may have a particular power given them to understand thoughts. The slenderness, the deliverance of the body from the encumbrance of much flesh gives us some conformity and likeness to the angels.

We may inquire of the nature of evil spirits as we do of poisons in physic,[26] of impure and revolted spirits, degenerate spirits.

The paralytic man which Christ had cured,[27] he was overloaded with himself. He had a soul in a sack, no limbs to move.

Dr. Hammond's Dream[28]

About the beginning of the troubles,[29] 1643, when ministers was put out of their livings,[30] though he was no valuer of trifles or anything that looked like such, he had so extraordinary a dream he could not then despise nor ever after forget it.

He thought himself and a multitude of others to have been abroad in a bright and cheerful day when, on a sudden, there seemed a separation to be made, and he with the far less number to be placed at a distance from the rest. And then clouds gathering, a most tempestuous storm arose with thunder and lightnings, with spouts of impetuous rain and violent gusts of wind, and what else might add to a scene of horror, particular balls of fire that shot themselves in among the

---

25. Austen adapts phrases from Eccles. 10:20: "Curse not the king, no not in thy thoughts; and curse not the rich in thy bedchamber: for a bird of the air shall carry thy voice, and that which hath wings shall tell the matter."

26. "The art or practice of healing" (*OED*).

27. Austen alludes possibly to Mark 2:3–12 or John 5:1–18.

28. Henry Hammond (1605–1660), Church of England clergyman and theologian (*ODNB*). Ross notes that this dream is taken from John Fell, *The Life of the Most Learned, Reverend and Pious Dr. H. Hammond* (London, 1661). *Katherine Austen's Book M*, 56n31.

29. England's civil wars.

30. In 1643, the House of Commons ejected from their positions of church leadership certain royalist ministers unsympathetic to the parliamentary cause; see Christopher Hill, *The Century of Revolution, 1603–1714* (New York: Norton, 1980), 139.

ranks of those that stood in the lesser party, when a gentle whisper seemed to interrupt those other louder noises, saying,

"Be still, and you shall receive no harm."

Amidst these terrors, the doctor falling to his prayers, soon after the tempest ceased. And then he heard began that cathedral anthem, "Come Lord Jesus, come away," with which he awaked. The correspondent event of all which he found verified in the preservation of himself and friends in the doing of their duty. The which

[31]{*See the dream of Lady Burton's*[32] *cousin that dreamed she should keep a coach and 4 horses, and she married at The Hague a lord and did so. In book of brown paper.*

It is certainly declared that there was a drop of blood fell from the ceiling at Greenwich upon the face of the statue old king[33] *and which spot or mark of it could never be got out at this day. This was when the old king and the nobles came to see the curiousness of the statue worth £1000.*

A man was murdered. One cut off his hand and hung it up in the castle of Cambridge. Some 10 or 20 years after, he that murdered him came into the castle and by accident touched[34] *that dry hand, and it bled. He confessed and was hanged: it was thought the soul of the murdered lay in the hand until the murderer appeared.*

---

31. Austen added the material represented here by italicized paragraphs in brackets on the verso folio facing the material concerning the dream experiences of Hammond, Donne, the Wotton family, and so forth (see Figure 5). These added paragraphs comment upon the dreams of famous men and their families.

32. Lady Frances Burton, Thomas Austen's aunt. Ross, *Book M, Perdita Manuscripts*, MS item no. 9.2.

33. Austen originally inserted "old k" above her line. Since she uses the phrase "old king" in the next sentence, "k" probably stands for "king."

34. Ross reads this word as "nicket"—that is, "nicked" in modernized form. *Katherine Austen's Book M*, 57. However, "tuchet"—or "touched"—is more likely.

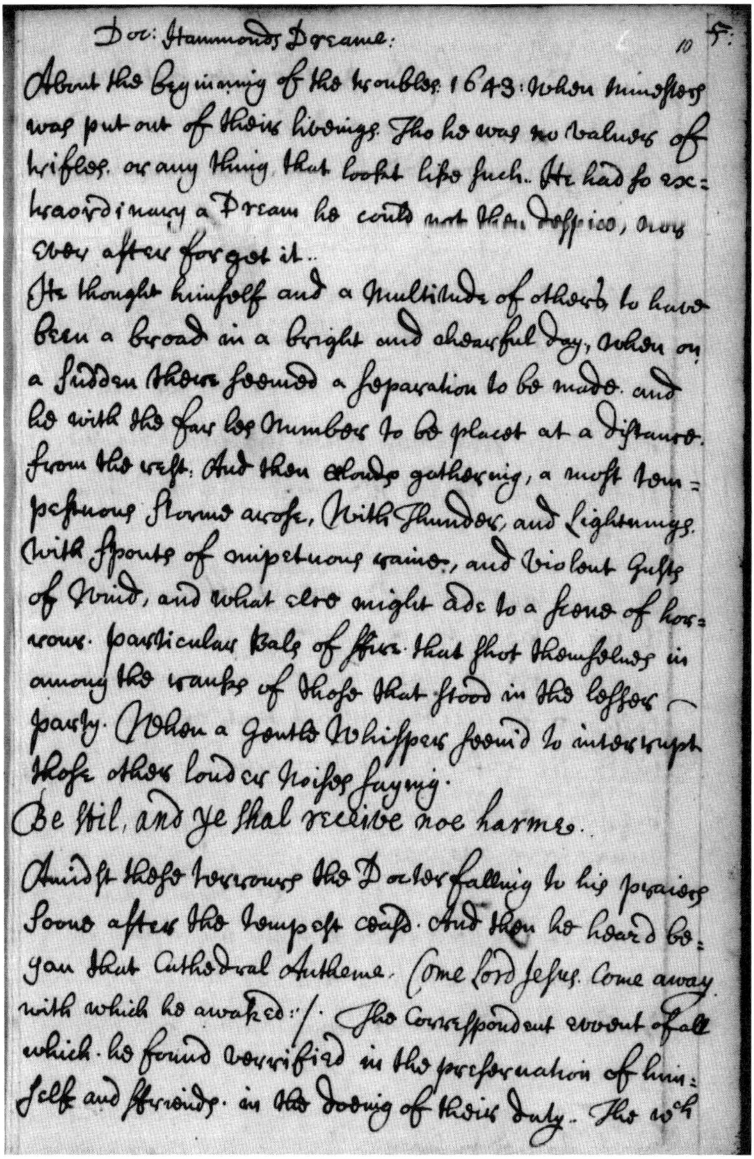

Figure 4. Folio 10r. Beginning of Austen's essay, "Dr. Hammond's Dream." © The British Library Board. Add. MS 4454.

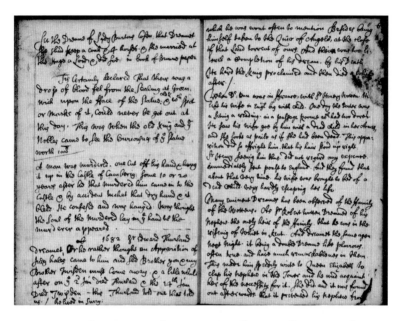

Figure 5. Folios 10v-11r. "Dr. Hammond's Dream" continued top
right page of *Book M*; writings on similar themes added on left page.
© The British Library Board. Add. 4454.

1682, Sir Edward Thurland[35] *dreamed, or he rather thought, an apparition of Judge Hale*[36] *came to him and said, "Brother, you and my Brother Twisden*[37] *must come away." And a little while after, on the 2d January died Thurland, and the 14th January died Twisden. This Thurland told one that told us. He lived in Surrey.*}

[38]he was wont often to mention. Besides being himself taken to the choir of angels at the close of that land torrent of ours, and then[39] was too literal a completion of his dream by his death. He heard the king proclaimed[40] and then died a while after.

When Dr. Donne[41] was in France with Sir Henry Wotton,[42] he left his wife in England big with child. One day the doctor was a sitting a reading in a passage room, which had two doors. He saw his wife go by him with a dead child in her arms, and she looked as pale as if she had been dead. This apparition did so affright him that his hair stood upright. Sir Henry, seeing him thus, did not regard any expense, immediately sent post to England, and they found that about that very

---

35. Edward Thurland was one of several legal investigators of the misappropriation of Highbury. Ross, *Book M, Perdita Manuscripts*, MS item no. 9.2.4.

36. Sir Mathew Hale (1609–1676), judge and writer (*ODNB*).

37. Sir Thomas Twisden (1602–1683), first baronet, judge, and politician (*ODNB*). Ross notes that Austen reverses Twisden's and Thurland's dates of death. *Katherine Austen's Book M*, 59n41.

38. Austen continues writing about Dr. Hammond's dream on a new recto page (see Figure 5).

39. Ross reads "then" as "their"—or "there" in modernized form. *Katherine Austen's Book M*, 59.

40. In 1660, the English monarchy was restored: Charles Stuart, son of the beheaded King Charles I, was invited to return to England from abroad and was officially recognized as King Charles II. Austen's dramatic, sympathetic portrait of Hammond points to her own royalism.

41. John Donne (1572–1631), poet and Church of England clergyman (*ODNB*). Austen certainly read Donne's sermons and probably his poetry too.

42. Sir Henry Wotton (1568–1639), diplomat and writer, lifelong friend of Donne (*ODNB*).

time, his wife was brought to bed of a dead child very hardly escaping her life.[43]

Many eminent dreams have been observed of the family of the Wottons, as Sir Robert Wotton dreamed of his nephew, the only heir of the family, that he was in the rising of Wyatt in Kent,[44] and dreamed the same again next night—it being a double dream, like Pharaoh's,[45] often true and have much remarkableness in them. This made him speedily write to Queen Elizabeth to clap his nephew in the Tower, and he would acquaint her of the necessity for it. She did, and it was found out afterwards that it prevented his nephew from taking arms with him, which, he professed, his intention was to join with him.

Another dream found out the thieves who robbed Eton College by his sending a letter to the college to know whether the college was not robbed by such parties, which they could not discover but by the intimation in the dream.

Henry, a German prince,[46] was admonished by revelation to search for a writing in an old wall which should nearly concern him. He did and found nothing but two words, "post sex": that is, "after six," whereupon he conceived his death was foretold to be within six days.

---

43. John Donne's dream appears in Izaak Walton's *Lives of Dr John Donne, Sir Henry Wotton, Mr Richard Hooker, Mr George Herbert* (London, 1675), but Todd suggests that Austen's reference predates Walton's published account. Todd explains that one of Austen's properties was "a house on Chancery Lane, tenanted recently by her father-in-law's friend, Izaak Walton" and notes that "Donne was rector of St. Dunstan's at the foot of Chancery Lane." "Property and a Woman's Place," 185, 197n39. Ross suggests that Austen's "sources are either manuscript or oral." *Katherine Austen's Book M*, 59n43.

44. Austen relates a story that also appears in Walton's *Life of Sir Henry Wotton* published in *Reliquae Wottonianae* by Sir Henry Wotton (London, 1651), but she misrepresents some details: Walton dates the dream from 1553, ascribes it to Nicholas Walton, and specifies that the queen in question is Queen Mary—the Catholic half-sister of Elizabeth I. Ross suggests that here, too, Austen's "source was manuscript or oral." *Katherine Austen's Book M*, 60n44.

45. In Gen. 41:1–57, Joseph successfully interprets Pharaoh's dreams. Austen refers specifically to Gen. 41:32: "And for that the dream was doubled unto Pharaoh twice; it is because the thing is established by God, and God will shortly bring it to pass."

46. Ross identifies the prince in question as Henry II, Holy Roman Emperor (973–1024). *Katherine Austen's Book M*, 60n50.

So he piously attended 6 days, 6 weeks, 6 months, 6 years, and on the first day of the 7th year, he was chosen Emperor of Germany.

I had no fore admonishment to look for the jewel I found.[47] Yet I found it out of an old wall, though by mere accident. What it may certainly import to me, I cannot surely determine. Yet sure I think it nearly concerns me. I wish I may as piously attend a circumspection of my days as this happy person in the story. 1662.

Story in Bishop Hall[48] of the writing of Laud[49] found out by a dream.

Of the emperor who, when he was a common soldier, was told by a cunning woman, when he killed the boar, should be emperor. He fell a hunting the boar, but as soon as he killed a great

[50]{*Lady Diana Holland*[51] *dreamed a while after the death of her mother, the Countess of Holland, that she was discoursing with her in the vault where she was interred.*

"Madame, why are you gone so far before? You are so far before I can't overtake and come near you."

"No, Di,"[52] *(said she), "You will quickly come after. Only your two sisters, Susan and Isabel, must come first. You have but two steps to come."*

It so came to pass her two sisters died first and then she two years after. After[53] *she had dined, she was took with an extreme shaking*

47. Austen believes the jewel she found has providential significance. It thus becomes the subject of later meditations and a poem celebrating its divine status. She considers it important enough to leave to her first son, Thomas, as part of his inheritance.

48. Joseph Hall (1574–1656), Bishop of Norwich (*ODNB*).

49. William Laud (1573–1645), Archbishop of Canterbury (*ODNB*).

50. Austen added the material represented by italicized paragraphs in brackets on the verso folio facing her entries concerning classical oracles and prophecies.

51. Possibly the daughter of Henry Rich, First Earl of Holland (bap. 1590, d. 1649), and Isabel Cope (*ODNB*).

52. Austen has the countess refer to Diana as "Die," but for the sake of consistent modernization, I have used the contemporary spelling "Di." In the context of this prophecy of death, Austen might have been suggesting that Diana's very name—"Die"—foreshadows her demise.

53. Austen crossed out "And" and started her new sentence with "After."

and cold, a week after that died of smallpox. She was discoursing of her dream at dinner and was then well.

About 1663, an apothecary at Westminster dreamed that he knocked at his wife's grave and had no answer (none came).[54] *He knocked a second time. His wife came, who was dead. She said to him, "Will, make room, and lie close, for your father is a coming." (A son that had been dead also.)*[55]
So a quarter of a year after, the apothecary had a fit of sickness and expected death. He recovered—that being the first knock without answer. He had a second fit of sickness a while after, and then he died, it being a summons to him indeed.[56]}

[57]person in hatred among the people whose name was the Boar, he was chosen Roman Emperor.[58] See:

The fathers observe of the Sibyls[59] and other oracles that they were possessed with such shakings and transports as bereaved them of their reason. But divine inspirations and oracles preserve the harmony of the soul.

The extraordinary manifestations of God to any are commonly very short, as we see in the scriptures, either external or internal: ex-

---

54. Austen appears to have first written "and had no answer." However, she then added, above the line, "(noen came)" and inserted parentheses around "answer." I have deleted the parentheses around "answer" and corrected Austen's transposed letters in "none." Ross reads "noen" as "no on," as in "no one." *Katherine Austen's Book M*, 61.

55. The dead wife addresses a son named Will, who is also dead. She tells her son to make room for his father (the husband who is listening), who will soon join his family in death.

56. Austen spells "indeed" as "endead," which, in a morbid pun, reinscribes the apothecary's fate. This pun seems all the more likely given that she sometimes spells "indeed" as we do today; see, for example, 30r in her manuscript.

57. Austen continues the story about the prophecy of the boar at the top of a new recto page.

58. Austen wrote "to" and "the" before "Roman Emperor" but crossed them out.

59. "Certain women of antiquity who were reputed to possess powers of prophecy and divination" (*OED*). Ross notes that Austen paraphrases from John Gauden, Jeremy Taylor, and John Donne in the following paragraphs. *Katherine Austen's Book M*, 62n55.

ternal of Elijah's transfiguration,[60] it was in a moment; or internal, by audible and articular expressions to Samuel, David, to Solomon, etc.[61] Oftentimes, it is hardly discernible but by the gracious effects on our spirits, as St. Peter's deliverance out of prison assured him of the truth of that vision that God had sent his angel and delivered him.[62]

God is not prodigal of these special favors, but for some great designs are they indulged, as I have been assured of some in great darkness of soul have had such visions of light as both cleared and cheered them ever after.

Dr. Gauden[63] was credibly informed that 20 years past, a very mild and worthy minister (Mr. Lancaster) that there was heard by him and all that stood by him so loud and sweet a consort of music for about half an hour before he died, that the good man owned it as a signal token of God's indulgence to him, thus to send for him, and with the close of which harmony, he gave up the ghost.

Dr. Brownrigg[64] told this story: that a Dutch minister, who was a most plain-hearted religious man, who coming from Ireland to England was cast upon the sea by a storm and floated two hours on the waves, despairing of life and half dead, lying on his back and

60. Elijah, an ecstatic prophet of the Old Testament, is miraculously taken to heaven by a whirlwind (2 Kings 2:1–12). The passage refers especially to 2 Kings 2:11: "And it came to pass, as they still went on, and talked, that, behold, there appeared a chariot of fire, and horses of fire, and parted them both [Elijah and Elisha] asunder; and Elijah went up by a whirlwind into heaven."

61. David, an Old Testament musician, poet, and king (see esp. 1 and 2 Sam.), is traditionally considered the author of Psalms and was a favorite point of reference (and personal identification) for many radical sectarian prophets of the English civil wars. Austen refers to David frequently in *Book M* and occasionally appears to identify with him as a figure associated with poetry, prophecy, and divine favor. Solomon, the son of David and Bathsheba, is also an Old Testament king (see esp. 1 Kings); he is traditionally associated with Ecclesiastes, Proverbs, and the Song of Songs and viewed as a figure of wisdom.

62. Peter, one of the earliest disciples of Jesus in the New Testament, is imprisoned by Herod but freed by an angel (Acts 12:1–19). The passage refers specifically to Acts 12:11: "And when Peter was come to himself, he said, Now I know of a surety, that the Lord hath sent his angel, and hath delivered me out of the hand of Herod, and from all the expectation of the people of the Jews."

63. John Gauden (1599/1600?–1662), Bishop of Worcester (*ODNB*).

64. Ralph Brownrigg (1592–1659), Bishop of Exeter (*ODNB*).

tossed at the pleasure of every wave, a vessel came by him under sail and took him up. Which when they were recovering and relieving him with dry clothes, upon the back of this man's coat was seen a print most perfectly of a man's hand, which by being dry and the rest of his clothes wet, was plainly seen by them all.

If any had told Socrates[65] that he saw a divine vision, he presently esteemed him vain and proud. But if he pretended only to have heard a voice or a word, he listened to that very religiously and inquired with curiosity. There was some reason in his fancy because God does not communicate himself to the eye to men but by the ear. "You saw no figure, but you heard a voice," said Moses to the people.[66] Now what a man pretends he has heard, we can inquire if it agree to God's word.

One rule in discerning and judging a miracle or of a revelation is to consider whether it be done in confirmation of a necessary truth. Otherwise, it may be suspected a delusion.

Was not one of my dreams the presagement[67] of blessing to the nation, as the dream of a poor stranger did confirm Gideon to go on with the more confidence to his victory?[68]

We are generally to receive our instructions from God's word, and where those means are duly exhibited in his church, we are to rest as being sufficient to instruct us without revelation. Yet we are not to conclude God in his Law as that he should have no prerogative, nor so to bind him up in his ordinances as that he never can or never does work by an extraordinary way of revelation.

65. Greek philosopher of classical antiquity.

66. Moses, a hero and prophet of the Old Testament, is called by the voice of God to lead his people out of bondage in Egypt towards the promised land of Canaan and receives the Ten Commandments from God on Mount Sinai (see esp. Exod. 20:1–17).

67. "A sign or indication of the future; an omen, a portent, a foreshadowing" (*OED*).

68. See Judg. 7:13–15; the passage refers especially to Judg. 7:15: "And it was so, when Gideon heard the telling of the dream, and the interpretation thereof, that he worshipped, and returned into the host of Israel, and said, Arise; for the LORD hath delivered into your hand the host of Midian."

Elisha begged a portion of Elijah's spirit, of his example and graces.[69] Give, Lord, thy servant to follow all good examples and all my life to have my dear friend's[70] upright and sincere inclinations and with Elisha to have a double portion of his spirit. But, Lord, that spirit is not enough. Elijah was subject to passions, subject to be too soon a weary of his race he was to finish. Give me, Lord, thy holy spirit I may with more courage and constancy, with less dejection and melancholy, steer on my course of life and not be a weary as Elijah, who was prone to fall into weariness of life.

Yet, when Elijah was in his distress in the wilderness, then was it God's time to show miraculous marks of his favor and frequently to send his angels to him; neither must he die an ordinary death.

Text: God, who at sundry times and in diverse manners spoke in times past to the fathers by the prophets, hath in these last days spoken to us by his son.[71]

Had God continued to us persons of infallible gifts and of extraordinary spirits, as heretofore the prophets and apostles were of, it had been a means to take us off from studying and searching the scriptures. Now God hath left us to hear what his son speaks, and we are to know the mind of God out of his word, which he hath spoken.

In the Church's infancy under the Law, the saints needed such dispensations of revelations and visions, and it was granted. But now they are in a better capacity of finding out the mind of God by industry and labor in the ordinary use of the scriptures.

Therefore, keep to the word of God, and that will keep you from delusions.

---

69. Elisha, an Old Testament prophet, is the disciple and successor of Elijah. Elisha accompanies Elijah before the latter is miraculously transported to heaven by a whirlwind (see note 60 above): "And it came to pass, when they were gone over, that Elijah said to Elisha, Ask what I shall do for thee, before I be taken away from thee. And Elisha said, I pray thee, let a double portion of thy spirit be upon me" (2 Kings 2:9).

70. Probably a reference to her dead husband, Thomas.

71. Cf. Heb. 1:1–2: "God, who at sundry times and in divers manners spake in time past unto the fathers by the prophets, Hath in these last days spoken unto us by his Son, whom he hath appointed heir of all things, by whom also he made the worlds."

And in things concerning sense and reason, reason and sense will be your guide that you do not err. Now if you neglect the study of the scriptures, expecting and seeking revelations extraordinary of the spirit, you are beside your business. For the spirit will never that way lead you into all truth.

The spirit teaches us by sanctifying us through the truth: "Sanctify them through thy truth: thy word is truth."[72] Thus while the spirit sanctifies us through truth, it begets in us a belief that it is the truth of God.

It was the mystery hid from ages and revealed to us, and all that we have to learn and inquire is from the son, to study what he hath taught and manifested to us.

Sermon: Dr. Featley's
"Whom have I in heaven but thee?"[73]

If we inquire the disposition of a man and what a man is, it is by knowing what he loves.

So a man may have faith and hope. But if not charity, he is never the near.

He may believe the truth and be a false man.

He may hope for good things and yet be bad himself.

But he cannot love the best things, but he must needs be good. He cannot affect grace, if he have not received some measures of it. He cannot highly esteem of God and not be high in God's esteem.

Our trust is that we shall not always walk by faith, and our hope is that we shall one day hope no more. We believe the end of faith, and we hope for the end of hope but love no end of our love but that it may be infinite.

"Whom have I in heaven?" Consider.

---

72. Austen quotes John 17:17 verbatim.

73. Ross identifies this entry as summarizing, in large part, Daniel Featley's 1613 sermon on Psalm 73:25, "Whom Have I in Heaven but Thee," in *Clavis Mystica*. *Katherine Austen's Book M*, 65n71.

All things under the sun are vanity.[74] Therefore, the verity of all things is above the sun, there where we shall go. Indeed, here we cannot reap the thousandth part we shall be partakers of. Here we have but a taste of the Tree of Life, a confused noise of the heavenly music, a glimpse of the sun of righteousness. Yet here the soul is refreshed and ravished with these glances more than a constant gale of prosperous fortune.

The world is no rooting place for a solid contentment. Who can aim steadily at a vanishing shadow or rest upon the wings of the wind? Such is the comforts of this life, which are emptiness itself. Therefore, "whom have I in heaven but thee?"

This speaks to our faith that it be resolved on God only. For true faith says, "Whom have I in heaven but thee to rely on?"

And speaks to our devotion that it be directed to God only. True religion says, "Whom have I in heaven but thee to call on?"

And speaks to our love that it be fixed on God only. True love says, "Whom have I in heaven or in earth but thee to settle upon?"

No papist[75] can bear a part with David—"whom have I in heaven"—in this song. For they have many there to whom they address their prayers: to saints and angels, as one for their diseases and another saint for childbirth and others for several their wants.

Doubtless, these monopolies was not granted to saints in David's time, nor the fathers had not any knowledge of these new masters of request in heaven.

We must know that invocation is the highest branch of divine worship.

Papists say we may pray to saints because we call upon the living to pray for us, and the saints departed are nearer to God, and if be no wrong to Christ's intercession to desire the prayers of our friends in this life, so it cannot be any derogation to his mediatorship to call on saints deceased. Bellarmine[76] brags that the heretics were never able to untie this argument. I believe him because there is no knot at all in

---

74. Cf. Eccles. 1:14: "I have seen all the works that are done under the sun; and behold, all is vanity and vexation of spirit."

75. A derogatory term for Roman Catholics.

76. Robert Bellarmine (1542–1621), Italian Jesuit cardinal and controversialist. "Bellarmine, Robert, St," *The Concise Oxford Dictionary of World Religions*, ed. John Bowker, Oxford

it. For to our friends, we desire them to commend us to God in their prayers, and a duty of Christian charity it is. But to pray to any saint, there's no precedent in scripture from the first of Genesis to the last of Revelations.

When we are come to the love of God, it will ravish us to seek God and to seek his face evermore and whom to desire is the fullest contentment and to enjoy everlasting happiness. For in God is all. If we thirst for grace to help us in our time of need, he is so full of grace that of his fullness, we all receive. For glory, he is the king of glory. For wisdom, in him are all the treasures of wisdom. For peace, he is the prince of peace. And for life, he is the well of life, and in his light, we shall see light.[77] For joy and pleasure in his presence is fullness of joy, and at his right hand, pleasure forever more.[78]

> That which is called "beauty" in us is "majesty" in God.
> "Life" with us is "immortality."
> "Strength" with us is "omnipotency."
> "Wealth" with us is "all sufficiency."
> "Delight" is "felicity."
> "Affection," "virtue"; "virtue," "Nature." And Nature all things:
> "for of him and through him and in him are all things."[79]

[80]{*Book L, p. 75*}

University Press, *Oxford Reference Online*. http://www.oxfordreference.com/ (accessed June 2012).

77. Cf. Psalm 36:9.

78. Cf. Psalm 16:11.

79. The passage quotes from Rom. 11:36: "For of him, and through him, and to him, are all things: to whom be glory for ever. Amen."

80. Austen included this cross-reference to another book on the verso page facing her account of her "Observation on My Dream of Monition," which starts at the top of the recto page. *Book L* might refer to Austen's writings chronologically preceding *Book M* or to a book on other themes or topics of interest to her.

Observation on My Dream of Monition[81]

Certainly, I may have an expectation, a dependence of something extraordinary to befall me at the period of that time, when I find stories from monitions and notices given to some persons years before it came to pass. Yet I have hardly heard of anything with so much plainness and certainty as what I have received. And yet in this certainty, I have found a contradiction. that "I shall not die but live and declare the works of the Lord."[82] As if that was the meaning, after the being exercised with diverse trials and afflictions, that I should continue to declare the works and manifestations of his goodness, which hath been in eminent preservations and most bountiful blessings and prosperous success of my endeavors; in the midst of infinite obstacles and plunges, often I was encompassed.

And if it be the will of heaven to enlarge my days as once to Hezekiah was known,[83] I beg of his Majesty a thankful heart to declare and tell the manifestations of his love to me, what he hath done for me, what great favor[84] showed to me a private, to me a particular person. Thou hast showed thy wonders to me, as well as to David, as well as to kings. Thy infinite goodness is my defense and protection, day by day, and surely if thy eye had not been over me, it had been impossible I should have sustained my oppositions. But I have seen the miracles of the kindness of my God to me, and though he leaves his children destitute, he does not deprive them of his gracious help nor of the safeguard of angels.

Not unto me, O God, not unto my weak help but to the arm of the Lord proceeds my daily succor and my help in time of trouble, that near help, which, though it be invisible to me and sometimes cannot apprehend, I have such aids as indeed I find.

---

81. "A (usually non-verbal) warning, sign, or intimation of the presence or imminence of something ... an omen" (*OED*).

82. Psalm 118:17.

83. Hezekiah, an Old Testament king, prays to God when he is ill and dying, and God extends his life (2 Kings 20:1–21).

84. Austen wrote a word with "b" as its first letter (possibly "bounty") and then revised that word by writing over letters to change them into "favor."

When I have little business to do, I praise God for giving me respite. When I have a great deal, I praise God for giving me strength and assistance, and I beseech him to bless me in what I am to do. The world may think I tread upon roses, but they know not the sackcloth I have walked on, not the heaviness and bitterness of my mind. Yet my God hath sweetened those bitternesses, else the gall would have been impossible to take.

[85]{*Sir, if you had been a gentleman, as you pretend to, you would have had civiler words in your mouth. I do*[86] *not deserve that odious, immodest character your rudeness was pleased to give me. Besides, I should be unwilling to call a woman of fourscore "old." "Ancient" is honorable; "old" is despicable. "Old" belongs to old shoes, old clothes—not to myself. For indeed, when I am come to the longest date and age in this world, I hope then to be as young as when I first came in it, shall be entered into a new spring, not to come within the compass of any change or decay more.*

Surely I have not deserved in my conversation among men his most abusive and scandalous speech. I ride in my coach, while I dare to let the way be so bad for them to walk. "Old goat." The rudest speech, not proceeding from a gentleman, as he pretends, but from a hind,[87] *a soughter.*[88]

I wish him no more punishment than to have such a shoe for him to cleanse, which it was not possible to prevent the dirt lying sometime

---

85. Austen added this angry response to a man who insulted her on the verso page facing her continued religious meditation on the recto page. Todd notes the practical and symbolic importance of Austen's coach: the vehicle not only transported her to the physical sites in London where she conducted her legal and economic business, but her use of it was also meant to signal gentle status. "Property and a Woman's Place," 184–85. Todd speculates that the unnamed man who insults Austen is her neighbor, Mr. Cruse, whom Austen lent money; the widow later recounts with outrage his mocking refusal to repay her (190).

86. Austen wrote "have," crossed it out, and added "do" instead.

87. "A servant; esp., in later use, a farm servant, an agricultural laborer" (*OED*).

88. "Soughter" is not defined in the *OED*; however, a "sough" can be "a drain, a sewer, a trench" (*OED*). Austen thus possibly uses "soughter" to refer to a laborer who digs drains, sewers, and so on. She uses "hind" to belittle the gentleman's professed rank, and she clearly means "soughter" to add insult.

until could be took away, which was carried away in carts nothing but water laded in.}

[89]Still look what God Almighty does for thee, and then thou wilt not regard what men does against thee. And see in this time of loneliness what a pretty, cheerful companion I have that knows not anything of the clouds and damps of melancholy: that God's gracious goodness allows[90] me my little daughter.[91]

I can't[92] but recite to myself my former sweetness of life: how I had one[93] that rendered me all the love and all the affection a person could possibly oblige his friend with. And God was pleased to give a conclusion of it. Yet, instead I have the favor and love of my most merciful God, and I cannot but persuade myself I have still influence by his desires for my perfection from him who bore me that regard when he was on earth. Nay, I cannot tell but that his love to his relative may not be of a far more excellent nature and effect to me than before. It is problematical; therefore, I dare not be too presumptuous in the belief, though some providences and marks have gave me some demonstrations. However, I am assured the blessing of heaven is more than ever was[94] in my prosperous condition, and this is the true sanctuary of refuge and rest. See page 85.[95]

Example of Joseph to His Brethren Not to Revenge

It was a lasting remembrance—the dread which Joseph's brethren was in—as after the death of Jacob, they were afraid he would retribute their cruelty showed him, as with all submission did acknowledge it and beg his favor. Joseph returned acts of love and tenderness to them and still told them their unkind act was to bring about God's abundant

---

89. Austen continues her religious meditation at the top of the recto page.

90. Austen wrote "appoints" but marked it out and added "allows."

91. Her daughter, Anne.

92. Austen traced new letters over old ones to rewrite the word as "can't."

93. Her late husband, Thomas.

94. Austen used a caret to insert "was."

95. Austen's original pagination.

mercy to be a help to them and to preserve them from famine and poverty.[96]

See what grace and a spirit sanctified and trained up in the road and observation of providence will do?

That which the world terms "greatness of spirit" cannot do this. That will prosecute revenge and wait for occasion to return evil actions with far worse, if a power can do it.

Learn in all the affronts you receive and unkindnesses meet with to have Joseph's temper to render kindness and love in the blows of injury. In the contumelies of men, be really ready to show favor and to do good.

The history of Joseph is full of remark to view it, as we cannot but conclude the ways which God's providence takes is[97] full of greatness and glory and by contrary way performeth his purpose. How many ways was poor Joseph distressed with? That there was little semblance of the performance of his dreams unless by contraries.[98] By contraries, it was a long time fulfilled. Instead of honor, he found derision, contempt, and danger and little hope of rising when he was near a cruel death. Then was his chastity assaulted and instead of honor brought to a prison by a shameful manner, appearing to his disgrace.[99]

---

96. Joseph, the favorite son of the Old Testament patriarch Jacob, is hated by his jealous brothers, who steal his coat of many colors, throw him into a pit, and plot to kill him. He is sold into slavery but eventually rises to a position of power and wealth in Egypt. Upon encountering his brothers again years later, instead of seeking revenge, Joseph shows forgiveness and generosity by rescuing them and their families from famine. After Jacob dies, Joseph's brothers assume he will take vengeance upon them for their past cruelties to him, but he still forgives them (see esp. Gen. 37:3–36, 45:3–28, 50:15–26). The passage refers especially to Gen. 50:20–21, where Joseph tells his brothers that God has transformed their former evils into good: "But as for you, ye thought evil against me; but God meant it unto good, to bring to pass, as it is this day, to save much people alive. Now therefore fear ye not: I will nourish you and your little ones. And he comforted them, and spake kindly unto them."

97. Austen wrote "if," marked it out, and used a caret to insert "is."

98. Joseph has prophetic dreams indicating that he will one day have dominion over his brothers; these dreams, which he reveals to his family, exacerbate his brothers' hatred (Gen. 37:5–11).

99. When Joseph is enslaved, his master's wife attempts to seduce him; although Joseph resists her, his master puts him in prison when his wife lies about what happened (Gen. 39:7–20).

Of the Fear of God[100]

No man is more miserable than he that fears God as an enemy. Then duty is intolerable, and therefore, of all the evils of the mind, fear is the worst and most intolerable. Anger is valiant; desire is busy and apt to hope; and credulity is entertained with appearances of success.

But fear is dull and sluggish, miserable and foolish. And from hence proceeds observation of signs and of unlucky days and *erra pater*.[101] If men do listen to whispers of fear and have not reason and observation enough to confute trifles, they shall be affrighted with the noise of birds and the night raven, and every old woman shall be a prophetess, and the events of our affairs—which should be managed by[102] the conduct of counsel, of reason, and religion—shall by these vain observations succeed by chance, by ominous birds, by the falling of the salt, or the decay of reason, of wisdom, and the just religion of a man.

And to these trifling superstitions may be reduced observations of dreams, on unsecure expectation of evils that never shall happen.

Dreams are without rule and without reason. They proceed very much from the temper of the body and trouble of the mind—though sometimes from some demon, good or bad.

The dreaming of teeth, they say, import the loss of a friend; though rather, it tells of the scurvy growing, and diverse things may point at diseases because the body being out of frame, the fancy may be vexed into a representation of it. Now if the events of our dreams do answer in one instance, we become credulous in twenty, and so we discourse ourselves into folly and weak observation and give the devil power over us in those circumstances we can least resist him.

---

100. Ross notes that Austen begins to paraphrase a sermon by Jeremy Taylor here. *Katherine Austen's Book M*, 70n96.

101. Probably a reference to a kind of almanac. Austen might be imitating the kind of scorn Joseph Hall displays towards such writings in sketching the character of "The Superstitious" in his *Characters of Vertues and Vices* (London: Printed by Melch. Bradwood for Eleazar Edgar and Samuel Macham, 1608), 89.

102. Austen wrote "by Reason," marked out "Reason," and added "the conduct of counsel."

Let the grounds of our actions be noble—beginning from reason and prudence and measured from the expectation of usual providence—and proceed from causes to effects.

Let us fear God when we have made him angry and not be afraid of him when we heartily and laboriously do our duty.

The 3 great actions of religion are to worship God, to fear God, to trust in him. Now the inordination of all these turns to superstition, the obliquity[103] of trust, the errors of worship, the excess of fear. God's word must examine all.

First, fear is a duty we owe to God, as being the God of power and justice, the judge of heaven and earth, the avenger of all injustice and oppression, a mighty God and terrible, and a severe hater of sin.

Now fear is the girdle[104] of the soul, the handmaid to repentance, the arrest of sin. It is the bridle to vice and making the soul to pass from trembling to caution and watchfulness, and by the gates of repentance, leads the soul to love and to the joys in God.

And fear is the instrument to religion and the only security of the less perfect persons, and God sends often to demand it by threatenings and afflictions and troubles upon us.

But this so excellent grace is soon abused in the tender spirits by infelicities or a sad spirit, and the devil often takes advantage to turn fearful natures to timorousness and scruple to sadness and suspicion of God. And thus he runs towards heaven, as he thinks, but he chooses foolish paths and takes anything as he is told or fancies. But fear, when it is inordinate, is never a good counselor nor makes a good friend.

And he that fears God as an enemy is the most miserable and completely sad person in the world. For there be some such perpetual tormentors of themselves with unnecessary fears that their meat and drink and all their actions are a snare to them, and every temptation—though resisted—makes them cry for pardon. These persons do not believe noble things concerning God, nor thinks how God delights in mercy. Such are either hugely tempted or hugely ignorant.

---

103. "Divergence from right conduct or thought; perversity, aberration; an instance of this, a fault, an error" (*OED*).

104. "That which confines or binds in; a restraint, limit" (*OED*).

Now he that is afraid of God cannot love him at all, and whom men fear, they hate certainly and flatter readily, and therefore, though the atheist says, "there is no God," the scrupulous, fearful, and superstitious man does wish there was none.

It is true in the Law: God used his people as servants and enjoined many hard things intricate and painful and

[105] [*Book Ar^X Soo p. 135 in Miracles of Divine Mercy.*]

[106]expensive. In the gospel, he hath made us sons and gave commandments not hard but full of pleasure and also for profit to our comfortable well-being and how many blessed promises in the gospel and few threatenings.

So that in the Law, they feared God as a severe Lord, dreadful unto death in threatenings. This the Apostle calls "the spirit of bondage."[107] But we have received the spirit of adoption and a filial fear, and our judge is our advocate, and our brother is our Lord.

Godly fear is ever without despair.

And to those who raise doctrinal fears concerning God, which if they were true, the greatest part of mankind would be tempted to think they have no reason to love God, as to say the greatest part are decreed to be damned. And they speak no good things concerning his name who say God commands us laws impossible, that think he will condemn whole nations for different opinions.[X108] We must remember God's mercies are over all his works, and he shows mercy to all his creatures that need it, and God delights to have his mercy magnified in all things and by all persons and at all times. And therefore, as he that would accuse God of injustice were a blasphemer, so he that sus-

---

105. Austen inserts this cross-reference on the otherwise blank verso facing a new recto at the top of which she continues her religious meditation on the fear of God.

106. Austen continues her meditation on the fear of God at the top of a new recto.

107. Cf. the words of Paul, to whom Austen refers as "the Apostle," in Rom. 8:15: "For ye have not received the spirit of bondage again to fear; but ye have received the Spirit of adoption, whereby we cry, Abba, Father."

108. Austen appears to have inserted this superscript "X" to indicate that this is the material to which her cross-reference to *Book A* on the facing verso page refers.

pects his mercy dishonors God as much and brings upon himself that fear which is the parent of trouble but no instrument of duty.

We must heighten our apprehensions of the divine power and his justice so it pass no further but to make us reverent and obedient. But that fear is unreasonable, servile, and unchristian that ends in scruple and incredulity and desperation.

Its proper bounds are humble and devout prayers, a holy piety, and glorifications of God. We must be full of confidences towards God, and with cheerfulness, rely on his goodness for the issue of our final interest.

For the presumptuous, let them know there is cause of fear because to the most holy and confident, his way is narrow and dangerous and full of pitfalls. We are tempted and do tempt ourselves. Therefore, to him that standeth, take heed lest he fall.

And they may fear, whose repentance is not an entire change of life, who can never get the dominion of their vice. They may fear lest God be weary of giving more opportunities, since their understanding is right and their will a slave, their reason for God and the affections for sin. Of these our savior[109] speaks, "Many shall strive to enter in and shall not be able."[110]

Of Our Zeal and Duty to God[111]

No man is zealous as he ought, but he that delights in the service of God. Else when he prays, it is as children go to school or gives alms as they that pay contribution and meditate with the same willingness as young men die. The fire of zeal must never go out. It must shine like the stars; though sometimes covered with a cloud, yet they dwell forever in their orbs and go not out by day nor night and set not when kings die nor are extinguished when nations change their government.

---

109. Christ.

110. Cf. Luke 13:23–24: "Then said one unto him, Lord, are there few that be saved? And he said unto them, Strive to enter in at the strait gate: for many, I say unto you, will seek to enter in, and shall not be able."

111. Ross notes that Austen again paraphrases from a sermon by Taylor in this entry. *Katherine Austen's Book M*, 73n103.

So though a Christian's zeal and prayers be sometimes drawn back by importunity of business, by necessities, by compliances, yet still the fire is kept alive; it burns within, when the light breaks not forth.

> See Book C: What the fear of the Lord is, p. 121.
> I will teach you the fear of the Lord.[112]

Observations of the Last Judgment: Dr. Taylor[113]

Whereas the general sentence is given to all wicked persons, to all on the left hand, to go to everlasting fire, it is answered that the fire indeed is everlasting, but not all that enters into it is everlasting but only the devils for whom it was prepared and others more mighty criminals, as St. John in the Revelations[114] speaks particular who shall be tormented forever and ever. Also, "everlasting" signifies only to the end of its proper period appointed by God.

The blessedness of the saints is that they shall indeed be forever and ever in immortality.

Whether the wicked shall have immortality is questioned by the old doctors of the church.

It is certain that God's mercies are infinite, and it is also certain that the matter of eternal torments cannot truly be understood. And when the schoolmen go about to reconcile the divine justice to that severity and considers why God punishes eternally a temporal sin, they speak variously and uncertainly and unsatisfyingly.

But the generality of Christians have been taught to believe worse things. And it is strange to suppose an eternal torment to those to whom it was never threatened or ever heard of Christ, to those that

---

112. Austen borrows from Psalm 34:11: "Come, ye children, hearken unto me: I will teach you the fear of the LORD."

113. Jeremy Taylor (bap. 1613, d. 1667), Church of Ireland Bishop of Down and Connor (*ODNB*). Todd notes that Austen's religious "thought seems to show the same eclecticism that marks the author she cites most, Jeremy Taylor." "Property and a Woman's Place," 191. She again paraphrases from Taylor here (also see Ross, *Katherine Austen's Book M*, 74n106).

114. The biblical book of Revelation is traditionally ascribed to John, one of the apostles of the New Testament.

lived probably well, to heathens of good lives, to untaught people, to young men in their natural follies.

There are two days in which the fate of all the world is transacted. This life is man's day, in which man does what he please, and God holds his peace. Man destroys his brother and himself and governments and sins and drinks drunk and forgets his sorrow, and all this while, God is silent, save that he is loud with his holy precepts and that God overrules the event but leaves the desires of men to their own choice and their course of life such as they will choose. But then God shall have his day, too. The day of the Lord shall come, in which he shall speak in terror and no man answer.

In April 1666, a boy was playing at St. Andrew's Church, and there was only the clerk[115] and he. He heard a voice say, "Go away." He asked the clerk what he had with him. He said he did not speak to him. The clerk, as well as he, heard it again say, "Go away." They both were afraid, and by that time, another came into the church and heard it say a 3rd time, "Go away." So presently the boy went to clamber up where was a monument, and it fell down and dashed his brains out.

It was a hollow sound, the voice.

Though many dreams have come to pass, yet when persons by an over-curiosity have anticipated their desires to know their fortune, it seldom hath been a good success to them, but they had reason to repent.

It incited Henry the 4th's[116] preparation to the holy war because it was told him he should not die until he had heard mass in Jerusalem. But he was fain[117] to take his leave of the world before he expected it and died in the chamber called "Jerusalem" in Westminster.[118] We may

---

115. A clergyman.

116. Henry IV, also called Henry Bolingbroke (1367–1413), King of England, Lord of Ireland, Duke of Aquitaine (*ODNB*).

117. "Necessitated, obliged" (*OED*).

118. Cf. William Shakespeare, *2 Henry IV* in *The Norton Shakespeare* ed. Stephen Greenblatt, Walter Cohen, Jean E. Howard, and Katharine Eisaman Maus (New York: W.W. Norton & Company, 2008): 4.3.360–68. See Ross, introduction to *Katherine Austen's Book M*, 32.

conclude this prophesy to be begotten by the Devil, and if be stopped at one hole, he getteth out at another like a fox.

The like story of a pope who was told he should not die until he came to Jerusalem, which was a church in Rome at the entrance of which he was slain.[119] [See?][120]

And so the equivocating Devil cozened[121] the monk that he should not die until he should find him sleeping between sheets. The wary monk, abjuring all such lodging, at last by over watching in his study, the Devil took him napping with his nose betwixt the sheet-leaves of his conjuring book.[122]

Hell's alphabet[123] must be read backward. Let Satan give an account of his own cozenage,[124] which is to save his credit. He takes mystical expressions that—in case he should fail in his answers—lays the blame on men's understanding him. Thus, they who are correspondents with the Devil have need when they have received the text to borrow his comments, too.

But men had need take heed of curiosity to know things to come, which is one of the kernels of the forbidden fruit.

Some dreams are not to be slighted, as that young man who dreamed he should be slain by a lion, which, because that beast did never come in their country, he was laughing at it, while he was in the temple of the gods, and there, out of a confidence of this impossibility, he put his hand into the mouth of a lion figured for ornament; a serpent bit him; and he died.

---

119. Austen squeezed "at the entrance of which he was slain" in small letters between two lines.

120. This unclear word was added in the margin. If it is "see," which is likely, then perhaps Austen thought she could find an appropriate reference but never did.

121. "To deceive, dupe, beguile, impose upon" (*OED*).

122. Ross notes that Austen here repeats an anecdote from Act 1 of Richard Brome, *A Jovial Crew; or, The Merry Beggars* (London, 1652). *Katherine Austen's Book M*, 77n116.

123. Ross observes that Austen begins paraphrasing here from Thomas Fuller, *The Holy State and the Profane State* (London, 1663). *Katherine Austen's Book M*, 77n117.

124. "The practice or habit of cozening; cheating, deception, fraud; the fact of being cheated" (*OED*).

The Lady Margaret, Henry 7th's mother,[125] a most pious woman (as that age went) and was esteemed in goodness the next to the Virgin Mary[126] (by those who too much adored her), she used to say if the Christian princes would undertake a war against the Turks, she would be their laundress. This lady had a[127] dream gave her a prediction of part of her fortune. See End History: Henry 7, Lord Herbert.[128]

Socrates was of opinion that none who are beloved of the gods but have some revelation.

The story of a Templar[129] a burning at Bordeaux spying Pope Clement and Philip, King of France looking out at a window at his execution said, "Clement, thou cruel tyrant, and Philip, King of France, I summon you both to appear at the tribunal seat to give an account for your cruelty within a year and a day, where I shall answer for your rigorous dealing."[130] And within that time, both died.

---

125. Margaret Beaufort (1443–1509), Countess of Richmond and Derby; Henry VII (1457–1509), King of England and Lord of Ireland (*ODNB*).

126. Mother of Jesus.

127. Austen first wrote "some" but crossed it out and inserted "a."

128. For details about Austen's confusion of Francis Bacon's history of Henry VII with a history of Henry VIII by Lord Herbert of Cherbury, see Ross, *Katherine Austen's Book M*, 77n119.

129. "A member of a military and religious order consisting of knights (Knights Templars, Knights or Poor Soldiers of the Temple), chaplains, and men-at-arms, founded c1118, chiefly for the protection of the Holy Sepulchre and of Christian pilgrims visiting the Holy Land: so called from their occupation of a building on or contiguous to the site of the Temple of Solomon at Jerusalem. They were suppressed in 1312" (*OED*).

130. Bertrand de Got, Pope Clement V (1305–1314), and Philip IV, King of France (1285–1314), collaborated to suppress the Knights Templars: "Returned from the Holy Land, they [the Knights Templars] were now large-scale bankers and property owners, and rumours (now largely discounted) circulated about their heretical ideas, blasphemous rites, and immoral practices. Philip, who probably coveted their wealth, had all of the Templars in France arrested on 13 Oct. 1307." "Clement V," in *The Oxford Dictionary of Popes* by J. N. D. Kelly, *Oxford University Press*, Oxford Reference Online. http://www.oxfordreference.com/ (accessed June 2011).

See Book J, page 260: of dreams and of prophecies

Story of Mr. Chainy, Near Chatham

Mr. Chainy, a gentleman in Queen Elizabeth's time when she was at Tilbury, he spoke words of treason against her at the Spanish invasion.[131] He, hearing she would send for him, prepared his petition. So, she sent her pursuivant[132] to take him, he being a horseback while he was pursued and coming to the place called the Hope near Rochester. He plunged into the sea and went to the ship where the queen was and held up his petition and swum on horseback three times around her ship and flung his petition to her. This extraordinary attempt in the sea drew her to pardon him, and he went back through the sea. As soon as landed, took his sword and run his horse through. He was asked why he would kill so brave a horse that not one in a thousand could do the like. He said it should never save the life of a traitor again. About a year after, he was riding by that place where the bones of the dead horse lay; his horse started upon the place and flung him upon the very horse's head and broke his neck. Upon his tomb near Chatham is the picture in stone of a horse's head in memory of this remarkable ingratitude.

Of Hildegardis[133]

God first humbles and afflicts whom he intends to illuminate with more than ordinary grace, and though she had afflictions, God gave her wings and raised her mounted soul in revelations, and St. Bernard[134]

---

131. Elizabeth I (1533–1603), Queen of England and Ireland (*ODNB*). Austen refers to events associated with the Spanish Armanda's attempted invasion of England in 1588. Elizabeth visited her troops at camp in Tilbury, where she delivered a famous speech.

132. "A royal or state messenger, esp. one with the power to execute warrants; a warrant officer" (*OED*).

133. St. Hildegard von Bingen (1098–1179), abbess and visionary (*ODNB*). Ross notes that Austen summarizes Fuller's *The Holy State and the Profane State*. *Katherine Austen's Book M*, 79n126.

134. St. Bernard (1090–1153), Abbot of Clairvaux (*ODNB*).

and the pope allow those revelations to be authentic. She prophesied of the mendicant friars[135] and diverse sins of covetousness and of the coming of those vermin into the world who would rob secular princes of their prerogatives and many things concerning the abuse of the papal church. She was of the pope's conclave[136] and emperor's counsel, to whom they had recourse in difficulties. Yea, the greatest torches of the church lighted themselves at her candle, and patriarchs and bishops sent knots as passed their fingers for her to untie.

Hildegardis was for certain a gracious virgin, and God might perform some great wonders by her hand.

Book J, page 87. Here add this to Book C, 131, or Book F, page 79.

Surely my God is preparing for me halcyon[137] days, for days of trouble and molestation I have found from men, who considers not afflicted widows. They take advantage of them, who has little help, and gives frequent occasion of more disturbance. My God, if it be thy will to consign[138] me quiet and repose, if not in this life, I am sure in another, for thy promise hath assured it. In thee there is peace to be comforted, though in the world trouble, and if I must taste of every variety of trouble in almost every concernment and if my neighbors must dart envy and unkindness to me, circumventions and injuries, my God hath strengthened me to this day. Continue thy help in all my crosses, O God of help and father full of pity. Amen.

---

135. "A member of any of the Christian religious orders whose members originally lived solely on alms" (*OED*).

136. "Any private or close assembly, esp. of an ecclesiastical character" (*OED*).

137. "Calm, quiet, peaceful, undisturbed" (*OED*).

138. "To make over as a possession, to deliver formally or commit, *to* a state, fate, etc." (*OED*).

Psalm: When Dr. Hobson[139] Preached at Twickenham[140]

Methinks this text speaks much to me.
What wait I for? My hope's in thee.
Then why disquieted? Then why oppressed?
While in the living fountain be refreshed.

[X141]Wait on God's time for thy deliverance out of troubles, either in this life or by a freedom by death.

And learn in afflictions, if God vouchsafe[142] to visit me, to preserve me in my being, in my subsistence in him that I be not shaked, disinherited, divested of him. Though I be not instantly delivered, yet this is a refreshing, a consolation to sit under the shelter of the love of God. And if God do not presently deliver, know, O Satan, how long soever God defers my deliverance, I will not seek the false and miserable comforts of this world.

Consider afflictions are the exercise of wisdom, the nursery of virtue, the venturing for a crown and the gate of glory.[143]

Afflictions are (also) oftentimes the occasions of great temporal[144] advantages. We must not look on them as they sit down heavily upon us but as they serve some of God's ends and purposes. If a man could have opened one of the pages of the divine counsels and have

139. Possibly a reference to Paul Hobson (d. 1666), Particular Baptist preacher (*ODNB*). However, as Ross rightly observes, "his politics (a Baptist) would make this a little odd." *Book M, Perdita Manuscripts*, MS item no. 24.

140. Todd notes that Austen's jointure properties included "a house in Twickenham on the south-west outskirts of London near the home of her sister, Lady Mary Ashe." "Property and a Woman's Place," 185.

141. This superscript "X" marks the beginning of the passage to which Austen's note, similarly marked with an "X," on Dr. Taylor's text refers. See notes 151 and 153.

142. "To show a gracious readiness or willingness, to grant readily, to condescend or deign" (*OED*).

143. Ross notes that Austen begins to paraphrase a sermon by Taylor here. *Katherine Austen's Book M*, 80n134.

144. "Of or pertaining to time as the sphere of human life; terrestrial as opposed to heavenly; of men's present life as distinguished from a future existence; concerning or involving merely the material interests of this world; worldly, earthly" (*OED*).

seen the event of Joseph's being sold to the merchants, he might with much reason have dried up the young man's tears.

God esteems it one of his glories that he brings good out of evil. Bear that which God send patiently, for impatience

[145]{*Of Affliction's Benefit*

Great are the riches that are hidden in tribulation. Adversity is sent them by the bridegroom[146] *to prepare them for his wedding.*

Prosperity is often contagious, and unfortunate indulgence abandons us to contagious prosperity.

To a Captive

Fortune knew no better way to raise you than by this fall. You must bid adieu[147] *to the resentment which the loss of your friends cause. That such was the order of the world and disposition of affairs as little losses were to usher in great advantages.*}

[148]does but entangle us like the flattering[149] of a bird in a net. Therefore, consider when God cuts off my weak arm of flesh from my shoulders, it is to make me lean upon him and becomes my patron and my guide, my advocate and my defender. Nay, and he may, if he will observe wisely, shall find so many circumstances of ease and remission, so many designs of providence and comfort, that it often happens in the whole sum of affairs that a single loss is a double blessing.

---

145. Austen includes these entries on the verso page facing her continued meditation on how to receive God's afflictions.

146. "Said of Christ in his relation to the Church" (*OED*).

147. Goodbye.

148. Austen continues her meditation on afflictions at the top of the recto facing the verso containing "Of Affliction's Benefit" and "To a Captive."

149. "To float, flutter" (*OED*).

God,[150] the great governor of the world, orders it by the variety of changes and accidents, and very oftentimes we see that which was a misfortune in the particular, in the whole order of things becomes a blessing bigger than we hoped for.

Stand still, and see how it will be in the event of things. Let God speak his mind out, for it may be this sad beginning is but to bring in and to make thee entertain and understand the blessing.

When a vehement calamity lies long, I can plead out of God's precedents that this will not last. David was not ten years in banishment, but he enjoyed the kingdom forty. Queen Elizabeth was 5 years in affliction; then it did appear God had mercy for her.

God will, if he sees fit, recompense my hours of

[151]{X *These two last sides out of Dr. Taylor, of Precedents of God's way for our help.*

We are apt to believe the first part of the covenant, blessings and mercies, but not the second part which belongs to us, resignation and obedience.}

[152] sorrow with days of joy, my years of trouble with those of quiet and deliverance.

And though God strikes, it is lest I should not know him, and again his hand strokes me that I should not faint under his hand correcting me.[X153]

Have I been preserved in my troubles as that good man when blown upon the water at the mercy of every wave and yet defended? Have not I been so, too, sunk down into the sea of grief? I was not drowned then, for thy hand, O God, saved me. I was tossed from

---

150. Austen wrote "And," crossed it out, and replaced it with "God."

151. Austen adds these sentences to the verso page facing the recto that continues her meditation on receiving God's afflictions. She uses her superscript "X" to show that the similar Xs above and below (see notes 141 and 153) refer to this text. Austen draws upon Taylor in her entries on afflictions. Ross, *Katherine Austen's Book M*, 80–81n134–38).

152. Austen continues her meditation on afflictions at the top of the recto facing her added notes on the verso.

153. Austen adds a superscript "X" to indicate that her note similarly marked with an "X" on the facing verso page refers to it as the end point of her paraphrase of Taylor.

one wave to another by unkindness, by aspersions, and lo, all along, thy hand held me fast. Thus wast thou pleased to suffer me to be distressed, yet not forsaken by thee. Nay, I may say for these 6 years that are passed, I have never been off from the waters of peril, from one danger, one violence, one oppression, one desertment,[154] one cross or another. And still, O God, thou hast converted every allay,[155] every rebuke to see thy mercy in, to tell me thou hast not forsaken me. Thou, O God, wilt do a miracle rather than forsake thy children in their distress. Hast not thou summed up all thy promises in one? "I will never leave thee, nor forsake thee."[156] Friends and estate may, and thou wilt never. See Book A, 143.

9 November 1664: it pleased God to take away an honest servant, William Chandeler, who had dwelled in my house almost ten years. He served me faithfully. I trust he is gone to a better service, though he had some infirmities I hope Christ hath forgiven. A long faithful servant is a breach in a family. I beseech God to assist me in every alteration, in the scenes of this world.

He was buried 11 November, aged 38 years. Four nights before he died, I dreamed I saw him fall down dead before us,[157] and[158] I did see him die. Though when I waked, I hoped he would not die. And he coming down the night before he died and thought himself pretty well.

Death came upon him in the space of 3 hours, when before that, he thought he might do well. But after the minister had prayed with him and he settled what he had to his friends, he died all the way and was apprehensive of every decay. His cough left him. "No," says he, "I shall bid you good night. The Lord Jesus receive all your souls."

154. Desertion, abandonment.

155. "Admixture of something that detracts from or diminishes the value, the intrusion or presence of any impairing element" (*OED*).

156. Austen borrows from Heb. 13:5: "Let your conversation be without covetousness; and be content with such things as ye have: for he hath said, I will never leave thee, nor forsake thee."

157. Austen wrote something else first but tried to reshape her letters into "us."

158. Austen appears to have written "Tho" (for "though") and crossed it out before "And."

Then after, began to sweat. Now the work is done and 1/2 an hour after died, speaking to the last minute.[159]

Upon Paying for the Fall of Mr. Rich's House[160]

May I as readily receive losses with patience, as thy bounty with gladness. The Lord hath gave me above my expectation or desert. I must look for accidents, which can have no foresight of me to prevent.

Surely after all the crosses and disappointments of this world, at last I shall find rest, and that shall be turned into joy. [Eccles.?] 6, 28.[161] If the Lord takes away or accidents and impositions falls out extraordinary upon me, let me remember as before how I have received plentifully and unexpectedly, which is a help to bear the burthens my estate gives a necessity to at this time as etc. Well does a many disadvantages look upon me this year (and the subtle evading of Sir T. R.), the staking[162] down of the house, etc., in such a time when I have a great building to do. Thus it pleases God to appoint it. And yet I may look a little further, and there I shall see before a 12 month is out how many advantages, what plentiful additions will accrue by God's favor to us. Let future expectation balance these seeming and present inconveniences. Thou satisfy thyself; if I live, I shall have enough. If I die, if I had all the world and all the wishes and accomplishments of

159. Austen's writing becomes smaller, and she writes increasingly in the margins as she begins to run out of room while she tries to finish this entry at the bottom of a verso page. This suggests that she wrote this entry after completing the material on the facing recto on another topic.

160. As Todd observes, this meditation "involves a landlord's problem"; Mr. Rich is apparently one of Austen's tenants. "Property and a Woman's Place," 191.

161. Austen appears to have written "Ecc" after "joy." If so, this abbreviation could refer to Ecclesiastes, chapter 6, but there is no verse 28 in that chapter. The first lines of chapter 6, however, seem relevant to this entry: "There is an evil which I have seen under the sun, and it is common among men: A man to whom God hath given riches, wealth, and honour, so that he wanted nothing for his soul of all that he desireth, yet God giveth him not power to eat thereof, but a stranger eateth it: this is vanity, and it is an evil disease" (Eccles. 6:1–2).

162. Ross reads this word as "stabing." *Katherine Austen's Book M*, 83.

every desire, I shall not have cause to need any of those thirsts and vast [infinite?][163] ambition.

My God, I beseech thee, let not the troubles I meet with make me a weary of my race I am to go on, but strengthen thy {27 November 1664}[164] servant I may discharge my calling and do the work thou putst in my hand.

And Lord, sanctify the afflictions thou hast laid upon me. O Lord, sanctify all that thy hand hath seen good to exercise thy servant[165] with. And prepare me, Lord, by all thy scourges, by all thy providences for that great mercy and blessing thou art making ready and preparing for me, which thou art providing for thy great blessings in this world or for great and eternal glories in a better, [which?][166] is the surest.[167]

Lord, fit me for thy mercy. Lord, prepare me for thy labor and blessing. Lord, sanctify me for thyself and for the accomplishing thy gracious will in my salvation. And then come life or then come death, I am in the hand of God, and that hand of love will crown me. Amen.

Lord, if it be thy will, say it is enough to thy servant—my days and years of sighing—and enter not into judgment with thy servant, for before thee, no flesh can be found acceptable.[168]

My God, grant I may begin that triumphant duty to praise thee on earth, which shall be performed to all eternity by thy saints and angels.

163. Ross reads this word as "finet." *Katherine Austen's Book M*, 83. However, Austen seems to have dotted an "i" at the word's beginning (as in "ifinet"), and this better fits the context with "vast."

164. Austen's page breaks after the word "thy." At the top of the next verso, she inserts the date in brackets before continuing her sentence.

165. Austen first wrote something other than "servant," marked it out completely, and used a caret to insert "servant."

166. Austen wrote over her letters to reshape them into a new word, probably an abbreviation for "which."

167. After "surest," Austen wrote several words—more than half of a line across the page—and then marked them out completely.

168. Cf. Psalm 143:2: "And enter not into judgment with thy servant: for in thy sight shall no man living be justified."

Thy mercy of creation to me is great, but the blessing of preservation is greater. O, let me magnify and bless thy name for that great mercy and blessing to me. Surely with David thy mercies are more in number than I can count.[169]

([X170] Writing this page 37 makes me think I am in the 7th year of my widowhood and in the 37th year of my age this November last 1664.)

I wish I may rightly understand of things and consider my condition may be happy if I will help to make it so, for surely I must put in my helping hand, or God will not aid me with his.

And let me consider whether it is not possible to be happy without a second marriage: I hear St. Bernard tell a great queen she was more[171] honorable in her widow condition as by being a queen.

It is unhappy in this world. If we have riches, so hard a matter to use them well, either too saving or too spending, and they are ordered so that unless you are rather frugal than the contrary, they will not stay with us but put the owners to hard necessities sometimes, as Henry 8.[172]

If the benefit of human learning and knowledge can bring such aids to the understanding and judgment of persons, what a far blesseder condition is it to be daily supported and directed by the aid of heaven, by the assistance of his mercy to me?

Wise Solomon, he tells me true,
There is a time for all things due:[173]
A time to spare, a time to spend,

---

169. Cf. Psalm 139:18: "If I should count them, they are more in number than the sand: when I awake, I am still with thee."

170. Austen's "X," inscribed halfway down the manuscript page, matches another "X" she marked next to the page number (37, in her original pagination) at the top corner of the same page.

171. Austen first wrote "as" but inserted "more" without marking out "as."

172. Henry VIII (1491–1547), King of England and Ireland (*ODNB*).

173. Cf. Eccles. 3:1: "To every thing there is a season, and a time to every purpose under the heaven."

A time to borrow, time to lend,[174]
A time of trouble, time of rest,   [5]
A time there is to be oppressed.[175]
A time of folly, time to be.

1.[176] Lord, lend me thy supporting grace,
May sustain me through my race;
Throughout my lonely pilgrimage,
Thy strong supportance do engage.
Help me when my emergencies   [5]
Do daily multiply and rise.
My life is stuck about with fears;
My best fruitions strewed with tears.
Thou'st tried[177] me, Lord, hast tried me young,
Hath exercised[178] me very long.   [10]
Yet, let it be a longer date,
If that I find thy love, not hate.
Thou see'st, O Lord, what sighs arise,
And I am apt to beg, "suffice."
If it appear unto thy will,   [15]
My often sighings mayn't refill.

O stay[179] thy hand, if sinners may implore,[180]

---

174. Cf. Eccles. 3:6: "A time to get, and a time to lose; a time to keep, and a time to cast away."

175. Cf. Eccles. 3:8: "A time to love, and a time to hate; a time of war, and a time of peace."

176. Austen numbered most, but not all, of her poems in *Book M*. Ross proposes that "the numbers seem to indicate some kind of selection process. Perhaps Austen extracted and collected the verses in another lettered volume, or a manuscript of a different, more formal kind—or she may at least have intended to do so." "And Trophes of His Praises Make," 199.

177. "To test the strength, goodness, value, truth, or other quality of; to put to the proof, test, prove" (*OED*).

178. "To harass, vex, worry; to afflict, make anxious, 'prove'" (*OED*).

179. "To stop, arrest, check" (*OED*). Ross interprets these lines as a continuation of the poem before it. *Katherine Austen's Book M*, 85.

180. "To beg or pray for (aid, favor, pardon, etc.) with tearful or touching entreaties; to ask for in supplication; to beseech" (*OED*).

And let thy sovereign balsam,[181] Lord, restore
My often uncomposed, afflicted mind.
And look to that same rock,[182] which has been kind,
That hath refreshed me, that hath sent relief,   [5]
When sinking in the burden of my grief.
Report[183] distinguishes of what griefs are:
Lean ones[184] deplor'd,[185] fat sorrows find no care.
That looking glass is false, for heaven can make
Fortune to tremble and earth's joys to quake.   [10]

My blessed Lord, I find thee still[186]
My safety's hold and my high hill.
Though sighs may discompose[187] awhile,
At the conclusion, use to smile.
When was I ever most beset[188]   [5]
That heaven his favor did forget?
Lord, keep me that I mayn't presume
On easy love lest it consume.
May thy revivements shield[189] despair,
I may not mantl'd[190] be in care.   [10]
Thy gracious pleasure does invite
To be refresh'd[191] with due delight.

---

181. "A healing, soothing agent" (*OED*).

182. Austen often uses "rock" as a figure for heaven, God, or Christ.

183. "That which is generally or commonly said; rumor, gossip; hearsay" (*OED*).

184. Austen appears to have reshaped other letters into an "o" to begin "ones."

185. "Lamented, mourned for" (*OED*).

186. Ross sees these lines as continuing the previous poem. *Katherine Austen's Book M*, 86.

187. "To destroy or disturb the composure or calmness of; to ruffle, agitate, disquiet" (*OED*).

188. "To encompass, surround, assail, possess detrimentally: said of temptations, dangers, difficulties, evil influences" (*OED*).

189. Austen first wrote "refreshes guard," put it in parentheses, and inserted "revivements shield" under the line. A "revivement" is "something which has a reviving or restorative effect" (*OED*).

190. "Covered with or as with a mantle" (*OED*).

191. Austen wrote "We should not" to start this line, crossed it out, began the line lower down the page, and substituted "To be refresh'd."

Infuse that tincture[192] most divine;
Thy[193] joys may vanquish my repine.[194]

See page 56.[195]

I know, O Lord, thou canst glorify thy name in the destruction and extirpation[196] of me and mine. Yet if it may stand with thy pleasure, magnify thy goodness in our preservation and continuance awhile to serve thee, and build up my children to honor thee. Let them be a family thou mayst delight to save them and deliver them from the many dangers and accidents, from their enemies and from the devices of supplanters[197] to them.

To My Children

The Almighty bless you all with his divine blessing and bless my blessing and that my hearty desires may confer[198] to your welfare and spiritual[199] and earthly prosperity. And think when you receive my blessing that you receive that of your dear father's also. (I representing him all.)

Lord, imprint every day more in me and my children the marks of thy bounty that we should receive so much and deserve so little.

192. "An imparted quality likened to a color or dye" (*OED*).

193. Austen appears to have written "That" to begin this line but then inserted "Thy" under the line as a substitute for it without marking out "That." She also appears to have written "voyes"—perhaps for "voice"—as the second word in this line but to have reshaped the first letter to make the word "joyes" ("joys").

194. "The action of repining, discontent; an instance of this, a complaint" (*OED*).

195. A cross-reference to Austen's original pagination in *Book M.*

196. "The action of rooting up trees or weeds; total destruction" (*OED*).

197. "One who dispossesses or displaces another in his position, esp. by unworthy practices" (*OED*).

198. "To collect, give, or furnish as a contribution; to contribute" (*OED*).

199. Austen wrote "heavenly" but used a caret to insert "spiritual" above "heavenly" without crossing it out.

To My Son, Thomas Austen[200]

A fellow of a college is made up of pride and unmannerliness (in diverse of them), and they that are fellow commoners learn those ill habits.

I repent me of nothing more I made you one. I had better have took the good counsel of Doctor [Wilbye?],[201] not for the charges,[202] as the diverse dangers is in it. What makes noble men to be so extremely civil but being used from all men to receive a great respect by observance and keeping their hats off in their presence?[203] Which does not exclude theirs by their dignity above others, but civility and good breeding obliges the same answerable return, as the Lord Manchester[204] to Cousin T. R. put off his hat all the time he had business to my Lord.

And truly in my observation, this very rude fashion creates abundance of pride in colleges, either all lordly—nay, kingly—or else vassals[205] and slavish in the royalty of colleges.[206]

And certainly for the ill breeding and unaccomplishments in colleges enforces gentlemen of quality to send their sons to travel to learn civility and sweetness of deportment.[207] For by the early habit of pride and surliness and stoutness of carriage, they hardly ever forget it while they live.

---

200. Ross notes that "Thomas Austen matriculated at Balliol College, Oxford, in 1664 and was admitted to Lincoln's Inn in 1669." *Book M, Perdita Manuscripts*, MS item no. 35.

201. Ross reads this name as "Wille." *Katherine Austen's Book M*, 87.

202. "Pecuniary burden; expense, cost" (*OED*).

203. Austen refers to the custom of "hat honor," removing one's hat in the presence of a social superior. For more on the practice, see note 19 in the introduction.

204. Possibly Edward Montagu (1602–1671), second Earl of Manchester, politician, and Parliamentarian army officer or his son, Robert Montagu (bap. 1634, d. 1683), third Earl of Manchester and politician (*ODNB*).

205. "A base or abject person; a slave" (*OED*).

206. Austen sees the practice of refusing hat honor as having an undesirable leveling effect on the social hierarchy.

207. "Manner of conducting oneself; conduct (*of* life); behaviour" (*OED*).

I suppose that fashion[208] commenced for a good end that the leaders of youth, by their gravity, might make an obedience in youth.

Yet I imagine civility and ceremony was in the first rudiments[209] scarce come into that time, and most sure there is a greater share of politure[210] and civility known in the commendable breeding of gentlemen than was at that time when colleges was first founded.

This custom, in my weak opinion, may be declined as the introduction to rudeness, to lofty and conceited carriage, and which renders yourself in your own esteem far better than your correspondent.

Tom, whatever the fashion is, I would have your demeanor otherways, and though you may go scot free, hat free, be not so rude in your carriage but if a beggar puts off his hat, give the like. And now I see the rise and original of Parson Wilson's surly nod from his pristine preeminence.[211]

Be conversant in civil law: I have heard say it will fit you for common law and is the foundation of law by so much reason in it.

You are very happy, Sir, you have received[212] your first education in the university, though it be for breeding gentlemen somewhat a clownish[213] place, and exactness of demeanor is not to be expected. But you have had a supply for that, being also happy to have had a conversation in the court, which has redeemed you from anything which relishes of that nature. Yet, I am of opinion they who have no other than court breeding come not to be principled neither in religion, nor solid learning.

There is nothing I adore more in this world than ingenuity, and an ingenious spirit is seen in all things.

208. Observing hat honor properly.

209. "The imperfect beginnings of some (material or immaterial) thing; an embryonic stage; those parts which are the foundation of later growth or development" (*OED*).

210. "Elegance; refinement; polish of style or manners" (*OED*).

211. Austen implies disapprovingly that the parson has puritan (esp. Quaker) tendencies.

212. Austen wrote "had," crossed it out, and added "received."

213. "Clown-like, rude, boorish; uncultivated, ignorant, stupid; awkward, clumsy; rough, coarse" (*OED*).

What is ingenuity?

I take it to be dexterity and aptness to undertake all things readily with life and apprehension, with judgment and solidity as suits with the undertaking. And for the proper derivation of the word, I am not a scholar to know from whence it comes.

Upon Sister Austen's Unkindness to Me upon All Occasions[214]

My punishment is for that sin, but surely, Brother, I did not mind my own interest at all, no, nor my relations, that I rejected her, my relation. But thy fortune, thy advantage, thy reputation I aimed at, although all was crossed, and thy fortune would have been as great and my contentment much and the unworthy aspersions[215] to me removed and had not been to appearance, and the unhappiness that attended on her, my friend, might have[216] been prevented.

But it was not I. For God appointed she that now persecutes me to be advanced by me, an instrument,[217] and to try her[218] humor how she would behave herself, how she would manage her prosperity. It was to try my humor, too, how I would receive the contumelies[219] of one I had been instrumental to raise and to give me the relish of an enemy, when I expected a friend, and perhaps deserved as to them

---

214. "Sister Austen" is Susanna Austen, the widow of Katherine's brother-in-law, John. Katherine and Susanna fought a legal battle over family properties, including the Red Lion Inn, on Fleet Street. Todd, "Property and a Woman's Place," 183, 186, 191. Todd explains that "Susanna repeatedly revived her quite reasonable claim to a life interest, but Austen … ultimately successfully defended her son as successor to his uncle John" (191). Also see Ross, introduction to *Katherine Austen's Book M*, 11–12.

215. "A damaging report; a charge that tarnishes the reputation; a calumny, slander, false insinuation" (*OED*).

216. Austen crossed out "not" between "might" and "have."

217. Austen used a caret to insert "an instrument."

218. Austen seems first to have written "her" unclearly and then to have used a caret to insert "her" again above the line.

219. "Insolent reproach or abuse; insulting or offensively contemptuous language or treatment; despite; scornful rudeness" (*OED*).

(though, they think otherwise). Yet not from my God, he raised them out of his wisdom to be my scourge,[220] blessed be his name.

And to my relation, as an aggravation to her greater unhappiness that she had been happy, this was for her good at conclusion, too. And as Mr. Raworth[221] said this day, the happiness of this world is not so much as we expect, nor the evils so great in adversity we need be so much afraid of. A poor condition God does afford contentment, as well as rich.

2. December 5th, 1664. Upon Robin Austen's[222] Recovery of the Smallpox and Colonel Popham's[223] Son, John, Dying of Them, a Youth of Very Forward Growth, Their Ages the Same, Popham 3 Years for Growth More

How does thy mercies still renew?
How does thy benefits pursue?
My child lay sick, while darts of death
Was ready to exhale his breath.
A dangerous, infectious dart   [5]
Might have seized upon his heart,
Expelled his vital powers in haste
And early in his nonage[224] waste.
His slender life then could not pay
His offerings by a longer stay.   [10]
His life was in the twilight sky,

---

220. "A thing or person that is an instrument of divine chastisement" (*OED*).

221. Francis Raworth (d.1665), a local vicar. "The Church of St. Leonard, Shoreditch," in *Survey of London: Volume 8: Shoreditch*, ed. James Bird, *British History Online*. http://www.british-history.ac.uk/report.aspx?compid=98299/ (accessed May 2013).

222. Robert Austen, Austen's second son.

223. Probably Alexander Popham (1604/5–1669), politician and parliamentarian army officer. Although a parliamentarian, he became increasingly moderate with age, distanced himself from the Crowellian regime in the late 1650s, and accepted the restoration. By 1663, he supported the restoration government loyally enough to entertain Charles II lavishly at his estate and to help stop a puritan uprising (*ODNB*).

224. "The state of being under full legal age; minority, youth" (*OED*).

Nor knew he not thy praise most high.
O, let him live and praise thee, who
Dost add more days and life renew.
Why was mine spared, and one so strong,   [15]
Whose lively health judg'd to live long,
A verdant[225] youth, in's growing spring,
The prime[226] of all the scholars, him
A jewel in his parents' eye,
And this so lov'd a youth did[227] die?   [20]
He strong by nature and mine frail
Was spar'd; the other did exhale.
Was it his sin or own[228] desert[229]
Made mine to live and him to part?
O no, my Lord, (my) hands uphold,[230]   [25]
It was thy will, nor dare be bold
To search thy secrets or ask why
My weak son liv'd, a strong did die.
Thy glory and thy mercy, too,
As well in death as life ensue.[231]   [30]

225. "Green with vegetation; characterized by abundance of verdure" (*OED*); used here to emphasize John Popham's seeming health and promising growth.

226. "The chief, choicest, principal, or most important member or members of a group of people or things" but also the "'springtime' of life, the time of early adulthood" (*OED*).

227. Austen used a caret to insert "did." She first inserted another word, but marked it out and replaced it with "did." This correction adds the missing syllable to complete her line of iambic tetrameter.

228. Austen wrote "my" but inserted "own" over "my" without marking out either one.

229. "That which is deserved; a due reward or recompense, whether good or evil" (*OED*).

230. Austen first wrote "with hands I do uphold"; she then inserted "(my)" above "with" and put parentheses around "I do." That she did not strike out any words suggests she was still deciding what to do. She might have realized that "O no, my Lord, with hands I do uphold" changes the meter from iambic tetrameter to iambic pentameter and thus might have tried to revise the line to avoid this change.

231. "To follow out (a plan, course of life, profession, etc.)" (*OED*).

Meditation on My Death

When thy stroke comes that will dissolve my breath
And shall annihilate me unto death,
Let thy eternal pity on me stream,
And by my savior's[232] merits, me redeem.
'Tis he hath paid the ransom of my sin;[233]   [5]
Else I, deplored I, had ever been
Condemned to the prison of despair
Nor been released by my effects of prayer.
In vain my verse, in vain what could invoke
Could ever give me the least dram[234] of hope.   [10]
But, in the union of that ransom paid,
My bleeding soul to joys shall be conveyed.
Here rest my heart in this assured balm:
My God holds forth all miseries to calm.
Th'impetuous tempests here I find to beat   [15]
Shall everlastingly find their retreat.
O fit me, Lord, and me prepare to come
Where mercy'll be unfolded in a sum,
A sum that brings perfection, brings repose.
So make it, Lord, when this dark light shall close.   [20]

232. Christ's.

233. A reference to the sacrificial death of the innocent Christ by crucifixion to atone for the sins of humans.

234. "A weight, orig. the ancient Greek drachma; hence, in Apothecaries' weight, a weight of 60 grains = 1/8 of an ounce" (*OED*).

Discourse to L. upon the Newington Barrow[235]

My Lord, when the king had this estate in his interest, it was of such a trivial value as he judged it not considerable at all, therefore parted with it.[236] In earnest, Sir, six and thirty years to come is the age of a man, nor does a man live a man longer than that time. Subduct[237] his first and his last time, where he acts the part of two children, and the next stage after his first childhood put into the scale of his life, where he is guided by irregular passions and desires, by folly and want of an experienced judgment to guide and command himself, and thus he runs in his ungoverned time to one vice or another as he can hardly redeem himself from ruin. Either he is the bondman[238] of a usurer or of his tyrant appetite taken in the fetters of a ruinating[239] love, so that until he has relinquished his vice and makes use of that refined faculty, Reason, he is no man. About the commencement of these[240] 36 years gave me my birth, I have grown[241] full into the world with many years, and though, Sir, the lease was an old one then (to thee), it is made young again to us, so cannot I be.

235. This letter refers to the large estate (900 acres) of Newington Barrow (also known as Highbury). Austen refers frequently, in both prose and poetry, to the political and legal battles she fought to secure Highbury for her family. For a thorough discussion of the complicated issues at stake in relation to this property, see Todd, "Property and a Woman's Place," 186, 191–94. As Todd explains, although Austen's father-in-law bought Highbury and "acquired the title to the lordship of the manor, the Austens were unable to take possession of the land until 1665 because of a long lease granted in King James's time." "Property and a Woman's Place," 192. Furthermore, there were competing economic and legal claims on the property, which led to the contestation of the Austen family claim. See also Ross, introduction to *Katherine Austen's Book M*, 9–11.

236. Todd notes that "[i]n the 1620s the manor [Highbury] had been granted by Charles I along with other estates to Sir Allen Apsley to use to settle debts for military supplies." "Property and a Woman's Place," 191–92.

237. "To take away (a quantity) *from, out of* another; to subtract, deduct" (*OED*).

238. "A man in bondage; a villein; a serf, slave" (*OED*).

239. "That ruins someone or something; destructive" (*OED*).

240. Austen first wrote "which time of," crossed it out, and used a caret to insert "the commencement of these."

241. Austen crossed out a word—probably "been"—between "have" and "grown."

[242]{*We are not come to the fruition of it*[243] *at this time, being still in lease.*}

[244]And now this lease becomes new to us. It would have been the same if the reversion[245] had not been parted with, too.

My L, I hope we shall reap the harvest at last of a long expectation, an expectation that everyone could not stay for only a good husband. Let us not receive interruption of this at last, which has tried the virtue of our disposition, and I hope we shall be better able to keep it when our family have lived in credit for this 100 years without it.

Of Honor: Contraries

Contraries and transcendents have a relation, though by opposition one to another. As I have found by good experience, the success of two thousand pounds hath been the growth of most of my fortune. So I desire never to find the contrary, as by the contracting a great debt upon an estate will eat and devour up a bigger estate than I have.

If I could have a fortune, could entice a person of honor, yet I am not so in love with it to be ready to part with that I know the getting of and know for what extravagance it was sold.

Of Honor

I esteem honor not anything worth unless it be well guarded with wealth that it ravel not out to a degree far meaner than yeomandry[246]

---

242. Austen added this marginal commentary on the verso page facing her continuing entry on the recto side about Newington Barrow (Highbury).

243. Possession of the estate of Highbury (Newington Barrow).

244. Austen continues her discourse on the estate at the top of a new recto page.

245. "The right of succeeding to the possession of something, or of obtaining something at a future time" (*OED*).

246. "The condition of a yeoman," which is "a man holding a small landed estate; a freeholder under the rank of a gentleman" (*OED*).

is. So that the fortune I judge to be the real honor, and the title is the ornament, the embellishing of that fortune, which makes it look a little brighter to dazzle common eyes.

And if the costliness and splendor of my title eats up my estate, I shall rather degrade myself of it by a privacy than degrade me of my real supportation or contrive unworthy detainings of any person's money, whereby I am made most really contemptible.

True honor consists not so much in those preferments[247] and titles of the world, which for the most part are vain like itself, but in holy wisdom, gravity, and constancy, which becomes a Christian either in well doing or in comely[248] suffering.

The honor of worthy actions brings not only peace of mind but makes the face of goodmen[249] to shine. p. 18, Gauden

Book I, page 12: of mediocrity and of honor

Perhaps I may change my condition[250] after I have answered some designs.

Then shall I not aim at honor. It is costly[251] to maintain honor in all its circumstances, nay, and it is scarce honor if punctiliousness[252] is not kept up. Besides, I somewhat dislike it, since I have a precedent before my eyes what the costliness of honor lost what I bought. Neither is it riches I want. Heaven has gave already most bountiful. It is a person, whose soul and heart may be fit for me, is the chief riches to be valued. Yet since this is more dispensable[253] in men, not so much

---

247. "An appointment, esp. to a position in the Church of English, which brings social or financial advancement" (*OED*).

248. "Pleasing or agreeable to the moral sense, to notions of propriety, or aesthetic taste; becoming, decent, proper, seemly, decorous" (*OED*).

249. "A man of substance, not of gentle birth; a yeoman" (*OED*).

250. Austen considers remarriage.

251. Austen wrote "(it is quiet)" before "it is costly"; she probably meant "quite" but accidentally transposed the letters.

252. "The quality or character of being punctilious; scrupulous attentiveness to fine points of procedure, etiquette, or conduct" (*OED*).

253. "Allowable, excusable, pardonable" (*OED*).

to consider terms, and hath a reflection of disrepute when women's inclinations are steered all by love, a rich woman must not marry with a person of mean fortune.

Surely mediocrity[254] is the happiest condition we can obtain, and yet, that is so disposed as the lazy man comes not near it, and the active man stays not at it but climbs far beyond it until he paces all the degrees from competency to superfluities,[255] and from thence, ambition tempts him with titles and eminency. And yet he may be as happy by a sweet peace without going up those additional steps, which creates obligations, etc. See Book C, page 50, The Ill Effect of Honor, page 73 and page 21, in that book. Arguments for it: Man is made to grow, page 63. Book [?],[256] Book C.

1664

I observe what a long and healthy age my Grandmother Rudd[257] lived, above 80, and Mr. Smith of Aldbury, 90, and Parson Wilson, about 80. All lived in the city and did not love the country. Their diet was temperate, their exercise little, a subtly pace ever went, not put Nature scarce ever in any violence by overstirring or heating, which makes a faintness oftentimes and a decay.[258] Yet I attribute the chief part of this long life to the quiet of their minds, never engaged in anything disquieted or disordered that peace within them. How was[259]

254. "Moderate fortune or condition in life" (*OED*).

255. Forms of "action or conduct characterized by or exhibiting excess or extravagance" (*OED*).

256. The mark after "Book" is illegible, but it might have been "C." If this is the case, then Austen tried to squeeze *Book C* into the bottom margin of the page but ran out of room and thus rewrote *Book C* more clearly in the bottom corner nearby.

257. Probably Austen's maternal grandmother, Anne Perks, wife of Richard Rudd of London. Todd, "Property and a Woman's Place," Figure 1, 183.

258. Austen added "and a decay" by squeezing it into the margin. Ross reads the following words differently: she sees "litle" as "lithe," "soubtly" as "souftly," and "overstirring" as "over striving." *Katherine Austen's Book M*, 94.

259. Austen wrote "did," crossed it out, and inserted "was."

my own mother's strong nature worn out by too much stirring and walking and the many cares and businesses which a great family gave occasions to her![260] That nature was spent, which, in likelihood, by indulging to retirement would have prolonged. The distractions of the times wherein she lived gave her many discomposures and crosses by abuses. Dear Mother, thou hadst a great estate and a great burden, too.

To My Children

Let the example following divert your wishes and your aims at the estate of friends.

Your Uncle Field[261] had an estate of £800 per annum and no children, so that your father's mother and her sister, Mrs. Duffield, had expectation of his estate to come to their children. When he died, he left to sister's younger son an estate of reversion[262] after his wife; Durhams fell to your Uncle Austen.[263]

---

260. Austen's mother, Katherine Rudd, first married Robert Wilson (Austen's father), but after Robert's early death in 1639, she married Alderman John Highlord (Austen's stepfather), who died in 1641. Since she outlived both husbands, Austen's mother managed her family's finances during both periods of widowhood; Todd estimates that she was younger than fifty when she died. "Property and a Woman's Place," 183, 196n18. Todd also notes that Austen's "mother valued real property and aggressively used her connections with members of the Committee of Compounding for Royalist Estates to acquire properties for her children." "Property and a Woman's Place," 185.

261. Her children's great uncle.

262. "An estate granted to one party and subsequently granted in turn or transferable to another, esp. upon the death of the original grantee; the right of succeeding to, or next occupying, such an estate" (*OED*).

263. "Uncle Austen" refers to Katherine's brother-in-law, her husband Thomas's younger brother John Austen, who died in 1659, leaving his wife, Susanne Winstanley Austen, a widow. Apparently, Uncle Field (brother to Thomas Austen's mother, Anne Field) arranged for his estate first to go to his wife after his death and then, after the widow's death, to revert to his nephew, John Austen, the uncle of Katherine and Thomas Austen's children (Thomas, Robert, and Anne) to whom this letter of warning is directed. See Todd, "Property and a Woman's Place," Figure 1, 183, for details about Katherine Austen's family; for the sequence of factors affecting the inheritance of Durhams, see 185–86. Also on Durhams, see Ross, introduction to *Katherine Austen's Book M*, 12–13.

Yet my observation took notice that if he had not left him any-thing, it would been better.

First, £2200 it cost the widow's life and so much in finishing it that had the purchase and finishing money been laid out on any new purchase would have come to as much, and it is thought might have prevented his [?].[264]

Suspend all craving and expectation. Go on in your own way of industry, and be the raiser of your fortune, and leave the rest to God, and he will do better than your own projects can.

These two last weeks have been weeks of discomposure to me, of troubles. Lord, carry thy servant through every week of danger, and does this week to begin with accidents, too, assist and keep me. Sprinkle, Lord, with thy blessing all my actions, if it be thy will, how-ever with patience and discretion to govern myself in all that shall befall me.

Upon Lending Mr. C[265] Money

His abominable rudeness for my kindness to him, I may learn a lesson from. Have I lived in the town for many years with that ungrateful person and judged him a man of credit? Therefore was deluded to lend him money. And now he hath it, does he contemn[266] me and upbraid[267] me and defy what I can do? Nay, is he ready to answer the law to my face, and like a knave,[268] tells me I have neither bill nor bond from him. Surely, as I was exercised in my first afflictions, with those trials and dejections to be instructions to teach me piety and holiness,

264. The letters here are unclear; Ross suggests "M," *Katherine Austen's Book M*, 95.

265. Todd identifies "Mr. C" as "Mr. Cruse," a neighbor whom Austen names later in *Book M*, and speculates that Mr. Cruse might be the man who insulted Austen (by calling her an "old goat") when she drove past him in her coach. "Property and a Woman's Place," 189–90.

266. "To treat as of small value, treat or view with contempt; to despise, disdain, scorn, slight" (*OED*).

267. "To reproach, reprove, censure" (*OED*).

268. "An unprincipled man, given to dishonorable and deceitful practices; a base and crafty rogue" (*OED*).

to cast my dependence on the God of comfort, to be[269] stayed by his consolations.

Now for this last year, I have had crosses from men, have known the affairs and dealings of them[270] that things hath not gone smooth and easy, full of rubs[271] and diverse cross emergencies. From these I am to be instructed in. And as I have found to this day, all that hath fallen is for my good, so may these several exigents,[272] if I will take them by the right handle. They are to instruct me in wisdom, to render my experience of the world fuller to me than without them and either to prevent for the future or to give a remedy in them.

I am not to be of so easy a credulity to think I shall not be deceived, when I may find too many persons are made full of circumvention.[273] I am also to put more regard, more inquiry and cautions in my dealings. And thus I may be glad I have met with some to prevent more.

3. On the Death of My Niece, Grace Ashe, 4 Years Old[274]

Sweet blooming bud
Cropped from its stud[275]
When growing up
Unto fair hope,
Thy pretty sweetness time hath hid.   [5]
As soon as shown, we are forbid

269. Austen inserted "be."

270. Austen wrote "men," crossed it out, and used a caret to insert "them."

271. "An obstacle, impediment, or difficulty of a non-material nature" (*OED*). Ross reads this word as "rules." *Katherine Austen's Book M*, 95.

272. "A state of pressing need; a time of extreme necessity; a critical occasion, or one that requires immediate action or remedy; an emergency, extremity, strait" (*OED*).

273. "The action of circumventing; overreaching, outwitting, or getting the better of anyone by craft or artifice" (*OED*).

274. The daughter of Austen's sister, Mary, and brother-in-law, Sir Joseph Ashe. Todd, "Property and a Woman's Place," Figure 1, 183.

275. "A stem, trunk (of a tree)" (*OED*).

To gaze upon that lovely hue
On which Time's shady curtain drew.

Yet, when we know
The best mayn't grow   [10]
In this dark vale,[276]
Where ills still ail,
The great disposer[277] sets them free,
Whose better character doth see,
And early in their nonage place,   [15]
Where[278] their chiefest part will grace.

---

276. Figuratively, "the world regarded as a place of trouble, sorrow, misery, or weeping" (*OED*).

277. "One who regulates or governs" (*OED*); in Austen's use, God, specifically.

278. Heaven.

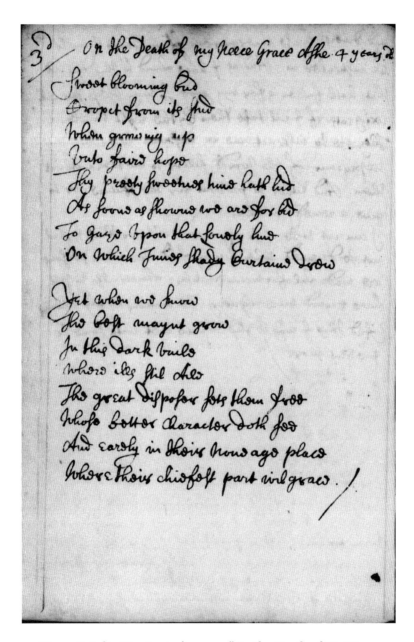

Figure 6. Folio 53v. Austen's poem, "On the Death of My Niece,
Grace Ashe, 4 Years Old." © The British Library Board.
Add. MS 4454.

On the Death of Mr. Francis Duffield, My Husband's Cousin
German.[279] Died December 18th, 1664 of Smallpox, Aged 33[280] at
Medmenham

How many young persons are dead since I had my dream gave me
intimation of mine! And when I related the time to them, it appeared
very short. Whether[281] I shall finish up my course then, I know not.
This I am sure: they have theirs who did not think should be so soon,
as my worthy friends, my Brother Austen, my Grandmother, Uncle
Rudd (though, they two were almost ripe; their years did necessarily
oblige them to look from this world to another). Then followed my
Brother Wilson, Sister Richard Wilson, a beautiful young woman.[282]
And of acquaintance: Doctor Broke, Mr. Chillingworth, Richard
Morecraft, Mrs. Cordivel, Cousin Sara Foulke and her 3 children died
within half a year one of another, and William, my servant. My Cousin
Duffield, the darling of the family, a lusty proper man, well and dead
in a week (about that time Colonel Popham's son died). His father, full
of infirmities of age and sickness, not come out of his chamber in 3
years, and he must die before death comes in his sorrowful affection
for his most hopeful son. Mrs. Young of Kingston, a lusty person dead.
And I am living. These may be preparations to me I may make myself
ready. And if my part is next to be acted, I may not shrink by fear but
learn to render up myself to the Almighty's pleasure.[283]

O, this day, in the multitude of things, I am a weary.
Yet then I cast my eyes on this 68 Psalm 28 verse revives me
again.[284] "Thy God hath sent forth strength for thee," and surely by a

---

279. "The son or daughter of (one's) uncle or aunt; (one's) first cousin" (*OED*).

280. Ross reads this number as "35." *Katherine Austen's Book M*, 96.

281. Austen wrote "And," crossed it out, and inserted "Whether."

282. On Austen's extended family, see Todd, "Property and a Woman's Place," Figure 1, 183.

283. Austen's writing becomes smaller in this passage as she tries to finish it on the same recto. There is an illegible mark squeezed into the bottom corner of the page; perhaps Austen attempted to insert "Amen" as a conclusion to her meditation.

284. Austen used a caret to insert "again" in the far right margin above "me." Cf. Psalm 68:28: "Thy God hath sent forth strength for thee: stablish the thing, O God, that thou hast

supply of that assistance of heaven, my ways shall be established with blessing.

Then being supported through my weariness, my strength (with David) will I ascribe to thee,[285] for thou are the God of my refuge. He, verily,[286] is my strength and my salvation; he is my defense, so that I shall not greatly fall.[287] Fall I may, but then the divine love will bear me in his arms. It shall not be a fall to ruin me.

Therefore, will I make still this repetition of this joyful suc cor[288] I meet with in my extremities.[289] God truly is my strength and salvation, my defense so that I shall not fall. Nay, I may assuredly believe as long as God is with me, I shall not fall, so fall as to be dejected or dismayed. If I fall by heaven's tuition,[290] I shall then rise to a blessed exaltation and favor.

That I may be held by his love, meditate on the 62 Psalm[291] of placing affiance[292] in him and drawing it off from all false retreats and wrong succors.

Still learn of David: he was as valiant as ever drew sword, yet in patient bearing and forbearing, he went beyond all men before him.

---

wrought in us." In this case, Austen appears to have used *The Book of Common Prayer* (New York: Oxford University Press, 1969).

285. Cf. Psalm 68:34.

286. "In truth or verity; as a matter of truth or fact; in deed, fact, or reality; really, truly" (*OED*).

287. Cf. Psalm 62:6: "He truly is my strength and my salvation: he is my defence, so that I shall not fall" (*BCP*).

288. "Aid, help, assistance" (*OED*).

289. "An extreme measure; the utmost point of severity or desperation" (*OED*).

290. "The action or business of teaching a pupil or pupils; the function of a teacher or instructor" (*OED*).

291. Psalm 62 emphasizes the believer's absolute reliance upon God.

292. "The action of confiding, or fact of having faith, in a person, quality, etc.; faith, trust" (*OED*).

On My Troubles in 1664

My troubles may be above the strength of nature—not above my spiritual strength—is of high joy to me. Lord, if it be good in thy sight, let not this rugged world always disquiet me, always render crosses and vexation to me. Give me the opportunities of serving thee from the perturbations and persecution of covetous men. My Savior, give[293] me that peace which thou promisest thy chosen that my heart be not troubled.

[X294]Although our life is miserable and extremely apt to be strewed with sadnesses in every condition and circumstance of it (as Doctor Taylor most fully relates in a perfect resemblance), yet here's the refuge for a Christian, which I have often found: I will fly unto my God, unto that God which hath performed all things for me, and I trust will not leave me now, but still his favor will shine upon me in this time of peril.

[X]This 5th May 1666, my multitude of business and of cross affairs, I do renew that petition that my God would strengthen me and waft[295] me over this ocean where I am.

To Obtain a Sweet Nature

The beginning of a gracious disposition is to be qualified with joy. The fruits of the spirit is joy, long suffering, gentleness, goodness.[296]

---

293. Austen began to write something else (perhaps starting with an "f" or "s") but reshaped the first letter of that word into "g" in "give."

294. Austen appears to have marked this part of her meditation on her troubles in 1664 with an "X" to indicate that the statement below it from 1666 is meant to comment on it.

295. "To convey safely by water; to carry *over* or *across* a river, sea, etc." (*OED*).

296. Cf. Gal. 5:22–23: "But the fruit of the Spirit is love, joy, peace, longsuffering, gentleness, goodness, faith, meekness, temperance: against such there is no law."

A cheerful disposition is the fittest to serve God and please him, also the most acceptable for a comfortable[297] society. Cheerfulness is ready to forgive errors. It is full of love, and Love can pardon a multitude. You may observe in some young persons who are of a cheerful nature of what sweet complying tempers they are of, and when age comes with infirmities that joys are unpleasant, what sour, peevish[298] dispositions ariseth in the temper of men and women.

To Spend Time

Consider how to spend my time, not trifling away, but with method, usefully and comfortably, and to weigh the hours of the day, to divide them in several studies, employments: in devotion, in soberness, in educating my children, in history, in a portion for retirement, in seeking knowledge. It is observed the ignorant man is compared to a beast, but he is far worse than a beast. Their nature is to be ignorant. It is man's fault if he be so.

January 28, 1664/5[299]

"Remember David and all his troubles";[300] remember thy servant and all her afflictions, too. And if be thy will, to say it is enough. Thou, Lord, knows how to deliver the godly out of temptation. O, my God, make me fit for thy gracious conduct, and then I shall come within the promise of defense. O, my Lord, be pleased to deliver me from

---

297. "Strengthening or supporting (morally or spiritually); encouraging, inspiriting, reassuring, cheering" (*OED*).

298. "Irritable, querulous; childishly fretful; characterized by or exhibiting petty bad temper" (*OED*).

299. Austen uses the old calendar.

300. Austen first wrote "afflictions" but inserted "troubles" over it without marking out either one. Ross takes "troubles" to be part of the essay's title. *Katherine Austen's Book M*, 99. The versions of Psalm 132:1—the line Austen quotes here—as given in the King James Bible and *BCP* differ precisely over the word Austen corrects: where King James has "afflictions," *BCP* uses "trouble."

temptation. Thou knowest, my Savior, how many ways we are beset with snares and dangers in this life and therefore did place this petition in that holy compendium[301] of our continual prayers to thee: "Lead us not into[302] temptation." Free me[303] from the perplexities of troublesome men who makes advantages of accidental casualties.[304]

February 10th

My gracious father, help thy servant out of the multitude of encumbrances that does beset me round. I thought my troubles grew to an end, now my 6 years is near at conclusion, but lo, I find them rather augmented. One perplexity arrives close to another without intermission to overcome one before I find another. Thus it hath been with me formerly—as soon as one was past, another came. But now I know not how to do any, so many assail and crowd in upon me together. O, my God, let my heart smite[305] me: what are the sins lie hidden and unrepented of that thy displeasure is so many ways upon me? O, that my heart might be a humble heart, that though I am in intricacies, my sins deserve far more. Blessed Lord, sanctify what is upon me, and give me courage and prudence, wisdom and patience to overcome them to thy glory. Then shall I lay thy deliverances or supportations either to ease me or free me, which, O my God, as may be most to thy will and thy honor. I shall lay them on thy altar of praise and thanksgiving all the days of my life. "Make thy face to shine upon

301. "An abridgement or condensation of a larger work or treatise, giving the sense and substance, within smaller compass" (*OED*). Austen probably refers to Matt. 6:5–13, which provides instructions regarding how proper believers ought to pray. By "holy compendium," she might also mean *BCP*.

302. Austen wrote "Deliver us from," put it in parentheses, and inserted "Lead us not into" above.

303. Austen used a caret to insert "Free me."

304. "A chance occurrence, an accident; esp. an unfortunate occurrence, a mishap" (*OED*).

305. "Of a heart, conscience, etc.: To discompose or disquiet (one); to affect painfully" (*OED*).

thy servant. Save me for thy mercies' sake."[306] "Make me to hear joy and gladness that the bones which thou has broken may rejoice."[307]

[2?]0[308] February

How does God Almighty comfort me that he relieveth the fatherless and widows? Then when cross men burden them with the weight of perplexities, the father of pity will bring them out of their power.

I hear the prophet David say the way of evil men shall be turned upside down.[309] Those projects which they think established with assurance shall be leveled and turned to the ground, and the top of their expectation to fail. And the Lord will save such as be of a clean heart, of a contrite[310] spirit. The Lord will reign in his compassion forever, even thy God, O Zion,[311] to all generations. Praise ye the Lord.[312] O praise the Lord, while I live, that hath been the help of the afflicted and hath been so to every generation.

See Psalm 6 and 7th.

306. Psalm 31:16.

307. Psalm 51:8. Austen wrote these last three sentences ("Make thy face ... broken may rejoice") at the top of a recto page in a way that interrupted her meditation (between "O" and "that my heart might be a humble heart"). She placed an "X" at the beginning of these sentences (next to "Make") and a corresponding "X" halfway down the recto page at the end of the meditation, possibly to indicate that they should be inserted as the conclusion to the entry. She might have squeezed in these lines at the very top of the page after having filled most of the page below her meditation. Ross suggests that the sentences beginning "Make thy face" constitute a refrain and that Austen meant to include them twice: first where they appear at the top of the page and then a second time at the end of the meditation where she places her "X." *Katherine Austen's Book M*, 100n221 and n224.

308. Although the first digit is hard to read, "2"—making the date "20"—is probable. Ross, however, reads it as "10." *Katherine Austen's Book M*, 101.

309. Cf. Psalm 146:9.

310. "Crushed or broken in spirit by a sense of sin, and so brought to complete penitence" (*OED*).

311. "The name of one of the hills of Jerusalem, on which the city of David was built, and which became the center of Jewish life and worship" (*OED*).

312. Cf. Psalm 146:10.

Now is Mr. Rich,[313] Mr. Symons, the Parliament,[314] Mrs. Pelhams unjustly taking advantage all upon me at once.

I hear David pray to be delivered from men which are thy hand, O Lord.[315] And surely I am the more satisfied that when I find troubles from men, that it hath pleased thee to make them the instruments of rebukes to me; by this allay,[316] they cannot smite me more than my gracious father permits for my good. And though evil men give offence, yet woe be to them by whom they come. O God, make me a passive sufferer far rather than an active doer of injury. And I beseech thee, O God, to forgive them who do me wrong, for this is my duty to pray for them who despitefully use me. I am commanded to be in charity with them. I pray God make me to be so and to overcome my passion, which these parties'[317] most despiteful usage creates in me, and ever to cast away revenge.

4. Read Psalm 27: Of Supportation[318]

In this time, Lord, support me through,
Who now have much, now much to do.
Lend me thy hand; lend me thy guide,
And if things fail, do thou abide.
Lord, compose my troubled mind;   [5]
Safety in thyself may find.
Then, if affairs do press and weigh,
My heavenly Father, be my stay.[319]

313. Austen refers in a previous entry to house repairs for which she must pay on behalf of her tenant, Mr. Rich.

314. Before writing "the Parliament," Austen wrote something else but marked it out. One deleted word appears possibly to have been "Scroop."

315. Cf. Psalm 17:14.

316. "Abatement, tempering of the force of anything" (*OED*).

317. Austen revised "by his most despiteful" into "these parties' most despiteful."

318. Psalm 27 begins, "The Lord is my light and my salvation; whom shall I fear? the Lord is the strength of my life; of whom shall I be afraid?"

319. "A thing or a person that affords support; an object of reliance" (*OED*).

Thou never layst so much on thine,
But thy succor will consign.[320]   [10]
Surely when we have much to bear,
Relief from thee will come and share.
Then pity me, thou heavenly aid,
And be my shield, now I have prayed.
Now storms of difficulties arise,   [15]
Give me wisdom; make me wise,
And that which is my part to do,
Assist with blessings do endue.[321]
I've often found thy shining beam
Then come and help in my extreme.   [20]
My strength is not compos'd so strong,
But subtle violence will wrong,
And in this world shall be a prey,
Unless the aid of widows stay,
Unless thy blessings do concur,   [25]
Shall find all comforts to demur.
And since thou wilt acceptance find,
When we quiesce[322] a quiet mind,
Such meek deportment to thy will
In every accident be still.   [30]
For then no cross can intervene
Where condescends[323] to thee are seen.
No cross, nor trouble can arise,
If thou beholds me with thy eyes.

320. "To give over or devote *to* a purpose or use" (*OED*).

321. "To invest *with* a power or quality, a spiritual gift, etc." (*OED*).

322. "To become quiescent"; that is, to be "in a state or condition of quietness" (*OED*).

323. This appears to be Austen's plural version of "condescendence"—"condescension; complaisance; compliance, concession" (*OED*). Because it would change the meter of her verse to regularize her idiosyncratic vocabulary (esp. in the plural) in this case, I have kept her term.

5. What need I fear? What need I hope?
This terrene[324] stage has little scope.
The ills we do endure not long;
Its flattering blisses are not strong,
Are like the water, like the wind.   [5]
Such is the fleeting joys we find,
Are like the sand or like a cloud,
So finite blisses find a shroud.[325]

6. And is this day, this day now[326] closed?
So shall my life be once reposed,
And all the tumults[327] that invade
A time will come shall overwade.[328]
They need not scare me or affright;   [5]
They're only sent for one short night,
As fleeting air, as winged Time.
Troubles and life will quick rejoin.
Suppose my life to be[329] a shade:[330]
This shadow the Almighty made   [10]
And hath appointed out my days,
Whether for short or longer stays.
Unto his glory, I resign
Whate'er I am and what is mine.

---

324. "Belonging to the earth or to this world; earthly; worldly, secular, temporal, material, human (as opposed to heavenly, eternal, spiritual, divine)" (*OED*).

325. "The white cloth or sheet in which a corpse is laid out for burial; a winding-sheet" (*OED*).

326. Austen first wrote "is" but then inserted "now" above the line without marking out either word.

327. "Great disturbance or agitation of mind or feeling; confused and violent emotion" (*OED*).

328. "To wade across" (*OED*).

329. Austen reshaped her original letters into "to be"; Ross reads "to" as "it." *Katherine Austen's Book M*, 104.

330. "An unsubstantial image of something real; an unreal appearance; something that has only a fleeting existence, or that has become reduced almost to nothing" (*OED*).

Upon[331]

7. Upon Courtiers at the Committee of Parliament Striving for Highbury, the 14th February That I Was There, 1664/5[332]

Wise Solomon, he tells me true,
There is a time for all things due.
A time to spare, a time to spend,
A time to borrow, time to lend,
A time of trouble, time of rest,   [5]
A time there is to be oppressed.[333]
Such is this time, now men of power
Do seek our welfare to devour,
Confederated in a league
By an unjust and[334] dire intrigue.   [10]

331. This is the first word in the title of a poem that Austen marked out completely. The title probably includes a February date. The poem appears to have contained thirty-eight lines and covered half a verso page and the entire recto facing it. Austen made a series of tight, swirling loops to mark out each line of verse carefully to the point of illegibility. It is unclear why she did not similarly mark out the first word in the title (that is, "Upon").

332. As Todd explains, Sir Allen Apsley had been granted the estate of Highbury by Charles I, but Thomas Austen, Katherine's father-in-law, later bought it. Regardless, Austen's family could not take actual possession of Highbury until 1665, when a lease granted during the reign of James I expired. The legal and economic situation of the estate remained complicated, however, and Apsley's other creditors persisted in making claims on Highbury. For the details of this property battle, see Todd, "Property and a Woman's Place," 186, 191–94. Many of Austen's poems and meditations refer to her ongoing efforts to free Highbury from competing claims, to secure her family's title to the manor, and to gain possession of it (in addition to holding the title). Her negative references throughout *Book M* to "courtiers" and to parliament and its committees often pertain specifically to the battle over Highbury. The title of this poem makes its context and focus explicit.

333. Austen borrows and recontextualizes these opening lines from the brief metrical paraphrase of Ecclesiastes she inscribed earlier in *Book M*; these are the relevant lines from Ecclesiastes: "To everything there is a season, and a time to every purpose under the heaven" (3:1); "A time to get, and a time to lose; a time to keep, and a time to cast away" (3:6); and "A time to love, and a time to hate; a time of war, and a time of peace" (3:8).

334. Austen wrote "oppressive," crossed it out, and inserted "unjust and" above it. She also wrote "intrigue" twice: once in the line and again more clearly in the margin.

Envy, thou base encroaching[335] weed,
Never did any noble deed;
We cannot be secure for thee—
O thou most treacherous quality!
No time in this same world secure,[336]   [15]
Alive nor dead a hold have sure.
A shovel throws us from our grave,
As Envy plucks from what we have.
'Tis better far on Heaven to place,
Where we are freed from Envy's chase.   [20]
No thief, no supplantation[337] can
Despoil[338] what is the best of Man,
Nor of thy favor, most great Lord,
In our huge straits[339] does aid afford.
Since I have seen the Lord, to six   [25]
Most saddest years my heart I'll fix,
And while I move upon earth's stages,
Fly to that same rock of ages.
All widows fall, all orphans bow
To our great God that smiles allow.   [30]
When in your plunges,[340] your distress,
When powerful wrong contracts[341] you less,
Fly to Heaven's sure help alone,
For Heaven will hear when men hears none.

335. "To seize, acquire wrongfully (property or privilege)" (*OED*).

336. Austen initially wrote something else—possibly "secure" with a different spelling—then marked it out and wrote "secure" clearly at the end of the line.

337. "The dispossession or displacement of a person ... in a position, esp. by treacherous or dishonourable means" (*OED*).

338. "To strip of possessions by violence; to plunder, rob" (*OED*).

339. "A narrow or tight place, a time of sore need or of awkward or straitened circumstances, a difficulty or fix" (*OED*).

340. "The point at which a person is precipitated into trouble, difficulty, or danger; a critical situation, a strait; a dilemma" (*OED*).

341. "To make smaller, reduce in amount, diminish the extent or scope of; to narrow" (*OED*).

Men never think their wives may be
Necessitate[342] by misery,
Or their children be a prey
When themselves are gone away.
I not resented widow's tears   [5]
Before I was distressed with fears.
This retribution do I find:
To meet with all the world unkind.

My sin forgive, let pity flow,
And comfort unto sad hearts show.   [10]
Most gracious Heaven, relieve sad hearts;
Be healing balsam in their smarts.
O Heaven, send down thy full relief,
Who art the help of all in chief.

My Dream on 2nd of January 1664/5

I dreamed I was going to a wedding and took my leave of my mother. Then I went up a high pair of stairs and came into a room where was a long table. In the middle at the upper end sat my husband a discoursing with a gentleman in a gown sitting at the side of the table. I looked upon them and went down. As I went down a few steps, I saw my husband again. I kissed him and asked him how he could come down before me, since I left him sitting. He told me by a back stairs. So, down I went, and then I, forgetting my muff,[343] I went up the back stairs for it. But I had not gone up above 8 or 9 steps, but I waked.

This ran in my mind diverse days afterwards, and I concluded: the first pair of stairs signified to me to the end of January, and the second was so many days in February, and then something would fall out to me. And indeed, I was troubled that some unhappy adventure would come, as I in dreaded every day, wishing February out. It came to pass that on the 9th of February, I was appointed to be that day at

342. "To reduce (a person) to want or need" (*OED*).

343. "A covering, often of fur and usually of cylindrical shape with open ends, into which both hands may be placed for warmth" (*OED*).

the Committee of Parliament.[344] And when I came into the room, it was the same as I saw in my dream, the situation of the room the same with the table. And as soon as I cast my eye on Sir John Birkenhead,[345] I was confident he was the very same man I saw my husband with.

This business was a wedding, for it was a contract, a confederacy to take away our estate.[346] And I shall no more be of that opinion generally observed in dreams that a wedding foretells a burying and a burying a wedding, but that it is danger of conspiracy against one, as this was to us. By my muff—going for it—I was to be lapped[347] warm; as it fell out, went in muff and velvet hood and mantle.[348]

And certainly something might concern Sir John by my husband's seeming to divert him, that if he acted in so just a matter, it would not be well to him, and by my husband's sitting at the upper end of the table, as if he would be his judge.[349]

It proved a very troublesome time to me, for I was sick of an exceeding cold in my head made me to be almost deaf and dumb, and going to Westminster about 6 times, I was exceeding ill and more unfit to contest with such a business than ever I had been before, God having continued my health all ways before, that now it was a huge burden. And how subtly carried they their design by resolving the committee they chose should make what report they pleased to the Parliament.

---

344. Due to legal matters pertaining to the Highbury estate.

345. Sir John Birkenhead (1617–1679), journalist, poet, staunch royalist, and member of parliament after the restoration (*ODNB*).

346. Highbury.

347. "To enfold in a wrap or wraps, to enwrap, swathe; hence, to clothe, to bind up, tie round" (*OED*).

348. "A loose sleeveless cloak" (*OED*). Austen squeezed this last sentence into a small space between paragraphs.

349. Austen squeezed this sentence, in which she used increasingly small letters, into a tight space. Perhaps this entire paragraph was added later to a blank area between paragraphs.

The 11 of February, my son was very ill, insomuch I had that day the tidings[350] he was in a consumption[351] and very dangerous[352] by a cake of phlegm backed at his stomach. That day also was discovered to me what potent trains[353] was laid to get his estate, and my own faintness and weakness became insupportable.

My Meditation[354]

If the Lord does not help me, I shall be like to them that go down to the pit,[355] this day that I have fears of the loss of my son, of the loss of his[356] land.

Meditation[357]

If the Lord is not on our side, now men rise up against us, [and][358] if the Lord takes not our part, now that we have great opposers, they will swallow our estate up quick, while their many devices are intended to overthrow us.

Help me, O Lord, now I am helpless; now I am weak by distempers of body, be strength to my body, be supportation to my mind. Endow that with fortitude and submission, and be pleased to send

---

350. "Reports, news, intelligence, information" (*OED*).

351. "Disease that causes wasting of the body, *spec.* tuberculosis" (*OED*).

352. "In danger, as from illness; dangerously ill" (*OED*).

353. "An act or scheme designed to deceive or entrap, a trick, stratagem, artifice, wile" (*OED*).

354. Ross reads what I interpret as "My Med:"—an abbreviation for "My Meditation"—as "my nied:" *Katherine Austen's Book M*, 107.

355. Cf. Psalm 28:1: "Unto thee will I cry, O LORD my rock; be not silent to me; lest, if thou be silent to me, I become like them that go down into the pit."

356. Austen appears to have initially written "my" but to have marked it out and put "his" instead, perhaps censoring herself for imagining herself as the owner of the lands in question.

357. Although Austen gives this section (at the top of a verso page) a title of its own, it could be the continuation of "My Meditation," which begins at the bottom of the previous recto.

358. Austen wrote "I," rather than "and," but the context suggests she meant to put an ampersand and wrote "I" by accident.

thy angel and deliver me. Vouchsafe[359] a conducting guardian angel to defend us. Thou didst send an angel to discomfit[360] vaunting[361] Sennacherib.[362] The Almighty can also frustrate the snares and trains laid by our unjust oppressors, if it seems fit for his glory, or if our adversaries have the upper hand, the Almighty can convert the loss received for our greater gain. And sanctified adversity is better than fortunes, where heaven denies it.

Sure if they take away our estate, three worlds would hear of it: Heaven, Earth, and Hell. Hell would gape; Earth would complain; and Heaven would judge.

Fly sin, for sharp revenge doth follow sin,
   And wicked deeds do wrathful dooms procure.
If God stay long ere[363] he to strike begin,
   Though long he stay, at last he striketh sure.[364]

While I am distressed with fear,
Grant thy favor, smile, and cheer.
While troops of discomposures rise,
God's former love may fill my eyes.

---

359. "To confer or bestow (some thing, favour, or benefit) *on* a person" (*OED*).

360. "To undo in battle; to defeat or overthrow completely; to beat, to rout" (*OED*).

361. "That vaunts or boasts; given or addicted to boasting" (*OED*).

362. In 2 Kings 19:35–36, God sends an angel to defend Jerusalem from invasion by the army of Sennacherib, King of Assyria:

> And it came to pass that night, that the angel of the LORD went out, and smote in the camp of the Assyrians an hundred fourscore and five thousand: and when they arose early in the morning, behold, they were all dead corpses. So Sennacherib king of Assyria departed, and went and returned, and dwelt at Nineveh.

363. "Before (in time)" (*OED*).

364. "Certainly, with certainty; without risk of failure" (*OED*).

Heaven can light my candle.[365] Heaven can make my darkness to be light by his sweet and blessed refreshment to my soul.[366]

X[367] I could not be at home the 14th February to rejoice in the favors of God in preserving me in 6 years of troubles, I waiting on the Committee, but I may have another day may give the relation of it.

Certainly, by the conclusion of this last 6th year, I had such accumulated[368] troubles and a many encumbrances, many businesses—with a weak disposed body—to go through, that if heaven had not in a most special, most eminent manner supported me, it had been my death. So that I was nigh[369] unto death, and my weakness and indisposition continued many days. Now it hath pleased God I have passed that time wherein I thought death might have been presented to me, I hope it will please him to comfort me according to the days wherein I have seen evil and the years of my trouble, that as[370] I do not yet die but live, so as I live, I may declare the conducting love I have found from my God. He hath been a sun and a shield, and no good thing he will withhold from them that trust in him.[371] O, that I may live to tell the singular providences of God to me that all widows and orphans, all fatherless and friendless, may put their trust in God, may set their hope in him, who hath been my ready defense in the years of my distress, then when the water floods were ready to drown me.

8. On 25th February 1664/5

Make me, my Lord, even this time see
How much thou hast defended me.

365. Cf. Psalm 18:28.

366. Austen used a caret in the right margin to insert "soul" above "my."

367. It is unclear to what part of *Book M* this cross-referencing mark (i.e., "X") refers.

368. Austen crossed out something before "accumulated."

369. Near.

370. Austen used a caret to insert "as" above the line between "that" and "I."

371. Austen adapts Psalm 84:11: "For the LORD God is a sun and shield: the LORD will give grace and glory: no good thing will he withhold from them that walk uprightly."

This year three months, five year beside,
Thy supreme favor was my guide.
Blessings on blessings did bestow;   [5]
Love in the cup of trembling[372] show.
Lord, if thou hadst not sometimes smiled,
My fears had rendered me exil'd.
The many waves did overflow;
Sometimes, I thought thy favor slow   [10]
In those disconsolated years,
So often strewed with sighs and fears.
Then came thy aid and succor down
And was my light, my life, my crown.
None but Heaven's all-seeing eye   [15]
Could cast[373] my discomposures by.
His sweetly moving providence
In sore afflictions was my fence,
Did lay their billows,[374] stop their rage,
Did my oppression's storm assuage.   [20]
Blest Succor, how hast thou consign'd
Revivements when in grief confin'd!
What shall I render to my God and pay
For his conducting and defending stay?
Eternity[375] itself's too small   [25]
To reckon up thy mercies all,
And to repeat my tongue is dumb.
No figures audit up the sum.
O no, my Lord, they're higher far

---

372. For the expression, "cup of trembling," cf. Isa. 51:17 and 21–22: "Awake, awake, stand up, O Jerusalem, which hast drunk at the hand of the LORD the cup of his fury; thou has drunken the dregs of the cup of trembling, and wrung them out," and "Therefore hear now this, thou afflicted, and drunken, but not with wine: Thus saith thy Lord the LORD, and thy God that pleadeth the cause of his people, Behold, I have taken out of thine hand the cup of trembling, even the dregs of the cup of my fury; thou shalt no more drink it again."

373. Austen wrote "lay" but inserted "cast" above it without marking out either word.

374. "A great swelling wave of the sea, produced generally by a high wind" (*OED*).

375. Austen added an "s"—which I leave out—to "Eternity."

Than the deep center[376] to the star.   [30]
None but archangels can declare
Thy ample glories what they are.
When thou hast made me like to those
And this same band of death disclose,
I shall triumph then with the skill,   [35]
In high perfection praise thy will,
And in thy hierarchy,[377] I shall
Innumerable acts extol.

9. Upon My Dream the 20th October 1664, When I Dreamt I Saw 4
Moons in a Clear Sky: Meditation

Will four moons more my fate declare?
Wait I in hope? Or in despair?
Does life or death my date unfold?
I know not, Lord; thou art my hold.[378]
Which state is fittest, Lord, for thee,   [5]
To that most willingly agree.
If through the pavement of the grave
Heaven's providence more beauty have,
My God, I do submit and know,
More glory unto me will show   [10]
Than this frail life can contribute,
When pleasures to our hearts most suit.
The meantime, Lord, prepare my heart
For what thy goodness shall[379] impart,
For what thy purposes intend   [15]
In embassage[380] of life or end.
Adorn my soul, and beautify
That chiefest part, I may comply.

376. "The centre of the earth" (*OED*).

377. Of angels.

378. "A fortified place of defense; a fort or fortress; a stronghold" (*OED*).

379. Austen wrote "purposes," crossed it out, and used a caret to insert "goodness shall."

380. "A mission" (*OED*).

O fit me, Lord, to die or live,
To do my duty while I breathe.   [20]
Then welcome life or death each one,
If thou entitle me thy one,
If thou convert this little sand,
To stand the shock of thy command.

    I dreamt—I think it was about the 20th August 1664, the last night before I came from Twickenham—that my Father Austen and my Brother Austen[381] was partners at one game at cribbage[382] and my husband and I. And as soon as the cards was dealt, my husband said he would deal again. I was unwilling and said I had a good game, for I had three aces, and I said that was six.

    And this, I thought, intimated to me six months and something would happen, which now that six months is passed, I think that and my 4 moons dream related to our[383] estate of Highbury, which then was called into a most dangerous question by persons who is[384] ready to do what they please, if[385] the special providence of God do not prevent[386] them.

    That troublesome business might well be compared to a game at cards, wherein my Father Austen and all of us have been concerned in the taking care of and defending. February 1664.[387]

---

381. Her dead in-laws, Thomas Austen (her father-in-law) and John Austen (her brother-in-law).

382. A card game.

383. Austen crossed out "that" between "to" and "our."

384. Austen marked out a word (possibly "was") and wrote "is" above it.

385. Austen marked out something illegible and inserted "if."

386. Austen changed this sentence from the past to the present tense but failed to correct "prevented"; I have used "prevent" to be consistent. "Do not" is squeezed into the margins in a way that suggests further revisions into the present tense.

387. Austen inscribed small circles to render illegible several entire lines of prose before and after "February 1664."

Our adversaries do see our cause is so apparently right, and yet[388] they will essay[389] to vex us more. I[390] beseech God, if it be his pleasure, to divert their unjust pretensions.[391]

I dreamt awhile before I had thieves come to my bedside, and there was my husband came and gave me two rings: one, his father's gold-sealed ring; the other, a diamond ring of his brother's. And his father was in the entry but did not come in, and thus I[392] was delivered from the thieves.

And when I waked, I hoped I should have the better of my father's estate of Highbury and of my brother's estate of the Red Lion, now at this time which I am in law with by my Sister Austen.[393]

I have had these two years in my house an unfaithful servant, and when I found out his knavery, was forced not to accuse him of it but to keep him, while my urgent occasions was passed. Yet he, at last discovered, told me he must be going into his own country in 3 days and could not stay—then, when my other man had broke a bone and could not stir in many days to do anything.

On Their Reporting Our Business to the Parliament the Day They Were Rising

Now I am sure this is the time all my monitions to me tended. This is the time of the greatest trouble for outward concerns of estate. I pray God it may be my time of trust and reliance in him.

I am in the hands of potent men, men skillful to destroy, of subtle men, who lay trains to ruin the widow and fatherless. But stay: I am in the hands of a gracious God can disappoint their projects and suffer them not to go further than his pleasure.

388. Austen marked out several words before using a caret to insert "and yet."

389. "To set oneself, undertake, try (*to do* something)" (*OED*); Austen marked out a word between "will" and "essay."

390. Austen marked out a word before the "I" beginning this sentence.

391. "The assertion of a claim as of right; a claim made; a demand" (*OED*).

392. Austen crossed out a word between "and" and "thus."

393. Her widowed sister-in-law, Susanna Austen.

And let me be assured that pleasure of heaven—if I and mine depend in him—can make our outward losses of this world turn to our greater gain in another. And let us be encouraged that God is able to give as much success to our remaining estate as if we had that, too. Of this I may be sure from my experience: God hath blessed me with success and prosperity in my estate as to all men it may appear a wonder, as if I had that estate in my possession they would deprive us of, to men's understanding could hardly increase to more. Therefore, will I commit the event of it to heaven, for he will dispose for the best. Therefore, in patience I shall endeavor to possess my soul, and then heaven will bless us, and I shall magnify his name, whether we have it or whether we lose it, for thy mercy hath and will endure forever.

10. Meditation, on.

I now have pass'd those years, did wait
From intimation of my date
Might then expire. I now march on
Longer in life, more time to run.
As Hezekiah was repriev'd,   [5]
I yet of life am not bereav'd.
Another space is lent to know
What I to my Creator owe.
His noble acts my tongue relate
Beyond all time, beyond all date;   [10]
His ancient favor adds his new.
Before heaven's firmament,[394] he drew
His love to Mankind; in that stream,
He did descend his gracious beam
On me, unworthy, that high grace   [15]
Most eminent in six year's space.
Those minutes, which I could not tell,[395]

---

394. "The arch or vault of heaven overhead, in which the clouds or stars appear; the sky or heavens" (*OED*).

395. "To mention numerically, to count, reckon" (*OED*).

In each of them did care[396] excel,
And all my time his grace was found.
But, in adversity, 'twas crown'd,   [20]
Tendered with peculiar[397] love
When I sat sighing, could not move,
Or make recovery of my loss;
I was upheld in every cross.
What are the stories I can tell?   [25]
Higher than mountains or seas' swell!
From Earth to Heaven is not so high
As my God's providences spy.
So great a God should me behold
In all my paths cannot be told.   [30]
No words I have that can indite[398]
Or while a mortal can recite
That his great glory should espy
And save a worm, not throw her by.
Low men would spurn, and when they tread,   [35]
Not value it but leave it dead,
And yet high Heaven's descends[399] still flow.
Lord, how much mortals ever owe
To thee, their Savior, in their grief,
Thy vial's powers of full relief.   [40]
What can I render unto thee
But that which floweth still to me
From thy influence, from thy rays,
Implant divine, eternal praise,
That I may pay thee what is thine?   [45]
For surely anything of mine
Is most unworthy to present
To thee, all pure, all excellent.

396. "Mental suffering, sorrow, grief, trouble" (*OED*).

397. "Special, remarkable, distinctive" but possibly also resonating with the connotation of "peculiar" as "a personal or chosen possession of God; a chosen or elect person or people" (*OED*).

398. "To put into words, compose (a poem, tale, speech, etc.)" (*OED*).

399. "A descent; a downward slope" (*OED*).

Infuse, O Lord, that spiritual flame
That I may offer thee the same.   [50]
But still I fear, while I am dust,
That heat abates and is unjust,
Will lose its weight and cannot shine
Thy praises forth, 'til made divine.
Fit me, by all thy dealings past,   [55]
For thy high joys shall ever last.
And when I'm made a perfect soul
Shall perfectly thy praises roll.[400] Amen.

Here join those 4 leaves out of parchment book of meditations
of praise, beginning October last, 1664.

11. Ap.[401]

Come, all my thoughts, awake, awake,
And trophies of his praises make!
Come summon forth his acts of praise,
How his rich conduct freely stays!
From secret[402] caverns of my breast,   [5]
Tell, O tell, how Heaven gives rest.
I fain[403] would of his glory sing.
My soul is narrow, cannot ring;
'Tis circumscrib'd and is confin'd.
I ready only am in mind;   [10]

---

400. "To record (a statement, fact, judgment, etc.), esp. in an official roll or register" (*OED*).

401. Ross speculates that this abbreviation refers to "Apostrophe" and finds the poem to be "the most reminiscent among Austen's verses of Donne's and Herbert's sophisticated religious lyrics." "And Trophes of His Praises Make," 196. She suggests, more specifically, that it echoes Donne's Holy Sonnet, "At the round earth's imagined corners." Ross, *Katherine Austen's Book M*, 114n282. Another possibility for the abbreviated title is "April."

402. "Of feelings, passions, thoughts: Not openly avowed or expressed; concealed, disguised; also, in stronger sense, known only to the subject, inward, inmost. Hence, said of the heart, soul, etc." (*OED*).

403. "Gladly, willingly, with pleasure" (*OED*).

Affection and my will is bent.[404]
My God, accept of my intent,
For nothing else I have to pay.
I dedicate my heart to stay,
And what I cannot, Lord, express,   [15]
Vouchsafe to read it out by guess.
No character[405] of human Art
So high a subject can impart,
Or while we fly on winged Time,
It is impossible to chime.[406]   [20]
Th'immense perfection of thy name,
Stupidity can never frame.[407]

On Report at Parliament

For this complaint of oppression, God hath punished the land formerly in the great calamities which fell upon the times, and surely if they pursue and commit the same crimes of injustice and injuries to poor men, and especially to act violence on widows and orphans, how will their cries and grievances pierce the ears of Heaven, who will hear and judge their cause against an unjust nation!

O God, hear thou in heaven, thy dwelling place, and have mercy upon us. O Lord, direct thy servant; O Lord, assist thy servant in this so weighty concern I have to overcome. I am weak as a child to contest with my potent adversaries. Yet, I have an Almighty God (and a just cause), who I trust will defend me.

---

404. "Determined, resolute, devoted, inclined, set" (*OED*).

405. "Writing, printing" (*OED*).

406. Ross reads "chime" as "clime." *Katherine Austen's Book M*, 115.

407. Austen first wrote "Stupidity must here refrain" as the last line of this poem. She then put this line in parentheses, wrote "or" next to it, and added "Stupidity can never frame" as a new last line. However, she never marked out the first version.

One day I shall be delivered from these inquietudes, from these molestations of law and trouble—when it pleaseth God—the which I have been encompassed with.[408]

O Heaven, be thou the judge of our just cause. Whoever has a hand in our overthrow, O Lord, forgive them all, and send some mark, some impression upon them, in mercy, whereby they may ask thee forgiveness.

O God, that hast heard the sighing of oppressed widows, of helpless orphans heretofore, hear me at this time.

Meditation

O merciful Father, let me never forget thy testimonies of conduct. Let them be perpetual assurances thou wilt not forsake me.

And what a mercy full[409] of allay and mitigation that God did not lay the trial and hazard of our estate at my first widowhood but hath forbore to six years, showing me six years of his blessing and tender care over me, greater than the affection of parents or of any relative. Surely by this sweet method of his correction to me, not laying more upon me than he enabled me by degrees to bear, let me still be satisfied that, as my God hath mingled mercy and protection through every chastisement, will in this also. And here I will acquiesce—not ceasing either my prayers or industrious diligence—that if it seems good in this sight of God, to lend us that pleasant and fruitful Canaan[410] to possess to his glory.

---

408. Austen wrote the following sentences but crossed them out with diagonal lines: "Surely if they take Highbury from us, what a happiness I continue a single life! My son's welfare may be reestablished again by God's blessing on my industry for him." Austen initially wrote "continue singly" but used carets to insert "a" after "continue" and "le" at the end of "sing." She also reshaped the "y" in "singly" to make "i"; she first wrote "for my industry" but marked out "for" and used a caret to insert "on." Perhaps Austen struck out these sentences when she gained possession of Highbury.

409. Austen wrote "merciful" but reshaped the "i" into "y" and used a caret to insert "full" above the line, thus changing "merciful" to "mercy full."

410. Austen conflates Canaan, the promised land of the Old Testament, with Highbury.

1665

Surely when I consider the passages of my widowed state, what a blessing I am to be thankful I made that resolution to continue seven years for the particular esteem to my dear friend and that I have continued almost to that time![411] And certainly if my son's estate be taken away, I shall begin to take a new lease of seven years more, if God Almighty spare me so long, for the good of my son, for his welfare and resupportation. No, no, Fortune, no self-interest I hope shall prevail on me for his prejudice.[412] If his estate do hold, he would not much know my kindness; if it fail, my love, my affection, my zeal, my honor shall be expressed both to him, his dear father, and worthy grandfather, who have a deep obligation ever imprinted in my memory, respects, and endeavors. Thus, friends are not known until adversity, yet happy it is not to have adversity to try the generosity of friends. But to have no friends in the crosses of the world is a double calamity.

The Lord continue to this poor destitute family friends, and above all, friends himself, the unfailing friend.

Let us still observe that which can never be too much observed: how divine providence never fails the innocent.

12. Meditation

Six bitter gusts blew for six years.
A heavenly hand bore through those tears,
The clouds of sorrow, and grief's storm;
By Heaven's support receiv'd no harm.
Rebukes are bracelets do enchain   [5]
Us fast to Jesus and obtain
His saving pity; then, when grief

411. Austen reflects upon her marital status as a widow almost seven years after the death of her "dear friend" (i.e., her husband, Thomas Austen).

412. "Harm, detriment, or injury to a person or thing resulting from a judgment or action, esp. one in which a person's rights are disregarded" (*OED*).

Does represent[413] us small relief,
We come into his shelter most.
When strong, oppressive rapine[414] boast,   [10]
God is not deaf, will surely pay
Revenge, who innocents betray.
O Lord, incline to save that dust
Who builds on thee, our only[415] trust.

O God, though my enemies seem to take advantage upon my weak and destitute and helpless condition—a woman without alliance of the family to help me—yet, O God, help me and make me overcome those bands that do environ me.

They curse when any friend speaks for me and band and threaten them with a court displeasure. But my God can wound with an arrow suddenly and suddenly can be removed. O God, how do they seek to get by violence and oppression under pretense to gratify the king's friends by such rigor and extortion! Surely, he that helps those that cannot help themselves will disappoint their devices.

In Answer to One Why Not Marry to Ease Me of My Burdens

O no, Cousin, marriage should be peaceable and not strewed with thorns and encumbrances. I do not know what regrets might have been by it. It is sufficient I am able to bear with patience myself the loss of an estate because[416] bigger afflictions. And if my children should find loss in their estates, by God's blessing, should be able to make a supply to them in their great disappointments, which I could never do by engaging myself away from them.

413. "To give, offer, deliver" (*OED*).

414. "The act or practice of seizing and taking away by force the property of others; plunder, pillage, robbery" (*OED*). Ross suggests that "repine" is another possibility. *Katherine Austen's Book M*, 117n292.

415. Austen first wrote "stay and trust" instead of "only trust." She then inserted "only" above "stay and" without marking out either option.

416. Although Austen wrote "because," perhaps she meant "besides," which would make more sense in this context.

You might be kind to them also.

O no, I cannot understand it. And as I am able to make requital to them without studying designs of entreaty and commiseration for them, when I have parted with my interest, can render a compensation.

Many women have had great afflictions, yet sometimes I think mine outgoes them all. But then I turn on to other side, to the favor and conduct of my heavenly guardian: his sweet converting every rebuke to a blessed love token.

Was there ever an estate had so many troops of enemies as ours have? And it may please God, their very multitude and diverse interests may overthrow one another, and they may conduce[417] to our safety.

My God, thy name I bless that gives me peace; thou art my sure support. These crosses come from thee for my good.

My poor sister is sorrowful, full of afflictions (she that is far better than I). Yet hers appears to present consideration sooner at conclusion than mine have been. Yet[418] she is like to pass, before she sits quietly down, with some disrelishing[419] disturbances, and then it may please God to give her refreshments and take off her fetters.

I pray God grant his peace may fill my heart and possess my soul, whatever the men of the world dispossess us of. Let my heart be filled with thee, possessed with trust and dependence, with faith and assurance in Christ; then will this disposition be assured peace in all the calamities that can befall me or mine. If we have thy peace, O God, it is a peace and joy which passeth all understanding (but what are filled with it).[420]

This divine peace, which God's children have in their bosoms, will allay the tempests and inquietudes of this life. It will give anchor in the violences of unjust actions of men. This is the peace my soul, above all, desires far rather than to be invested in peaceable posses-

---

417. "To lead or tend towards (a result); to aid in bringing about, contribute to, make for, further, promote, subserve" (*OED*).

418. Austen used a caret to insert "yet."

419. "Distasteful" (*OED*).

420. Cf. Phil. 4:7.

sions: to possess thee, God the Father of peace,[421] God the Son, the[422] Prince of Peace, God the Holy Spirit, the[423]

Upon the Interruption of Highbury

Blessed be the Lord that hath given me a rebuke in this so near expectation of ours.

And if the monition I received tended to the death of our estate, instead of me, his name be blessed. I have found the sweet favor of my God in all his sharp strokes, and the result of this will be converted for the best, let the event be seemingly displeasant.

26 March 1665 at the Sacrament

The light of heaven's divine providence hath hitherto been my splendor, my luminary.[424] Therefore, shall I not doubt in the darkest eclipses of this world; he will still be my assured confidence. This day, O Lord, I have begged at thy altar of mercy for a renewed supportation from thy power. And then let the issue of things be what they can, if I have thy light to lead me, I am safe, even in the midst of all my enemies. O God, strengthen my understanding and judgment and patience, and if thou hast strewed my way with thorns, yet those thorns will be roses, if they be strewed by thee. Nay, if all my way is hedged with briars and thorns, if they grow up by thy appointment for my good and if I depend on thee, wilt preserve me from being scratched and tore by them. They are to make me cautionary and watchful, not to dismay me. For, while I am upon this vale of tears, my breathing must be sighs. O, my God, speak peace to my soul, while men do detraction and injuries to us. Let me not balk any way thou hast chalked out[425] for me, still go on with courage whatever the difficulties are.

421. These words are squeezed into the right margin of a verso page.

422. "The" is written over an illegible word.

423. Austen stops abruptly without finishing her sentence.

424. "A source of intellectual, moral, or spiritual light" (*OED*).

425. "To trace out, mark out, as a course to be followed" (*OED*).

O, let me glorify thy name in all the paths of thy providences is the unfeigned desire of my soul. Come life, come death, come adversity or prosperity, still I may serve thee and perform thy will.

Begin this discourse, p. 33; ending, 39. Begins at page 56 to 84.[426]

By the perpetual changes we see in this world, God will prepare us for those durable constancies we shall find forever in the next.

Out of Poem of Doctor Corbett's to His Friend When She Might Be a Widow[427]

And as the Paphian[428] queen by her grief's show'r
Brought up her dead love's spirit in flow'r,[429]
So by those precious drops rain'd from thine eyes,
Out of my dust, O may some virtue rise!
And like thy better Genius[430] thee attend,   [5]
'Til thou in my dark period shalt end. See page 16.[431]

426. Austen cross-references other parts of *Book M* (following her original pagination) similarly focused upon afflictions.

427. This is the only case in *Book M* of Austen explicitly attributing a poem to someone else. As Ross explains, Richard Corbett was known as an "Oxford coterie poet and Arminian bishop," and his poems "were enormously popular in manuscript commonplace books—in particular, those associated with Oxford and the Inns of Court in the 1630s and 1640s—and misattribution is frequent in these sources." "And Trophes of His Praises Make," 188. Ross has discovered that these lines are not from Corbett but from Henry King's poem, "The Legacy." Introduction to *Katherine Austen's Book M*, 32–33. I agree with Ross that Austen's misattribution of these lines suggests that she had access to poetry in manuscript sources; for more on the specific social networks through which Austen likely encountered verse in manuscript circulation, see Ross's introduction, 33.

428. "Of or relating to Paphos in Cyprus, a city believed to be the birthplace of Aphrodite or Venus and formerly sacred to her" (*OED*). "Paphian queen" refers to Aphrodite or Venus, the goddess of love.

429. These first two lines invoke the story of Venus and Adonis in Ovid's *Metamorphoses*. Adonis, an extraordinarily handsome boy whom Venus loves, is killed by a boar; the mourning goddess then transforms her dead beloved into a flower.

430. "The tutelary god or attendant spirit allotted to every person at his birth, to govern his fortunes and determine his character, and finally to conduct him out of the world" (*OED*).

431. Ross reads this cross-reference to an earlier page in *Book M* as "18." *Katherine Austen's Book M*, 120n306.

Certainly, if there was such a story of that queen's grief which brought the comfort of her lover to her, I may also believe some virtue is derived to me from the spirit of my dear friend[432] and that that emblem did convey an influence to me, which my mournful laments and meditations drew, not only heaven's comforts, but his intelligence also.

O Heaven, that has been my guardian and sent me assistance to a miracle, leave me not now in this encumbrance on me. And I shall resolve to sanctify to[433] thy great Majesty by all thou dost afford me and to make them (by thy grace) ladders to climb up to my eternal possession. I desire thy blessing they may not anchor my affections and love on the sandy foundation of this world's instability but serve for a far more noble intendment.[434]

Make me, Lord, to know why I should live, the end it tends to, and how I should live that I may be well instructed, informed, and directed how to perform that end which is commanded by my creation, my redemption. O, thou Holy Spirit, my {*See page 170*[435]} sanctifier, sanctify thy servant to discharge thy will.

The last week, I attended a friend of mine (Cousin Birkenhead's wife, Mr. Prier's daughter) to her grave. And when I recollect my distemper[436]—which began in February last about the beginning and continued until the middle of March—by a violent cold in my head, took away my hearing, my speech, my eyesight, and vapors flew up almost continually, as dossed[437] me in that manner I had scarce the benefit of my understanding. This cold and illness, meeting with troublesome business, the more discomposed me that I could not tell

---

432. Her dead husband, Thomas.

433. "To" appears to be inserted above the line.

434. "Purpose, design" (*OED*).

435. Austen added this cross-reference to the bottom margin of a verso page; she finished the last line of her prayer at the top of the facing recto page.

436. "Deranged or disordered condition of the body or the mind (formerly regarded as due to disordered state of the humours); ill health, illness, disease" (*OED*).

437. "To butt, toss, or gore (a person) with the horns" (*OED*). Ross reads this word as "dessed." *Katherine Austen's Book M*, 121. "Dess" means "to arrange in a layer or layers; to pile up in layers" (*OED*).

whether my occasions I had augmented my illness or my illness made my business so tedious to be endured. And coming upon that time I sometimes had the persuasions I should die at. And yet the Lord was pleased to let my glass[438] run longer and give a final stop to this sweet, good woman, adorned with the graces and true, humble virtues of a Christian and a wife. The original[439] of her illness—only a cold in her head—caused the same effects as fell to me in my head. Yet, Death became in earnest to her, and after 3 or 4 days, the sickness was contracting at her outward senses; in 2 or 3 days more, grew violent by convulsions, which deprived her of her life the 3rd of April 1665.

God hath spared me and my two sons, all three having felt severe effects of the sharp winter. And how many gone and withered as grass, and their places know them no more.[440] The 5th March 1664/5, my brother-in-law, Sir Edward Cropley, died; the same month, little infant Rowland Walteres and Sir Thomas Bide's eldest son of 13 years. The 21 April, Aunt Wilson, aged 73,[441] died, mother to Cousin Samuel Wilson.

Of Newington Barrow Hazard, 1665

If there is such a power can take away that which the laws of the land does affirm to us, I know no other remedy than to prepare myself to work for my living,[442] for I must expect all that I have may be gone. And I bless God I shall be able to do it. They cannot take away the peace and content of my mind and that disposition to dispose of my time in a peaceable contentment.

438. Hourglass.

439. "The thing or person from which something springs or is derived; a source, cause; an originator, creator" (*OED*).

440. Cf. Psalm 103:15–16.

441. The odd position of "aged 73" at the bottom of fol. 72r makes it unclear whether it refers to Aunt Wilson or someone else. When the book was closed, ink from the facing verso page bled onto this number; as a result, the "3" appears at first glance to be "9."

442. Working for a living would be at odds with Austen's upwardly mobile social aspirations.

God's care hath been over me, and it will be over me still, I trust.

How many enemies have I to contest withal, and how many parties to satisfy and to behave myself obliging to? Direct me, my God.

"Lord, how are they increased that trouble me! Many are they that rise up against me."[443]

Lord, hide thy servant from the insurrection of unjust men, who whet their tongue like a sword to divide and cut away our just estate. They encourage themselves in an evil matter and lay snares by a secret combination.[444] But thou, O Lord, art a shield for me—my glory, my riches, and the lifter up of mine head against them all. So that in thee I will not be afraid if they multiply to ten thousands that set themselves against me round about. If thy gracious providence arises and saves me, then am I sure of thy best blessing. And lead me, O Lord, in thy righteousness because of mine enemies. Make the way straight before my face. Thy way of thy wise providence let me understand, which can convert the victory my oppressors may have to see thy favor leaves me not. To exercise my faith, thou wilt "be a refuge for the oppressed, a refuge in times of trouble."[445] Let me ever trust in thee, since in all ages thou hast not forsaken them who depends on thy promises and seeks thee with a true, sincere heart. Read 27 Psalm.[446]

What shall I say of my foregoing felicities I found of that joyful intimation of my sovereign's restoration[447] in a dream? Book K, page

---

443. Austen quotes Psalm 3:1 verbatim.

444. "The banding together or union of persons for the prosecution of a common object: formerly used almost always in a bad sense = conspiracy, self-interested or illegal confederacy" (*OED*).

445. Psalm 9:9.

446. Psalm 27 is also an inspiration for Austen's fourth numbered poem, "Of Supportation." In this prose meditation, she returns to Psalm 27 for spiritual consolation and reassurance and echoes it in several places (e.g., Psalm 27:6, 9–10, 13).

447. Austen refers to her previous anticipatory happiness (and apparently, to what she sees as her prophetic dream), as a royalist, about the return of King Charles II, and her disappointed surprise that the new regime is implicated in her battles over Highbury.

207.[448] And shall it be that my lord and king's coming in must prove a fatal blast to our estate? It cannot be. Yet, if we are condemned by his clear judgment (and not by the violence of our craving adversaries), I submit. Since he is returned in peace, I sacrifice life and fortune, and let that blessing on a dying nation take all that I can offer.

Of English and Dutch Quarrel, 1665[449]

I pray God compose an agreement and union between both nations.

It is pity that honest industry should receive a punishment, and it is also unworthy that that nation should prove a viper to eat out the bowels of the mother which has fed and nourished it, the English nation having been the instrument of the Dutch's subsistence and greatness. (And) How did they in their deplored condition when the Spaniard governed them under bloody masters, who made spoil of their people by[450] the cruelty did by Duke D'Alba,[451] who bragged he had executed eighteen thousand by the hand of the common executioner, and yet it was their opinion they did not use cruelty enough? Then it was they made their miserable laments known to Queen Elizabeth (who was the balance to turn the scale of Europe). She adhered to their party and delivered them from the Spanish insultment.

448. Another example of Austen's practice of cross-referencing her other books.

449. This entry and the next refer to the Second Dutch War (1665–7), about which, see Christopher Hill, *The Century of Revolution*, esp. 167, 181, 185, 231. Todd convincingly relates Austen's concerns about the war to her own personal economic interests. "As an informed investor," Todd writes of the widow, who invested in the East India Company, "she must have been alert to conditions of trade, and to the marvels of the products of the East on which the company profits were based. When she discussed the Dutch war of 1665, for example, her remarks about the 'ungrateful' Dutch ... hint at resentment of their competition in the 'honest industry' of Eastern trade." "Property and a Woman's Place," 188.

450. Austen wrote "insulting over" after "people," crossed it out, and used a caret to insert "by."

451. Austen refers to events that happened during the reign of Elizabeth I in the last decades of the sixteenth century as part of the historical context for the current war in 1665; D'Alba was Spanish governor of the Netherlands serving under Elizabeth's enemy, Philip II, King of Spain.

O Ingratitude, well mayst thou be termed a monstrous vice! Now prosperity hath outworn those humble submissions and received benefits; now you, unworthy Nation, are become injurious and insolent to your obliged benefactors, who created you.

On the Battle at Sea, June 1666[452]

Everyone in these sad encounters prays and desires a particular prosperity: one that the Hollander and French prevail, and we that the English. My prayer is that a universal victory may be obtained and that all parties may be ready to comply to amity and detest the fury of blood and slaughter of Mankind.

Upon God's Giving Me Health

Surely, O God, when I was attended with discomposing infirmities and had a multitude of occasions, I complained with a kind of despair I could hardly overcome what was upon me. Well might it be very burdensome, for when we consider the weight of sickness, it is the greatest affliction of Nature, and when attended with another weight of difficult matters to negotiate in a season of sharp weather, was an accumulated heap of trials. From these, God hath gave me a suspension and restored me to my health, hath exceedingly assisted me and delivered me (though for a time) out of the perplexities and made my way easy to me again and laid aside those agitations of my mind.

Praised be the God of my help.

Read 7 Psalms called the "Hallelujahs," before 119.[453]

452. Austen added this essay later. She not only dates it 1666, but she also squeezes its last word, "Mankind," in the bottom margin of the facing page instead of continuing (as she often does) at the top of the next facing page, which must have already contained her meditation, "Upon God's Giving Me Health."

453. Austen refers to psalms that include the phrase, "Praise ye the Lord," which stands in for "hallelujah" in the King James Bible. Austen's note, "before 119," probably refers to seven

How shall we hide ourselves under those storms of calamity and scenes of these miseries of Mankind but under thy wings, O Lord?[454]

Upon My Jewel[455]

Surely in the sparks of this gem, I can see the sparks and shinings of God's love dart out to me. O, that I may wait at his altar all the days of my life and pay my vows, which I have made to him when I was in trouble.[456]

And though I have passed that time I expected some issue of divine providence would particular attend me and be explained to me, I may still wait and still learn to be assured, as a propitious hand hath been my attendant all the years of my afflictions and in a most supporting manner at the conclusion of that time when sickness and opposition meet together (and then I was defended).

O, that I may find the same protecting guard in every remainder moment of my life; then shall I not only find this emblem as an ambassador of peace to me formerly but in the future, too.

Nor let me think my observations have been vain and fruitless, not significant and useful to me. The issues[457] all along hath been gracious and the event full of the good pleasure of my God, and God hath spared me my life and gave a countermand that he would spare it, that he would exercise me with afflictions for the trial of my submission

psalms organized in a significant way poetically around the phrase "Praise ye the Lord" or "Praise the Lord" that appear before Psalm 119, probably Psalms 111–13 and 115–18.

454. This statement probably comments on Austen's meditation, "On the Battle at Sea, June 1666." It appears at the bottom of the recto upon which Austen squeezes the last word of that essay and is located—despite ample blank space above it—so that it is directly across from that essay, which is on the facing verso.

455. Austen refers to the jewel—which she believes to be a divine, providential gift—that she found near an old wall; see note 47.

456. Cf. Psalm 66:13–14.

457. "The outcome of an action or course of proceedings or the operation of something; event, result, consequence" (*OED*).

and reliance on him, that with Job[458] I might trust in him. And it may be God hath a further end to serve of me, that[459] I should live to praise his name as Job and Hezekiah[460] did. Although Satan endeavored to make the faith of the first to fail and Death brought ill news to the latter, God was glorified in both.

And as Isaac[461] lay at the altar, so did[462] my life lie a sacrifice at the will of my God. And if it had pleased him to take it away, my children lay almost helpless and their fortunes at the arbitrary will of enemies and encroachers. This was to try my faith, to[463] surrender them and myself to him, to him[464] the blessed guardian of orphans, to him that hath spared my life for his glory, to him that could have raised up[465] Isaac out of the dust unto Abraham.

To that most merciful God that hath chastened me sore but not given me over unto Death by its weight, that hath countermanded I should not die but live and declare the works of the Lord:[466] let my heart, O God, be fitted and set in tune to chant the acts of thy favor showed me and to bring forth the fruits of amendment of life, since thou hast enlarged a longer date to it. Nor was Hezekiah's death foretold to him by a plainer demonstration than I had. For what could be more certain to persuade myself of the reality than the agreement there was of my husband's age and mine to be the same at the period of the time limited to live? So was the counter-intimation the same as to Hezekiah. Nay, I received it by a wonderful providence ascertained

---

458. Job, a patriarch whose story is told in the Old Testament book named after him, remains pious, patient, and loyal to God despite repeated, severe tests of his faith and immense suffering.

459. Austen crossed out "and" before "that."

460. On Hezekiah (and his interaction with the prophet Isaiah), see note 83 above.

461. On Isaac and his father, Abraham, see note 18 above.

462. Austen initially wrote something else—possibly "was"—but reshaped the letters into "did."

463. Austen crossed out "and" before "to."

464. "To him" is deliberately repeated: Austen used a caret to insert the second "to him" above the line between "him" and "the."

465. Austen used a caret to insert "up" between "raised" and "Isaac."

466. Austen adapts Psalm 118:17–18 to serve her own purposes here.

to me in the words the prophet David spoke, corresponding to those of the prophet Isaiah, which were sent to Hezekiah.[467]

Has my God lengthened out my thread of life, and am I to tell his wonderful works that others may see them as well as I? "Open my lips, O God, and my mouth shall show forth thy praise."[468] Direct me I may spend my time thankfully and usefully, yet since it is not in the power of Man to direct his way, not in the ability of my frailty to exalt[469] thy goodness, not in my weak[470] courage and constancy to go over[471] the briars and thorns, the snares and temptations of this life, which if we pass over them with patience and courage, with weakness and resignation, with acquiescement[472] and address,[473] then we come nearest to the commands of God. O thou, the helper of the destitute, instruct me to those ends.

See Book J, 89.

Some persons may think me void of ordinary understanding to make so much of a trivial thing of so small extern[474] value, yet it cannot invalid[475] my eminent esteem. For sure I may very well place that emblem as a hand and[476] figure that relateth and expresses adversity and prosperity.

In adversity that therein a divine hand will send me relief and supportation, strength and patience. It looks at prosperity, too, notwithstanding so many occasions of incumbent[477] expenses, so much

---

467. See Psalm 118:17 and 2 Kings 20:1.

468. Austen quotes Psalm 51:15 almost verbatim.

469. Austen wrote "set," crossed it out, and inserted "exalt."

470. Austen used a caret to insert "weak" between "my" and "courage."

471. Austen wrote "overcome" but inserted "go over" above it without striking out either option.

472. "Acquiescence; passive acceptance" (*OED*).

473. "The action of making ready or getting prepared; preparation" (*OED*).

474. External.

475. "To render invalid; to invalidate" (*OED*).

476. Austen crossed out several letters (possibly "tha" or "the") and wrote "and."

477. "Falling as a charge or pecuniary liability" (*OED*).

as if all that I had coming in might been to the defrayment[478] I had not been accounted prodigal.[479]

But—to my own admiration[480] how it could be—have I been blessed with bountiful, increasing portions in the midst of obstacles.

Much of this in the beginning was insinuated to me. But the event declares plainer, and as I have passed extraordinary troubles and grievances, as what woman more, and go through with so little outward dismay or did not seek a shelter by a second marriage. Also, for blessings what woman—nay, or man—can tell the like (without[481] merchandise help or a trade), as I. But not to me, but the great God hath done it.

Who knows but[482] God in his providence sent me 6 years of trouble to prepare and fit me for the bountiful and prosperous blessing God was making ready for me and for my son: an estate that might well be six and thirty years in waiting for and six years in learning how to receive and entertain the blessing to enter into the land of Canaan, a rich soil flowing with milk and honey, silver and gold. And to me, who had once the interest to enjoy it longer than I shall, God thought fit to put me by, but hath provided for me another plentiful fortune. O, that I may know how to be sufficiently thankful and know how to manage so great favors of God's providence.

See meditation in parchment book, page 73, on my 36th year.[483]

478. "Payment of expenses or charges, discharge of pecuniary obligations" (*OED*).

479. "Extravagant; recklessly wasteful of one's property or means" (*OED*).

480. "Wonder, astonishment, surprise" (*OED*).

481. Austen used a caret to insert "with" in "without."

482. Austen first wrote "Perhaps" but then inserted "Who knows but" above it in the top margin of a new verso page and put "Perhaps" in parentheses without marking anything out. She might have been deciding between them, or she might have meant "Who knows but (perhaps)."

483. This cross-reference connects a previous meditation Austen apparently wrote on the occasion of her last birthday to the birthday meditation immediately following this cross-reference.

This on My 37th, April 30th 1665, Being Sabbath Day

God Almighty hath been pleased to add another year to my life and made my 36 now thirty-seven years. We know[484] time passed looks like the arrow that is flown, like the similitudes[485] of swiftness, frequently recounted. And though my years are[486] gone and I can never more recall a day back again—much more a year—yet, O my Soul, every day resolve with the Psalmist[487] to bless thee (O God). And every year for this patient forbearance of me, for thy bounty, for thy tender providence over me, therefore, will I praise thy name forever and ever.

And as in that 147th Psalm[488] of the recital of God's acts of munificence to David, so in the last psalm but one,[489] in one of those victorious psalms of praises which crowns the whole book, he incites to give praise for our birth: "Let Israel rejoice in him that made him: let the children of Zion be joyful in their King."[490] Nay, and let my soul and my body, too, every faculty of soul, every member of my body sing unto my God that hath made me. (And) whereof this day is the annual commemoration[491] of my birth and being, blessed be my God; he hath done so much for me, whereof I am glad. O, that the high praises of my God ever be in my mouth, that hath lent me another year, ending upon his day of praise.[492] Nor does it only finish up this last year, this day which my redeemer hath celebrated for his praise. This day is the commencement of a new year to me, which, as it represents my birth,

484. Austen originally began this sentence with the phrase, "And though those years are passed," but she drew a line through it and used a caret to insert "We know."

485. "A comparison drawn between two things or facts; the expression of such comparison; a simile" (*OED*).

486. Austen used a caret to insert "are" between "years" and "gone."

487. David; see note 61 above.

488. Psalm 147 begins, "Praise ye the LORD: for it is good to sing praises unto our God; for it is pleasant; and praise is comely."

489. She refers to Psalm 149, which begins, "Praise ye the LORD. Sing unto the LORD a new song, and his praise in the congregation of saints."

490. These lines quote Psalm 149:2 verbatim.

491. Austen first wrote "memory" but used a caret to add "com" and "ation" to the word, changing it into "commemoration."

492. Cf. Psalm 149:6. His "day of praise" is Sunday, the Sabbath; see the title of her meditation.

my coming into this world, so let this new beginning incite my living well and usefully in the world, whereof I now am incorporated into it by so many years past and am become an obliged person to perform those duties commanded from my Creator to my soul, my body, to my particular relatives and general.

Nor let me be troubled, O God, my years spin so fast away and are increased to more than half the age of Man, which—how few arrives to this account passed and how fewer number to that which Nature in some have attained of this later date!—no art, no certainty, no assurance, no positive demonstration can make out to me for another year. No, they cannot command the casualties,[493] the constellations of one day, of one hour to be confined.

My conclusion to this meditation shall be, with panting desires, that every day of my life may redound[494] to the glory of that great God, whose[495] I am (by his grace) and who hath made me. Then, if my time is concluded sooner or later, I know it shall be in the most proper and seasonable time finished, when it comes by his appointment who hath all times in his hand, who hath my particular determination in his keeping, to whom be the glory and honor of all his commiserations to me and of this year passed. On this day of his praises, bless the Lord, and forever more praise his name.

The[496] one and thirtieth year of my life was at the first year of my widowhood, and now, the 37th year of my life is in the seventh year of my widowhood.

This 30th of April 1666, in the recital of the dangers this year, I may well add and apply to that observation of the last year, for the casualties I have passed in this is a clear demonstration to me that it was not possible to foretell what might be or to prevent the dangers

---

493. "A chance occurrence, an accident; esp. an unfortunate occurrence, a mishap" (*OED*).

494. "To have the effect of contributing to some advantage or disadvantage for a person or thing" (*OED*).

495. Austen wrote "who hath," squeezed "se" onto the end of "who," and struck out "hath."

496. Austen first began this statement with these words: "Within the compass of a year, I could reckon that." However, she crossed out this phrase to start her sentence with "The one and thirtieth." This statement reflects upon the meditation immediately before it.

depending[497] on us. O God, we cannot: it belongs to the glory of thy providence; our deliverance is wrought by thee.

And in

[498]{*To Rejoice in God: A Duty in All Conditions*

My God, let me be assured whatever rugged path thou hast designed and dictated for me to pass, if I trust in thee, thou wilt make that hard way pleasant.

If I do not trust in thee, I shall be consumed.

O Lord, possess my heart, my affections with that cheerful disposition of joy, which thou requirest and commandest, to deport myself in every estate always to rejoice. And though sin is bitter and hath a weight to sink into the greatest sadness, although afflictions are grievous and what is grievous must be displeasant, yet since, O[499] my Savior, thou dost afford so gracious a remedy for sinners—thy most precious blood to absolve and reconcile to thee—since in our greatest sufferance[500] in this world, in our most sharp rebukes, thou dost afford faith and patience and hope, how can it but there must needs be joy, joy in the forgiveness of our sins, joy thou dost convert sorrows of this life to fit us for a crown of glory?

A true[501] Christian has these two grounds for his joy and that he is of the true faith.

Who was a greater sinner than St. Paul?[502]

Who was a greater sufferer than he? And what saint did ever exceed him in his joys in Christ?}

---

497. "Hanging or inclining downwards; pendent" (*OED*).

498. Austen started this essay on the verso facing the recto page at the top of which she continues her meditations on her birthday in 1666.

499. Austen marked out a word—probably "of"—between "since" and "O."

500. "The suffering or undergoing *of* pain, trouble, worry, etc." (*OED*).

501. Austen used a caret to insert "true" between "A" and "Christian."

502. On Paul, see note 19 above.

[503]that day of my near dissolution was thy ready safeguard found. I now can add another record of the favor heaven allows to me: to bless his name for this year's mighty preservation to me and to mine. Lo, death was strewed all the way before me, accidental and epidemical. We have been rescued from the raging pestilence that devoured thousands. We are surviving monuments of heaven's particular love.

Let me and mine make it a birthday to us all: growing in obedience, growing in thankfulness. Or if we do not, those heaps of mortality will rise up and be our condemnation. We might have been part of their admonition. They now are ours.

O God, give us grace to improve all thy monitions, my particular deliverance from apparent death and from contagious plague. Let us remember how eminently thy favor hath been our hiding place.

May 20: If the Parliament Takes Away Our Estate Who Are to Sit in June Next

Blessed Alderman (Highlord),[504] how do I revere thy memory, who wast the foundation, in a great part, of my second and later fortune (my own father's[505] being the happy instrument to raise me to my marriage without other assistance)?[506] Yet, by God's prosperous blessing, by the second addition I received, will make repair, if the violence of unjust persons bereave this family which I am grafted in[507] of what is their just due and honorable expectation. If they take away

---

503. Austen continues her meditation on her birthday in 1666 at the top of a new recto page facing her essay, "To Rejoice in God: A Duty in All Conditions."

504. Austen's stepfather, Alderman John Highlord, was the second husband of Austen's mother, Katherine Rudd; he died in 1641. Todd, "Property and a Woman's Place," 183.

505. Katherine Rudd's first husband, Robert Wilson, a draper who died in 1639. Todd, "Property and a Woman's Place," 183.

506. She never closes the parentheses; ending it here is conjecture.

507. Austen figuratively invokes the practice in gardening of inserting a graft, "a shoot from one tree ... into another tree" (*OED*). The family into which she is "grafted" is that of her dead husband, Thomas Austen, and his father (her father-in-law). Her essay discusses the different financial resources to which she has had or will potentially have access through her natal family and stepfamily versus her marital family.

40 pleasant fields from us, situated in a fertile soil,[508] we have about 40 considerable houses placed in an advantageous ground standing in a plot of the same likeness as that land is.[509] I may well esteem it parallel in situation to it: that land hath fields of each side a road or lane, and this hath houses of each side a lane or street.

Let our enemies do their worst, I cannot but infinitely wonder (how) God Almighty only makes exchange to us, both coming in their profits out together. My building[510] may be perfected at Michaelmas[511] next, when Highbury was to come to our possession (if we should hath both given to us, surely it would be a blessing bigger than we could receive).[512] Fortune, do thy worst: I am not in thy power, not in the hands of hab nab,[513] of thy blind lottery that cannot destine anything to the virtuous. No, I am in the hands of an especial providence, which differs as much from thy gifts as virtue does from vice, as truth from falsehood. This shall truly satisfy me, as what I have did come by the blessing of God, so what may be lost comes by his permission, too. I shall not murmur nor procure[514] curses—whoever is possessor of what was ours—that a blast[515] and caterpillar may devour it. It is sufficient he that wrongs the fatherless, the widows and oppresses in-

508. The Newington Barrow or Highbury estate.

509. Austen refers to small rental houses she built in an area known as Swan Yard in London. As Todd explains,

> Swan Yard had multiple meanings in Austen's exterior and interior worlds. It meant hope for ongoing income, the excitement and satisfaction of imposing her will to create a new neighbourhood and then, briefly, the anxiety of delayed completion and unlet properties during the Plague. As the contest with other claimants for Highbury mounted … Swan Yard came to be her particular achievement; paralleling the acquisition of Highbury by her father-in-law, it elevated her to his level. "Property and a Woman's Place," 188.

510. At Swan Yard.

511. September 29.

512. Austen first wrote "we were fit for"; however, she added "or we could receive" and put "we were fit for" and "or" in parentheses.

513. "Get or lose, hit or miss, succeed or fail; however it may turn out, anyhow; at a venture, at random" (*OED*).

514. "To contrive or devise with care" (*OED*).

515. "A sudden infection destructive to vegetable or animal life (formerly attributed to the blowing or breath of some malignant power, foul air, etc.)" (*OED*).

nocent persons heaven has made laws from the world's creation, and since that time (from the cruelty to Abel),[516] hath been enforced by all the violences committed that no true prosperity is entailed to unjust attainments. I may be sure that a little which the righteous hath is better than the proud revenues of usurpers. X 107[517]

O Heaven, give me thy especial grace, whatever my condition is, I may demean[518] myself with sobriety and patience, I may see what thou hast bountifully bestowed on me may retard all unevenness of spirit, may vanquish that unquiet temper of revenge and molestation, may conquer all weaknesses of passion, all clamors of discontent, and the frailty of my sex, knowing God is my advocate, God is my portion and my inheritance, not only my eternal but, by his exceeding blessing, my temporal also, to the wonder of all spectators.

O, that I may have that true charity not to pray against my enemies but for them, since God is ready of himself to hear oppressed persons. Though they make no colloquies,[519] though they vent no sighs, though no[520] tears of distressed orphans water the grounds which the power of violences commands away, God will hear in heaven. And O, that he may hear to convince the wrongdoer of that most heinous sin of oppression (the sin and scourge of all ages), that our thirsty, craving adversaries may not violate justice and devour[521] that which the just laws of purchase hath assured unto[522] us.

---

516. Abel, a shepherd, is the second son of Adam and Eve; his older brother, Cain, a farmer, murders him in a jealous fit of sibling rivalry when God prefers Abel's sacrificial offering over Cain's. God punishes Cain for his fratricide by condemning him to wander in exile and cursing his efforts to farm the earth (Gen. 4:1–16).

517. Austen marks the end of this paragraph with an "X," cross-referencing this material to a later page in *Book M* (i.e., her original page 107), where she adds a comment on this material and then marks that comment with a corresponding "X" and her number for this page (i.e., her page 102). See note 540 below.

518. "To behave, conduct or comport oneself" (*OED*).

519. "A talking together; a conversation, dialogue" (*OED*).

520. Austen marked out "they" between "though" and "no."

521. Austen used a caret to insert "devour" between "and" and "that."

522. Austen used a caret to add "un" to "to," making it "unto."

O, that God may hear to convince the wrongdoer into a reconciliation to himself, and however they succeed in this world, it may not be a snare to their family or ruin to their eternal estate.

Lord, now I walk in the midst of trouble, do thou revive me; stretch thy hand out against the unjust purposes of my enemies, and let thy right hand save me, thy gracious providence that in many former trials hath been merciful to me.[523] O, now be merciful to thy poor creature!

Upon 25 May 1665, the receiving a writ to go to trial at the suit of Sister Austen against me for the compassing[524] the Red Lion[525] to her and to make me pay £600 her husband hath tied that estate to pay it withal. Awhile after, I was reading the 120 Psalm: "In my distress, I cried to the Lord, and he heard me."[526] And do these words relate anything to me in this occasion; is a suit of law properly a "distress"? Truly, it might have been a great distress, if it had been all that we have. Yet, while we have so many pretenders to take away far more than that, does increase a bigger regard to this, and while it is one of those troubles which Job reckons[527] springs out of the dust,[528] may come within that comprisement,[529] since it is from those persons which, a few years since, was in confederacy and amity with me, from them which could the testator who conferred a present interest to them known their persecuting unkindnesses, they could not have exercised their will.[530] But

---

523. Austen adapts to fit her own situation Psalm 138:7, which states, "Though I walk in the midst of trouble, thou wilt revive me: thou shalt stretch forth thine hand against the wrath of mine enemies, and thy right hand shall save me."

524. "To contrive, devise, machinate (a purpose). Usually in a bad sense" (*OED*).

525. On the legal battle over the Red Lion Inn fought between Katherine Austen and Susanna Austen, the widow of Katherine's brother-in-law, John, see note 214 above.

526. Austen quotes Psalm 120:1.

527. Austen used a caret to insert "Job reckons" between "which" and "springs."

528. Probably an allusion to Job 5:6–7: "Although affliction cometh not forth of the dust, neither doth trouble spring out of the ground; Yet man is born into trouble, as the sparks fly upward."

529. "Comprehension; compass" (*OED*).

530. Austen first wrote "anger" but crossed it out and used a caret to insert "will."

it must suffice me he could not discern how they would be injurious; neither can they discover who will rise up hereafter to be their molestation. These troubles, these enemies, they spring out of the dust, and we cannot discern them. Yet though we cannot see them, he that orders and disposes for the good of his children does know of them, and if we learn to salute the chastisement, it will be a beneficial one. Now, surely it is by this way holy David prescribes me if I would have a blessing in my distress, it is to cry to the Lord that he may hear me and order it to his glory:

"In my distress, I cried to the Lord, and he heard me."

My God hath heard me in my many former distresses that were ponderous and weighty, and if he brings new, how may my confidence depend, my God will order it for the best, however it succeed.

Verse[531] Not without ground may I continue my prayer with David to be delivered from a deceitful tongue.[532] Who hath made more fair promises to do good to this our[533] family than he (Winstanley)?[534] And by flattering words deluded me into a friendship to serve some avaricious design, which lasted but a little while, and now breaks out into open treachery and injustice, encroaching all that he can to his family, which is the propriety belongs to the right of another, invading the interest of an orphan and, I may say, robbing the dead and the concernment of three persons in their graves (viz.,[535] father-in-law, husband, brother-in-law[536]). The living think they see them no more and therefore may do as they please. I know not how to dispute it, yet

---

531. Austen leaves a blank space and two colons with space between them after "Verse"; perhaps she meant to insert a specific biblical reference at some point.

532. Austen borrows from Psalm 120:2 (possibly the reference she meant to insert after "Verse"): "Deliver my soul, O LORD, from lying lips, and from a deceitful tongue."

533. Austen inserted "our."

534. This is a reference to Susanna Austen's father, James Winstanley; see Todd, "Property and a Woman's Place," Figure 1, 183; and Ross, introduction to *Katherine Austen's Book M*, 12.

535. An abbreviation for "videlicet": "That is to say, namely, to wit" (*OED*).

536. Austen writes three letters here (i.e., "F: H: B") with superscripts, suggesting that the letters stand for contracted words. Given the context, she almost certainly means her father-in-law, husband, and brother-in-law.

for my part, I am afraid of my actions and therefore jealous[537] they may be such as all may behold them. And I am sure the God of heaven sees all.

The CXXI Psalm tells me what I shall find if "I lift up my eyes to the hills, whence cometh all my help,"[538] a help that "will not suffer my feet to be moved" if I stand in his ways; a keeper will preserve me when I cannot see to defend myself. And in the shades of darkness will be light, in the heat of day be my shelter. In all those perils and evils which is for his glory, which is for my benefit—he will preserve my soul out of them. For temporal deliverances, they are not comparable to his gracious supportations through those dangers and temptations to be sustained.

I would fain know, upon this trial my sister and her father hath with me, whether with a good conscience and upright intentions they can lift up their hearts for a blessing for the success. I dare not judge it a self-accusing act; I shall have that charity to my sister-in-law (though cannot have to her father, by reason of his protestations to do all the offices of love and friendship to our family, when his actions speaks a ruin to it). For her, her judgment may be falsely informed and her duty wrongly enforced. I shall construe it an error in judgment.

O God, pardon the mistakes and unkindnesses in her, and forgive also the errors in my actions; in some things, when I do ill, I think them well and am not ready to see their depravity so run into them with a consent.

On the Trial

My heart desires to resign the events of this world to God's blessed pleasure. O God, give me more patience, more resignation and charity, more of those humble graces of submission and obedience, for these

---

537. "Zealous or solicitous for the preservation or well-being of something possessed or esteemed; vigilant or careful in guarding; suspiciously careful or watchful" (*OED*).

538. Austen adapts Psalm 121:1–2: "I will lift up mine eyes unto the hills, from whence cometh my help. My help cometh from the LORD, which made heaven and earth. He will not suffer thy foot to be moved: he that keepeth thee will not slumber."

will defend me and[539] regulate me from murmuring and envy at what she hath or may have. The issue of their pretensions is now at hand. They may have more from us, and their desires may be granted. Let me not have less of thy favor and protection, nor my son. And how happy I hear this day from his tutor of his sobriety and temperance! Rather, O God, let him lose all that this world can give than lose that or thy grace to carry and fit him to a heavenly inheritance.

{*X page 102*[540] *It is possible to be wronged and defeated and put by his right by injustice, fraud, or a strong hand.*

Isa. 10: "Woe unto them that decree unrighteous decrees and that write grievous things which they have prescribed to take away the right from the poor, that widows may be their prey and that they may rob the fatherless."[541]}

The 30th May: The Day before the Trial

O, thou natural vice of Envy! How ready to be filled with it, especially to a competitor, to one of yesterday started up in our family to intercept a fair fortune from us? How ready will this ill temper carry us out to disrelishes, to prevail more and more by evil wishes and desires?

But, O, thou Spirit of Sanctity, Spirit of Peace and the Dove, possess and fill and govern every disposition; drive away all rancorous and swelling grudges from me. Let me truly say, "Thy will be done in all the affairs of this world."[542]

If their design is bad, I may the better hope for success, yet it is not the first time a good cause was known to suffer.

539. Austen used a caret to insert "and" between "me" and "regulate."

540. See note 517 above. Austen put an "X" on her original page 102 to cross-reference it with this material (on her page 107).

541. Austen's quotation from Isa. 10:1–2 silently revises the verses as given in the King James Bible: "Woe unto them that decree unrighteous decrees, and that write grievousness which they have prescribed; To turn aside the needy from judgment, and to take away the right from the poor of my people, that widows may be their prey, and that they may rob the fatherless!" Austen's adaptation sharpens the focus upon widows and fatherless children.

542. Cf. Matt. 6:10.

But yet, my God, if I sin not against thee by my taking offense at the victory my unkind disturber may receive, she can have no triumph over me, nor I can have no loss.

On the Success to Us of That Suit

The judges this day have sentenced for us.

And such is the long progress and art of law that, after twelve terms' formality and business to exercise that trade, the case was dispatched by six lawyers and the judges in a quarter of an hour. Yet surely I may conclude if that Universal Judge above had not at the beginning prevented, they might have obtained their desire. But far may it be from me to rejoice in the death of that infant.[543] The real esteem to her father[544] denies it, and I hope no evil desire in me was to her, for I was ready to deliver those writings which was her due when the grandfather[545] came and demanded them the day before she died, and I had promised him he should have them when he sent[546] for them. But before that time, came a messenger brought word of her death. Thus, by the prevention of a few hours, the obtaining the lease, which was the ground of the quarrel, remained in my hands. And the law presently decided that the lease was fit to continue with me for the preservation of his interest to whom it did belong.

13. June 16, 1665: On L. Bark's Suit with Me for Highbury: Meditation

Thy favor, most great Lord, thy favor show:
Then will my[547] frequent troubles overblow;

543. Catherine Austen, the daughter of the widowed Susanna Austen and her late husband, John, died before 1663. Todd, "Property and a Woman's Place," Figure 1, 183.

544. Austen's brother-in-law, John Austen.

545. James Winstanley, Susanna Austen's father and the deceased Catherine Austen's grandfather.

546. Austen marked out a word—possibly a less legible version of "sent"—before "sent."

547. Austen first wrote "these" but inserted "my" above it without marking out either one.

Then will these molestations, which I find,
Turn to a peaceful harbor in my mind.
No perturbations ever can remove   [5]
My chief affections from thy sublime love.
Come then, my Lord, and sanctify what falls;
A low submission fits me for thy calls.
So shall all crosses weave into a crown,
If thou, my Jesu, styles me for thy own.   [10]
O, do not leave me when I am depressed
With human deluges; in thee have rest.
No weight so heavy but can make it light,
When thy supportment bears me in the fight,
And strong temptations then with all its darts   [15]
Not wound my soul when thy bright aid imparts.

14. What makes me melancholy? What black cloud
Does intercept my peace, does me enshroud,
And entertains[548] me with the shades of night?
Is all thy splendid favors darkened quite?
Where is the signal[549] smiles[550] did oft display?   [5]
In great eclipses, joy did reconvey
Those radiant marks,[551] which, when I sat alone
Did seem a heaven so much glory shown.
And am I now enveloped in fear
And former ravishments forget to hear?   [10]
O God, my sin 'tis my declining soul
Flies from thy altar, to the world's does roll—

---

548. "To engage, keep occupied the attention, thoughts, or time of (a person)" (*OED*).

549. "That constitutes or serves as a sign or symbol; symbolic" (*OED*).

550. Austen wrote "marks," crossed it out, and used a caret to insert "smiles."

551. Austen inserted something above "marks"—possibly "signs of"—but crossed out her insertion and kept "marks." Perhaps she noticed that she had used "marks" twice in three lines. She seems to have considered changing the second instance of "marks" (line 7) but ultimately changed the first one (line 5) to "smiles" instead.

A Lethe[552] stupefaction from that snare,
Creating much unnecessary care.
Restore me, Jesu,[553] that live saving balm,   [15]
As[554] these discordances may ever calm.

Not to Doubt of a God

Let us not be startled by the variety of religions and opinions in the world. But let a believer that hath God and Christ and the Holy Spirit go on in a firm assurance of comfort and not doubt of his religion that the ground is tradition and education. For by[555] the lively and infallible assurances of the Almighty's succors and assistances, of his favor and tender regard over them who fly to him for refuge, may convince of the truth of such religion, which I have found, as well as Abraham and Isaac, as well as David and St. Peter and St. Paul, as well as Esther and Judith and Deborah.[556]

One Troubled His Friend Was Like to Die, Answered

To die is not to be lost; our conversation and union hereafter will be more entire and inseparable.

    But, Sir, to live to serve God.

    There is no comparison betwixt a saint and a sinner.

552. "A river in Hades, the water of which produced, in those who drank it, forgetfulness of the past" (*OED*).

553. Austen seems to have first accidentally written "Iesy" (i.e., for "Jesu"), to have struck out her mistake, and to have rewritten "Iesu" again more clearly.

554. Austen started the last line with "That" but inserted "as" beneath "That" without marking out either word.

555. Austen used a caret to insert "by" between "For" and "the."

556. Esther, whose story is told in the Old Testament book named after her, is a queen and heroine who saves her people from persecution. Judith, whose story also appears in a biblical book named after her, is a beautiful widow who famously seduces a general, Holofernes, into letting down his guard with her, whereupon she decapitates him in his sleep to protect her people. Deborah is an Old Testament prophet and judge who leads her people to victory (Judg. 4–5).

15. On the Sickness[557]

O, let me fly to thee, unto thee still,
A rock of shelter in approaching ill;
Such have I found thee, my great God supreme.
In seven long winters, thy light was my beam
To guide my way and poise[558] me in my strait,   [5]
Paphed[559] in obscurity, a ponderous weight.
Still was thy glory such a staff of rest,
As every accident became the best.
I cannot be dismayed when have thy guard:
It is a convoy in what seemeth hard;   [10]
It is a ship, though rolling on the waves,
Steers to a harbor and avoids its graves
My part on providence to anchor still,
Nor can these billows of this world be ill.

O God, send the voice of joy and health in those sad dwellings that have it not, and continue joy and gladness in those dwellings which yet have it.

On Sickness

O God, thou hast exercised thy servant long in sorrows, yet thou hast more darts—the darts of pestilential death—which, if it be thy will, deliver us from.

---

557. The plague.

558. "To steady or make stable by or as by adding weight; to ballast" (*OED*).

559. Although the letters in this word are legible, "paphed" is not in the *OED*. Ross notes that Austen's "meaning here is not clear." *Katherine Austen's Book M*, 136n401. Perhaps Austen adapted this word from "Paphian" in the poetic fragment above authored by King that she misattributes to Corbett. On "Paphian," see note 428 above. Perhaps Austen misunderstood "Paphian" and thought it meant something other than referring to Venus. Given the context of "Paphian" in King's poetic fragment and that of "paphed" here, perhaps Austen mistakenly thought these words were related to being in a state of emotional distress, especially mourning.

That putrid disease, which infects the air and makes the air breathe death and mortality on us, which in its nature does health and refreshment! O God, direct thy servant where I should be and where my children for their safety.

O God, give us thy grace, and thy grace will give us thy glory.

Stay thy hand, O Lord, and let not thy judgments be dispersed in the air that every breath we receive may not be a destructive breath.

Here is a time of trial of our faith, of resigning myself to God. Hath not God been a hiding place and security to me in almost 7 years of my solitariness? Surely in this public distress, I am encouraged to trust in him, to fly to him. God can make this place I am in to be a Zoar,[560] a defense to me, yet I must know that in this world all things falls alike to all men.

The plague is the more immediate hand of God than any correction. O God, let me not think to shun thy hand but that it can find me out in all places. Nor let me dread thy hand, since this world is a weeping place, and joys are in the next.

Does this present time of general calamity threaten loss of our lives? And then the loss we may receive from men will not be sighed for.

Surely if God's eminent providence do guard us from the destroying angel and from the usurping devil of this world and that he bring us to confidence again after terror, O God, let us not think we have cut the wings of our temporal adversaries or of Death. For God can bring us—as long as we are in this life—to conditions full of uncertainties, and we shall be insecure and tossed on the point of danger until we do arrive at that everlasting haven of peace.

---

560. In Gen. 19:19–30, Zoar is the small city to which Lot flees to safety to escape God's annihilation of the cities of Sodom and Gomorrah and their inhabitants by raining down fire and brimstone on them. Lot's wife notoriously disobeys the divine command not to look back at the burning cities and is turned into a pillar of salt.

The Lord have compassion on these multitudes of people that are took away daily[561] in whole families and swept by troops[562] to a sudden grave. Exchange their toilsome condition in much mercy; then will they be happier than if they were transferred to be kings and princes in this world.

God's time of deliverance is the best, the most seasonablest that he chooseth from that sharp temporal calamity of plague and pestilence. And so is that time the fittest when he rescues from oppression of men.

I know not whether I or mine shall escape this trial, this general scourge. Surely if we do not, there will be a period of a long contention.[563]

Yet, the Almighty's hand is not shortened, but he can save and redeem us from a violent, disconsolate death.[564] And when his time is come, we can be freed from this rod of oppression hath been on our family these many years and that hath lain upon my back by all the violence my adversaries could invent by might and by aspersion, making me a fanatic,[565] that by such forged pretensions the readier might devour the prey God in his good time can give us dismission[566] from.

And "the rod of the wicked shall not rest upon the lot of the righteous."[567] No oppression that makes a wise man at his wit's end shall not last[568] always because of the extremity it reduces to. Trust in the Lord and wait patiently is the Psalmist's direction.[569] See Exodus 12:41: "at the end of the 430 years, even the self same day, all the hosts

---

561. Austed used a caret to insert "daily."

562. "Used to indicate a great number; a lot" (*OED*).

563. "The action of straining or striving earnestly; earnest exertion, effort, endeavor" (*OED*).

564. Cf. Isa. 59:1.

565. "A mad person" (*OED*).

566. "Release from confinement; setting free, liberation, discharge" (*OED*).

567. Austen quotes from Psalm 125:3.

568. Austen marked out "have it" before "last."

569. Cf. Psalm 37:3, 5, 7.

of the lord went out of the land of Egypt."[570] Abraham[571] had been[572] told him in a dream: Genesis 15:13.[573]

91 Psalm: 12 July 1665

"I will say of the Lord, he is my refuge and my fortress. My God, in him will I trust. Surely he chall deliver thee from the noioomo[574] pootilonco, etc. If a thousand fall at thy side and ten thousands at thy right hand, it shall not come nigh thee."[575]

O, Lord God, now that we fear thy judgments that is among us, and as it lies now, we are afraid that ten thousands may fall on our right hand and a thousand on my side by me. How, Lord, can I think myself better than they, but that thy dreadful scourge will find us out also? But, O my God, if it be thy will, accept of my contrition and create such an affiance on thy merciful compassion that we may be delivered and that we may rejoice and be glad in thee all the days of our lives. "Spare us, O Lord, spare thy people, whom thou hast redeemed with thy precious blood, and be not angry with us forever. Spare us,

570. Austen quotes almost verbatim from Exod. 12:41: "And it came to pass at the end of the four hundred and thirty years, even the selfsame day it came to pass, that all the hosts of the LORD went out from the land of Egypt."

571. Austen marked out several words before "Abraham"; Ross suggests that the marked out phrase is "Yet it was 30 years more than what." *Katherine Austen's Book M*, 138.

572. Austen used a caret to insert "been" between "had" and "told."

573. See Gen. 15:13–14: "And he said unto Abram, Know of a surety that thy seed shall be a stranger in a land that is not theirs, and shall serve them; and they shall afflict them four hundred years; And also that nation, whom they shall serve, will I judge: and afterward shall they come out with great substance."

574. "Harmful, injurious, noxious" (*OED*).

575. Austen quotes selectively from Psalm 91: 2–3, 7: "I will say of the LORD, He is my refuge and my fortress: my God, in him will I trust. Surely he shall deliver thee from the snare of the fowler, and from the noisome pestilence.... A thousand shall fall at thy side, and ten thousand at thy right hand; but it shall not come nigh thee."

good Lord."[576] And commit us to the charge of thy holy angels to stop the currents of danger to us.[577]

My God, set thy love upon us, and then thou hast promised to deliver us. If we know thy name, know thy all powerful majesty, know God, our Redeemer, know the Holy Spirit, the comforter in our sorrows, and know to call upon thee, and then shall we find thy ready answer to us, to be with us in trouble, and we shall be delivered either temporally but most surely from eternal destruction.[578]

David composed this 91 Psalm when 70,000 died in 3 days.[579]

16. My God

Whose all sufficient mercy I have found
And by whose brightest glory I am crown'd,
That lofty favor and refulgent light
Still be transparent in despairing night,
And while environed with sharpen'd arrows   [5]
Of fierce contagion, send thy saving [carouse?].[580]
'Tis thy peculiar hand and stretched out dart,

576. Austen quotes almost verbatim from part of the Anglican Litany: "Remember not, Lord, our offences, nor the offences of our forefathers; neither take thou vengeance of our sins: spare us, good Lord, spare thy people, whom thou has redeemed with thy most precious blood, and be not angry with us for ever. *Spare us, good Lord.*" *BCP*, 69.

577. Cf. Psalm 91:11: "For he shall give his angels charge over thee, to keep thee in all thy ways."

578. Cf. Psalm 91:14–15: "Because he hath set his love upon me, therefore will I deliver him: I will set him on high, because he hath known my name. He shall call upon me, and I will answer him: I will be with him in trouble; I will deliver him, and honour him."

579. 2 Sam. 24:15 and 1 Chron. 21:14.

580. Although Austen's spelling of this word is clear enough (i.e., "carrowes"), what she means by it is not obvious. According to the *OED*, a "carrow" is "a gambler" (adapted from an Irish term), but this meaning does not fit the overall context of the poem. It is possible that Austen used a phonetic spelling for "carouses" to refer instead to "the action or fashion of 'drinking carouse'"—in other words, drinking liquor, toasting one's health, and so on; in fact, the *OED* lists "carrowse" as one spelling variant for "carouse." Perhaps she understood "carouse(s)" to mean a drink or drinks that improved, protected, or invigorated one's health or that had medicinal value (e.g., cordials), in addition to having the celebratory connotation associated with "carouse." This possibility seems reasonable, given her reference

'Tis thy preventive balm can shield my heart.
No antidote from men that can prevent,
Only that providence divinely sent.   [10]

My God, grant I may not be taken with these worldly enjoyments, which, if I have the greatest fullness, cannot render me a full satisfaction. Disunite, untie, and divorce my affections from the love of whatever thy blessing hath lent me, and totally attract them on thy glory, on thy will.[581]

July 30, 1665

O Lord, in mercy spare this slender family in this populous contagion, and remove thy dreadful judgments, which hang over our heads, that hangs over the city, over the country, over the kingdom, over the town I am in, over my house, and is not yet, by thy especial providence, in my house. Yet who am I or mine better before thee than the meanest beggar or than those whom thou hast taken whole families away? Be entreated, O God, to give a cessation to the destroying angel, to stop the rigor of the calamity.

Psalm 76

"Thou dost cause judgment to be heard from heaven."
"He[582] shall cut off the spirit of princes. He is terrible to the kings of the earth."

---

to "preventive balm" in line 8 and an "antidote" in line 9. A less likely option is "carus," which can refer to "various forms of profound sleep or insensibility" (*OED*).

581. Austen's language recalls John Donne's Holy Sonnet 14, "Batter my heart, three-personed God," especially line 11: "Divorce me, untie, or break that knot again." *John Donne: The Complete English Poems*, ed. A.J. Smith (New York: Penguin, 1986), 314.

582. Austen marked out a word before "He."

"The remainder of thy wrath," O God, do "thou restrain." For deliverance: "vow unto the Lord, and pay thy vows."[583]

"The righteous hath hope in his death."[584]

May not the thoughts of death dismay me or be troubled if God take me away from my possessions I have expected to enjoy. (No) for remember, Christ Jesus came not to redeem me for them—not for temporal possessions—but for eternal inheritances, which I hope by his merits to be partaker of: such as eye hath not seen nor ear heard of.[585]

For Highbury and for the Swan, my buildings, may they never possess my desires or swallow my heart.

O, my God, that hath kept me all my lifetime, keep and defend me in this temptation now, when a person of a most subtle insinuation,[586] of a most complying temper, of frequent opportunities seeks all the advantages to take my affection by acts of readiness and assistances to me and by his helpful offices of preservation to my health in the time of this great danger, doth by all ways that a great experience diving into my temper and inclination and deep contrivance can possibly act.

I bless God I early see at what all his addresses and winning, flattering discourses tends to.

---

583. Austen quotes almost verbatim from but significantly rearranges the order of verses in Psalm 76; cf. 76:8, 10–12: "Thou didst cause judgment to be heard from heaven; the earth feared, and was still.... . Surely the wrath of man shall praise thee: the remainder of wrath shalt thou restrain. Vow, and pay unto the LORD your God: let all that be round about him bring presents unto him that ought to be feared. He shall cut off the spirit of princes: he is terrible to the kings of the earth."

584. Cf. Prov. 14:32: "The wicked is driven away in his wickedness: but the righteous hath hope in his death."

585. Cf. 1 Cor. 2:9.

586. Austen probably refers to Alexander Callendar, a Scottish physician who became her friend and courted her, despite her resistance to a second marriage. Several later entries record her interactions with her persistent suitor. On Callendar, see Todd, "Property and a Woman's Place," 187.

O God, do thou shield me as with a garment and give me a cautious prudence to behave and acquit[587] myself that I may not do a dishonorable folly to sully and disparage the fair prosperities of my life.

May my carriage (in this intervene) be watchful, resolute, and yet not contemptuous or ungrateful, but if he doth oblige me by kind offices[588]—such as a friend may receive—that I may return civility and a fair requital.

And not give so great a satisfaction as the reward of myself and all my estate for that which I am in a capacity civilly to requite by[589] a lesser reward.

Most unhappy women, how many are your snares and trains laid for you! I no more wonder how soon you are won to another affection. There is a just cause you should design yourselves with the most discretion you can to prevent the dangers may unworthily surprise you in the race of a long widowhood.

My retreat is to fly to my ever-watchful guardian in heaven. And who can be safe without that special aid,[590] which I depend on in all my surprisements, and will not leave me if I go not from that Father of my spiritual and temporal conduct?

114, see 131[591]

The most remarkable points I have observed out of the works of Dr. Donne I do refer to two points, which are prosperity and adversity.[592] Not withstanding that[593] great adversity and crosses attend us in

587. "To meet standards of good conduct" (*OED*). Austen used a caret to insert "and acquit" between "behave" and "myself."

588. "A service or kindness done, or attention shown or given" (*OED*).

589. Austen appears first to have written "a" but reshaped that "a" into the "b" in "by."

590. Austen wrote "providence" after "special aid" but crossed it out.

591. These numbers appear to refer to Austen's original pagination of *Book M*. In her pagination, 114 contains the poem she numbers 15 and entitles "On the Sickness" and 131 contains a prose meditation against remarriage.

592. Ross notes that Austen draws in this entry from Donne's funeral sermon for Sir William Cokayne. *Katherine Austen's Book M*, 142n435.

593. Austen used a caret to insert "that" between "withstanding" and "great."

this world, we are not to slacken our duty of industry and usefulness in the course of our race.

Afflictions have a most excellent virtue.

And industry is established by a strict command of honoring God in upholding his works and doing his will. These have an instance in the[594] precedent of Sir William Cokayne,[595] to whom God gave two great lights: the sunshine of prosperity and the moonshine of affliction. Honor and fortune crowned his industry; crosses and troubles did the same to his graces, which fitted him for his highest and eternal crown.

[X596]Adversity and prosperity: both conduce for good. And the place of rising and the place of falling is most at courts, etc. See page 13, Book C; page 26, Book I.

Thomas

I purpose to leave you, my Son, my great jewel and a greater than that—my providential jewel.[597] I confess I present a temptation not to prize the first before the other, since reason demonstrates that more valuable before the other little rarity, which must have its worth imposed by imagination and fancy, by effects of the mind, by constructions. And I am sure when you go to a goldsmith, the one is a jewel, the other a pebble; one the ornament for an eminent person, the other no higher than a gem for a child. Yet could I, dear Son, impress in thy fancy some resemblances of mine, the value and esteem would hugely transcend the first. Well, I give them both to thee: in the one,

594. Austen used a caret to insert "courts" between "in" and "the" but crossed out her insertion. There is a small "X" next to the deleted "courts," which appears to correspond to an "X" at the bottom of this same page that marks a note on adversity and prosperity at court. She also marked out an "s" at the end of "instance." See note 596.

595. Sir William Cokayne (1559/60–1626), a merchant who became wealthy and rose to numerous positions of political importance across his lifetime (*ODNB*).

596. Austen uses this "X" to indicate that the material following it refers to a corresponding "X" in her text immediately above it; see note 594.

597. The jewel she once found near an old wall and regards as a divine gift.

look on my fortune to this world; in the other, as an emblem of a more lasting riches. And if I enjoin you anything, keep that which I chiefly regarded, and know it was once a means to ease me in[598] many storms of trouble and to mitigate a violent grief.

To My Son, Thomas, if He Lives to Enjoy the Blessing of His Estate

Dear Son, now you come to possess a comfortable estate, think not that you must entertain and welcome it with the thoughts that it is flung upon you by the hands of Fortune, for if you have no farther considerations, Fortune will put on a pair of wings and fly from you, just as the goddess Fortune in old Rome and their other gods, who could fly away to their disadvantage and transfer their favors to others.

You have a further duty by recollection and gratitude. You are not to think—though your father and grandfather are out of sight and out of your knowledge—that your respects are canceled. You must know an honor and duty is to be performed to the ashes of your most worthy father, from whence your being sprung and who did surpass conferring nature to you while he was with you by an ardent affection for your education. Also, you are to pay a gratitude to the memory of your honored grandfather, whose industry and just qualifications provided a fair possession, and in him, to the former predecessors, who brought a blessing to him and from them all derived prosperity to you. One part of duty is performed by a civil prudence, by a free charity, and by an industrious oversight that you may rather commendably augment, than riotously or carelessly impoverish or diminish, their estates descended to you. And it is easier and with less pains to spin the web out longer than to ravel it out. I say "with less pains" since, where is prodigality and vicious demeanor, is more study to fling an estate away than there is prudence to carry and manage it with virtue and usefulness to all the intentions and purposes of nature, of liberality, and reputation. There is more trouble to provide for pleasure because there is so great dissatisfaction in the least intermission of pleasure as it must be carried on with more solicitation to create that vanity and keep it to the height.

598. Austen used a caret to insert "in" between "me" and "many."

And we may observe to keep up those virtues of liberality and[599] to be useful and noble, to serve oneself and others, too, and to arrive at honor is by way of augmentation and enlargement of our patrimony, which enables to perform any lawful designment.

To My Son, Robert Austen

This lesson is related to you: to revere your predecessors in your heart. Nor can I be persuaded it wants a notice or go without a blessing but that very much we do receive by a reverent memorial and respectful regard. And you are to look back to the springs of your fortune, and though they have glided by your worthy father and Grandfather Austen, yet for as much as your estate came particularly from my portion from my good father, your Grandfather Robert Wilson, and my unparalleled father-in-law,[600] Alderman Highlord, it is fit you pay a homage to their memory and merit. This is practiced by imitation of their virtues, by enjoying your blessings, by thankfulness to God that blessed you with a good possession from virtuous honesty and praiseworthy industry. It may be a precedent to command the same good endeavors and fair qualities in you. And if they obtained it by their own faculty of industry (assisted by God's blessing), what may you then do by a ready help and supply from two foundations?

I dictate this lesson to you of prudence since I know it is so acceptable to our great patron[601] and its contrary, careless profuseness, the original of all the unhappiness that attends on[602] ourselves and posterity in this world.

---

599. Austen marked out "of" before "and."

600. Her stepfather (her mother's second husband), not her father-in-law.

601. Ross notes that this word—"Patteron" in Austen's original spelling—might instead mean "pattern" or "pater" (i.e., for "father"); however, in the given context, "patron" seems most likely. *Katherine Austen's Book M*, 144n443.

602. Austen first wrote "to," struck it out, and inserted "on."

To My Daughter, Anne Austen

Nor are you, my daughter, to be left out in this duty. Look you with honor on these predecessors mentioned, and take along with you your grandmothers. Have your Grandmother (Anne) Austen's virtue and goodness, yet may you be defended from the passion of her melancholy and bear with more courage the encounters of endeared[603] separations, which must necessarily attend us; her too great love occasioned much unhappiness to her by it. And remember my dear mother, your grandmother (Katherine Wilson Highlord). Take industry from her and me, and as I have practiced virtue and employment (I hope to be useful in my life) from my dear mother, be you an example and pattern to your children. And in this I shall conclude to you, all my three dear children, my wishes[604] that the blessings descended to you from the integrity and worthiness of all your predecessors be a blessing to descend in channels to your children and to many generations. And if you do your parts by leading commendable[605] and useful lives and that you set virtuous examples, God will to every generation continue his favor—who is the fountain of all blessings and happy contentment here and who has better blessings to crown our low and weak endeavors with—which that to all you and yours may obtain is the unfained prayers and blessing of your affectionate mother.

Katherine Austen[606]

August 28th, 1665

On going to Essex the 28th August: the day before I went there, there was dead that week before I went 7,400.[607]

---

603. "Affectionate, cordial" (*OED*).

604. Austen used a caret to insert "my wishes" between "children" and "that."

605. Austen first wrote "a" before "commendable" but struck it out.

606. Austen ended her notes to her children by signing her name in letters much larger than her normal writing.

607. This information appears in the form of a marginal note written alongside Austen's large signature and the poem that follows. Both the note and the following poem are in

17. Heaven's goodness was my ready stay;
May not that kindness go away.
Thy former conduct now appear
In this mournful, dying year.
Alas, my Lord, thy direful[608] hand,   [5]
What potentate[609] that can withstand?
And whither can I go or fly,
But thy severity is nigh?
'Tis near me, Lord, yet I have found
Th'effects of mercy to abound;   [10]
Those, now I supplicate, may attend
To the last period of my end.

We must not run into weak conditions and consent to a dishonorable marriage and then lay it upon the appointment of heaven.[610] I think no such thing ought to be imputed. Not but that there may be singular virtue in a person of a low fortune; there may be also the same in one of a considerable. And I think it is a great folly—of which myself[611] is the only accessory, by impairing the prosperity God hath given use—to cast myself and a future issue into meanness, when I may arise to better. When fond affection and deluded judgment is thus ensnared into error, the unhappiness I[612] must own as the contriver and carver of and not lay it on Destiny (for we must know if we will consent to unhappy choices, Destiny will not contradict it), and we must sit down under the burden of that grievance our own weak

---

smaller handwriting than that which Austen used in her letters for her children.

608. "Fraught with dire effects; dreadful, terrible" (*OED*).

609. "A monarch, prince, ruler, esp. an autocratic one. Also: a powerful or influential person; a magnate" (*OED*).

610. Austen's meditations on resisting the temptation to remarry probably relate to her interactions with her suitor, Alexander Callendar; see note 586 above.

611. Austen initially wrote "one's self" but added "my" above "one's" without marking out either one.

612. Austen wrote "we," put it in parentheses, and inserted "I" above it. In an essay about taking personal responsibility, her revisions increasingly acknowledge her own agency; also see note 611.

choice makes. Yet,[613] if we are in the care of God, with our endeavors will prevent our unhappiness.

The best way is not to stay by the temptation, which may insinuate into a weakness of consent and bring an undervaluing alteration of life.

Now, if it is urged there is extraordinary virtues and endowments does contract affection, without relation to fortune, and it is not so mean a thing as that does make to be beloved, it is answered. if there is such a thing as virtue to be loved for itself, let my Amoret[614] entertain me as his friend and not vitiate[615] a noble friendship with interest or any other respect but pure amity. Yet, certainly because it is rare and scarce—such a thing as virtue to be esteemed[616] for itself (especially in single men and single women)—I do rather hold the converse of such is not without great caution to be neither of married persons, lest a vicious end ensues, since men adore their company for advantage to themselves, nor can I believe when they say that men had rather be in the society of women and women loves better that of men.

No, I do discover by a comparison not to give credit to words: the king courts the city and loves it because it is rich, and then it will be safe[617] to the king, as a rich, wise woman is loved. And if she does not love again, it is no matter, if she is not wise and rich.

For my part, I do no injury to none by not loving, but if I do, I may do real injuries where I am already engaged to my deceased friend's posterity.[618]

As for my body, it can be enjoyed but by one, and I hope it is the worst part of me and that which every servant maid and country wench may excel mine and can give the same satisfaction as mine. But that which my desire is should far excel my body is my soul and the virtues and qualities of that, and this, I think, may be useful to more

613. Austen wrote "And" but added "Yet" above it without marking out either option.

614. Sweetheart, lover (an indirect way to refer to her suitor, Alexander Callendar, without naming him and while giving both a literary and hypothetical quality to her meditation).

615. "To render corrupt in morals; to deprave in respect of principles or conduct; to lower the moral standard of" (*OED*).

616. Austen crossed out "loved" before "esteemed."

617. "Secured, kept in custody; unable to escape" (*OED*).

618. That is, to her children (Thomas, Robert, and Anne) with her late husband, Thomas.

than one and not confined to a single person, and if anything in me is to be loved, I hope it is my mind, and that I deny not a friendly correspondence to you, nor any beside. Thus, all my friends may partake of me and enjoy me and be married in the dearnesses[619] and usefulness and benefits of friendship, and more than one can be satisfied with those lawful intimacies of friendship and correspondences of lawful, public, safe conferences, which is the better part of me and which true virtue should most affect. And thus I may be partakers of the nobleness of your parts by an open and free amity.

And[620] thus that person which pretends to so great affection to me may be satisfied with an[621] honest conversation and such lawful, allowed conferences.

I was in discourse with a gentleman. He had many arguments to prove the papists had not idolatry by their pictures. "This," he said, "Monsieur Amaruth[622] did prove in a book he set out, wherein he shows the idolatry of several nations, as the ancient Egyptians to be perfect idolatry but of the papists not to[623] be such." I answered diverse things to it, and though at last I did not disapprove according as it might be […][624] the having a[625] picture of Christ or of saints, yet let Mr. Amaruth say what he pleased, I must condemn the Romanists[626] of superstitions and idolatrous adoring theirs.

He then said to me and protested, if I was a very beggar woman, if I would have him, he would have me, and he would discourse with me all day, for he never talked with me but learned something of me. I told him he was mistaken, and if I was so indeed, he would not.

---

619. "An expression or token of affection" (*OED*).

620. Austen inserted an ampersand in the far left margin before "thus."

621. Austen marked out a word before "an."

622. Ross speculates that Austen refers here to Moise Amyraut, a French theologian. *Katherine Austen's Book M*, 147n455, 456.

623. Austen inserted "to" between "not" and "be."

624. Austen leaves an unusual blank space—in which a word or two might fit—after "be."

625. Austen inserted "a" between "having" and "picture."

626. Roman Catholics.

For my part, I declined all things might give him a vain encouragement and told him I was like Penelope[627]—always employed. "Aye," says he, "her lovers could not abide her for it."

When I was returning home from Mrs. Al., he said, "You would not take pity if one should grow distracted for you." "There is no fear of that," said I. Then, as[628] he took me by the hand, he said, "What a hand was there to be adored!" I answered him, looking upon a tuft of grass which had growing in it a yellow flower, "That there spire of grass was fitter to be adored than my hand." "Aye, alas," says he, "we are all but grass, but shadows, and whenever we see the grass, we are to adore the Creator in it."

I think at that time he was not very well, for afterwards, he said that on that evening, he first began to feel his head ache, which grew for 4 days very painful, so that eleven days after, he ended his life on the 7th of October[629] 1665 at Tillingham in Essex.[630]

He was one that much observed dreams, yet he had seldom any that boded any good to him but foretold him of disasters, which I took notice of. The night before he died, he told a very long dream of many circumstances in it—how that he was in a great place like a church and saw many friends and Mr. John Austen,[631] and he was in a habit all in white and over that long, white garment a short, black coat and his hair short and a little hat, and people said he was in orders.[632] "'No, but I am not,' said I. 'Then I kneeled on a stone and prayed a great while.'" Then he said he met me walking with a gentlewoman, and I told him I had a mind to go to such a lady's house, if I could get in. He said he would go and help me to accommodation there, and so I did. And it was a very curious house, where the lady did govern and order

627. Penelope is the loyal wife of the epic hero, Odysseus; for more on the significance of this classical allusion, see the introduction, 19–20.

628. Austen used a caret to insert "as" between "Then" and "he."

629. Austen wrote "August," marked it out, and used a caret to insert "October."

630. Todd explains that "[i]n October 1665, Callendar accompanied her to Essex as they fled the plague in London and he died in Tillingham, one of the villages in which Katherine had jointure properties." "Property and a Woman's Place," 187.

631. Her dead brother-in-law.

632. As a member of the clergy or a religious fraternity.

everything in a[633] most exact order and prudence. "And then I waked, being called by another name, called 'Kingsman.'"

I then asked him, after he had repeated this dream, what he thought of it. "Nothing at all," yet at first said it was a very strange dream, and he had had many strange ones of late. Then I said, "I am to go to the king at Oxford about my business, and you will be well and go with me." Says he, "I had rather go to the king of heaven," and I hope he is, who departed the next day.

His eminence in learning and in all the accomplishments of a gentleman, for his prudence and parts, might well make him arrive at high places, and to aim at promotions in England was the occasion he left France, a place where he had dwelt 18 years and found much contentment, a place which, when he found by changing from it, could not meet with preferment in England (much obstructed by the cloud and disrelish of his country) (being a Scot). This made him often, as he said, "sigh that he was parted from his beloved country, France," and this, among other frowns of Fortune, did give depression to his spirit that, on[634] the last night he had in this world, did express how he had passed through many checks[635] of Fortune. It is supposed made some impressions on his mind, together with late apprehensions at the place where he went with me to be freed from the danger of the pest,[636] and there he took notice of night birds, of screech owls,[637] as he concluded one in[638] the house would die. Nay, when his sickness did increase, my own fears suggested his end was nigh and revolved to me a dream in its full meaning. Book K, page 213.[639]

And in that place and room where I was then at Mr. Wood's was the very same fashion and situation as I saw in my dream: the gravestone I bought in such a corner was represented as Tillingham Church stands and that place where he was buried. And surely his

633. Austen wrote "with," crossed it out, and inserted "a."

634. Austen wrote "at," marked it out, and inserted "on."

635. "A sudden arrest given to the career or onward course of anything by some obstruction or opposition; a rebuff, repulse, reverse" (*OED*).

636. Pestilence, plague. Austen started to write a "b" but reshaped it into a "p."

637. Bad omens.

638. Austen wrote "of" but inserted "in" without marking out either word.

639. Another cross-reference to one of Austen's other books.

worth and merit deserves to have a memorial of stone infixed over his grave, he lying buried in such a remote place from his friends. He found his death in that country, and I was nigh meeting with mine there also at that time he had lain about 5 days ill.

How shall I be able to recite this act of commemoration by the escaping immediate death on a surprise, I being the moment before in perfect health? A fall off a tree—where I was sitting in contentment—that had seats on the tree easy to go up in! Yet, in return, I fell from a height about 3[640] yards to the ground, which bruised my face of the left side and my right thumb put out of joint, so that I lay dead at present and had not the least sense of my falling. Yet, it pleased my God to send two women who saw me fall, which if they had not seen me fall, the hedges and bushes would have made me undiscovered to any, and I do not know but I might have lain more than a day in that very lonely place. These women had then come a mile from their dwelling, (and) one of them was unwilling to come because that tree had frightened many a person, that it was haunted with spirits, and the fearful woman took me to be one. Yet, by the confidence of the other, they came and found me without any sense. They took me up, and I fell down again, being all in blood by my fall at the nose; at length, I began to speak yet could not in a good while recover to know how I came by that hurt and much amazed to see myself in that disorder. They brought me to the house where I lodged, two fields from the place I fell. There, by God's blessing, I recovered my great illness by cordials, which the sickness of vomiting up blood diverse times by the way had weakened my spirits. My temples had laid upon it 4 leeches, yet my face and head was in a numbed manner for a fortnight.[641]

Thus, it pleased my God to be my deliverer. Then, when I had a sensible impression I was but a wind, a puff, and if the Almighty had not sent and helped me, I had been blown out and should no more returned until the Great Day. (on the 2nd of October 1665, my fall)

---

640. Austen appears to have initially written "4" but then traced over it to make it a "3." It is also possible that she tried to do the reverse (that is, to reshape "3" into "4"); both numbers are still fairly visible, given that one is superimposed upon the other.

641. Two weeks (fourteen nights).

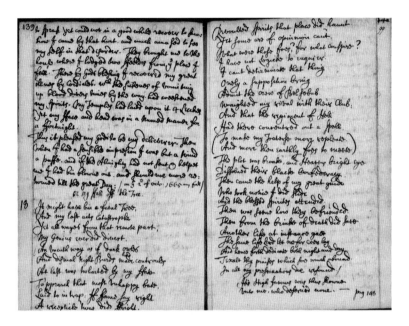

Figure 7. Folios 98v–99r. Austen's poem, "On My Fall off the Tree." ©
The British Library Board. Add. MS 4454.

18. On My Fall off the Tree

It might have been a fatal tree
And my last act's catastrophe,
Yet all ways from that remote part
My Genius ever did divert.
An uncouth[642] way, as if dark owls   [5]
And dismal night birds had[643] controls,
At last was thwarted by my fate
T'approach that most unhappy bait
Laid to entrap. If Fame say right,
A receptacle[644] 'twas did fright: [10]
Revolted spirits that place did haunt,
Yet some are of opinion can't.
Where were those foes? For what conspire?
I have not logic to inquire.
I can't determinate that thing,   [15]
Only a supposition bring,
Admit the crew of Beelzebub[645]
Weighted my rival[646] with their club
And that the regiment of hell
Had there concentered[647] out a spell   [20]
(To make my traverse more replete
And more than earthly foes to meet).
The plot was broke, and Heaven's bright eye
Dissolved their black confederacy.
Then came the help of my great guide,   [25]

---

642. "Not commonly known or frequented; solitary, desolate, wild, rugged, rough" (*OED*).

643. Austen first wrote "made" but inserted "had" without marking out either one.

644. "A place into which a person, animal, ship, etc. is received and sheltered; a haven" (*OED*).

645. Satan, the devil; see Mark 3:22–26.

646. Possibly in the sense of "a bank, a shore; a landing place, a port" (*OED*).

647. "Brought to a common center; concentrated" (*OED*). Ross, who reads the unclear fourth letter in this word as "v" rather than "c," suggests that Austen "coined a verb here from 'conventicle,' the term for a clandestine meeting, associated with Nonconformist sects and with witchcraft." *Katherine Austen's Book M*, 151n470.

Who took notice I did slide,
And the blessed spirits attended:
Then was seen how they befriended,
Then from the brink of death did save
Another life at instance gave. [30]
The same life, Lord, let me forever lay
And henceforth dedicate both night and day
T'exalt thy praises, which so much abound,
In all my preservations do resound.
His high favors was thus shown [35]
Unto me, who deserv'd none. Page 148.[648]

Meditations on the Sickness and of Highbury

Through six afflictions, God has promised to carry his children, and in the seventh, they shall be delivered.[649] Six I have passed, six years of diverse mixtures full of accidents and encounters extraordinary for a single woman to pass. And let me repeat the diverse emergencies I have been put to for the supplying great undertakings and how I have passed through, notwithstanding my preventions.
    Since August 1664 to Michaelmas 1665:
My expansions[650] in my building
Every term's bills of expense
William's burial
Mr. Cruse's cheat
A tenant's cheat
The vexatious suit of Symons   40-0-0
The renewing the lease of Deane Hardy   80-0-0
The expense at Parliament
The losing by a pickpocket   14-0-0

648. Austen cross-references this poem about her fall (from her original pages 139–40) to a short paragraph near the bottom of her page 148, where she contrasts her experience to that of a boy who fell from a tree and died. See note 669 below.

649. Cf. Job 5:19.

650. Austen's spelling is "expentiones"; it is possible that she means "expenses" instead of "expansions."

The lending money to Cousin William in necessity only for 2 months and unpaid yet	336-0-0[651]
Expense to maintain my son at Oxford	
My help to Cousin Varney in his urgent need	40-0-0
Giving Cousin AR	5-0-0
	£
My helping Sir T with	200-0-0
Then when I was to get and did get for them builders[652]	300 0 0
All these sums I raised, which found somewhat difficult by reason of hindrances, viz.	£
The not receiving at Mid. 1665 of the king	700
Not receiving Cousin William's money in May	250
Rent of arrear expected in Essex	150
Of Cousin Parnam	50
Of fines of houses	200
And the abating of the rent of a house I had let	£20 per annum
And the losing for the time of building the Swan	£100 per annum

At this time is arrived that most bounteous blessing of Highbury, which I hope will well wade me through the residue of my expensive buildings and disappointment of rents from a general stroke.[653]

Far be it from me to imagine I have had those helps and deliverances from my difficulties by the conduct of my own understanding, not possible to been defended without a greater help. And I have found by reliance on my good God an interest in those promises that all things work for the best. And I have found the assistance and ministry of angels; I have been comforted by the spirit of divine comfort and mercy—to whom be ascribed the full glory of every deliverance

---

651. According to Todd, "in February 1665 Austen's kinsman, William Williams (husband or son of Elizabeth Rudd Williams, Austen's maternal aunt), borrowed £336 from Austen, mortgaging the lease as security.... Like many other mortgagors, she had trouble getting her money back. 'Cousin William's' inability to repay the loan was one of the financial woes she listed in early 1666 and, family or not, in 1669 she began foreclosure proceedings." "Property and a Woman's Place," 186.

652. Austen used a caret to insert "builders."

653. Austen inserted "stroke" above "cause" without marking out either option.

and blessing—that helps one through intricacies by a miracle, and when he sends me losses, does also send me helps to a wonder. O, that I may be fit for such aids and mercies and that my children may grow up to honor the God of their fathers! By the deliverances I have received from my most gracious God, my faith, my hope does promise his future mercy for my eternal good. And my God is able to deliver me in this dreadful seventh year—a year where the angel of his displeasure conveys darts of speedy death.[654] Yet, I trust (to those who are smitten[655]), it is only a temporary anger, that anger which will end in everlasting favor. Now from this temporary, momentary stroke, God Almighty, if he pleases, can free me, his most unworthy servant, and my children and relations.

Surely this seventh year, wherein I am involved in this[656] general calamity, may well reckon completes out seven afflictions.[657]

O Heaven, if thy gracious will manifests thy praise and good pleasure by deliverance from this seventh, this lamentable calamity that strikes so terrible in all places, and give a rescue and freedom from our threatening adversaries and a stop to their unjust trouble, how shall I endeavor to live a new life? O, if Heaven will give to me the greatest providential perfection of time[658] to me in the dispensing his

---

654. The plague.

655. From "to smite": "Of the Deity, in or after Biblical use: To visit with death, destruction, or overthrow; to afflict or punish in some signal manner" (*OED*).

656. Austen wrote "a," marked it out, and inserted "this."

657. Several factors in Austen's life appear to have led her to ascribe special importance to a period of seven years. According to Todd, Thomas Austen indirectly constrained Katherine to avoid remarriage for the first seven years of her widowhood. Although Thomas's will did not explicitly prohibit Katherine from remarrying, it "did effectively prevent it by stating that Katherine would cease to be executor if she remarried, naming his son Thomas as the alternative. Thomas finally reached age seventeen (minimum age to be executor) in 1664. That, plus her husband's heavy charitable gifts over seven years, framed Katherine's sense that seven years was the limit to her imposed widowhood." "Property and a Woman's Place," 196n24. Ross argues that Austen's fascination with seven years related both to her belief that she would live only until the same age that her husband reached at his death and to her providential worldview, in general, which was profoundly influenced by the stories of biblical figures such as Job, Hezekiah, and David. Introduction *to Katherine Austen's Book M*, 15–17.

658. Ross reads this word as "mine"; given the similarities between how Austen writes "m" and "t" at the beginning of a word and "m" and "n" in the middle of one, "time" and "mine"

strokes and send deliverance to me—as now I am sure will be, either in this life or a better—what a heart ought I to have to be disposed and devoted to his glory!

19. Some work of piety go then and show.
A life of purity I ever owe,
All humble thanks, a life of full address[659]
Unto thy altar pay, from me that's less
Than the least mite[660] of what thy goodness throws.   [5]
Still streams of [bounty?][661] sure a mountain owes;
I never can discharge so great a sum.
Lord, teach me what to do. Thou bidst me come,
Come to that ocean, where I still have found
Exalted mercies in its triumph crown'd   [10]
With rais'd devotion and with ardent zeal.
Declare me what to do; something reveal,
Since grace and glory all high things wilt give.
Teach me with circumspection how to live.
From special favors begs enlarged desire;   [15]
My soul in all its motions may move higher
That Heaven and Earth, to all, I may display
The love of Jesu and his sovereign stay,
And by an outward and an inward story,
Render my praises to that immense glory.   [20]

---

are both possible here. *Katherine Austen's Book M*, 153. However, Austen's focus in this passage upon a seventh year as a time of deliverance suggests that "time" is more likely.

659. "An approach directed to God, etc., esp. expressing gratitude or praise; a prayer" (*OED*).

660. "A minute fragment or portion; a tiny amount" (*OED*).

661. The middle letters in this word are unclear. Austen appears to have written over them to reshape them into new letters or clearer ones, but in this effort, she blotted them out partially. "Bounty" best fits the context and meter of the poem. Ross suggests "poverty"; however, the "b" beginning the word is clear, and "poverty" seems unlikely in context. *Katherine Austen's Book M*, 154n487.

Let me ever give praise to thy name for thy mercies and receiving the satisfaction of my hopes from thy plenteousness and loving kindness. Let me never ascribe to myself any honor or the glory or thanks of any good action or prosperous success but to thee, who art the author of and giver of all good things. And preserve me from worshipping or loving any vain imagination and making anything be my confidence besides thee.

20. This is indeed a copious theme;
I have not words enough can speak
These acts of conduct and of grace.
To celebrate my great preserver's praise,
Some angel write that never hath decays.   [5]
My imperfections does admit no skill;
There's so much vanity and so much ill.
Most glorious Lord, send out thy brightsome ray:
Then my stupidity shall shine like day
And be unveiled from its gloomy night,   [10]
And thy unparall'd[662] favors shall indite—
Me, a weak woman, in my dangers strong,
Conducted by thy blessing all along.
In all my straits, when dangers sunk me down,
God was my castle and my high renown.   [15]
I am, alas, I am so weak a thing,
Neither assistance or can merit bring.
Thy supreme mercies mercies do unfold,
Can never with the tongue of Man be told.
O Fountain of immeasurable love,   [20]
What vast degrees transcendent goodness move!
Heaven, Earth, and Hell all speak what thou hast done.
Earth thy full blessings from th'abyss thy Son
Ransom'd from terror, and at last provide
A hill of glory never to divide   [25]

---

662. I.e., unparalleled; Austen wrote "vnparral'd" to keep within the line's meter.

Ravissant[663] happiness at glory's throne;
There know thy praises without learning one.

21. Has conduct carried me through seven great years,
Great in perplexities and great in fears?
Great griefs with Job[664] could hardly be expressed,
Neither by sighings or by tears redressed.
Six folded trials and a seventh as great   [5]
By a particular and general weight
Hard knot negotiates by oppression knit.
A dread, consuming sickness came, and yet
Mercy outshined all those dark-eyed clouds
Design'd[665] to me in seven years' rugged folds.   [10]
The wise Egyptians deemed six complete;
The divine scriptures does the same repeat.
Six hardest trials, and to give renown,
There comes a seventh: this is affliction's crown.
My gracious Lord, wilt thou admit to me   [15]
Thy special[666] favors, so much glory see?
O, that upon thy altar I may lay
A contrite heart and perfectly obey,
That every day and minute be confined
Thy bright memorials to bear in mind   [20]
And to the future generations tell
How high, how excellent thy glories swell!

    O God, that art worthy to be praised with[667]

---

663. "Ravishing, delightful" (*OED*).

664. On Job, see note 158 above.

665. "Marked out, appointed, designated" (*OED*).

666. Austen first wrote "dearest" but inserted "special" beneath it without marking out either one.

667. Austen ends this sentence abruptly. A large blank space (about one-third of the page) follows her unfinished sentence, suggesting she meant to write more there but never did.

A week before I had my fall, I heard of a boy in that hundred[668] that was a plowing, and when his fellow plowman went in for some occasion into the house, he went up a pear tree and presently fell down and broke his neck and never stirred more. It might have been the same to me.[669]

On That Day Highbury Came out of Lease, Michaelmas 1665

Am I the person am to reap the first fruits of that long expectation and enter into those pleasant fields of a fair inheritance? And that it should be appointed for my children—it is a blessing I know not how to receive! Yet, let me and mine ever remember that we receive our prosperity and enter into a large revenue through the jaws of death and by the heaps of mortality that we may be instructed always to be ready to part from it as readily as we do receive it and not to set up a rest in an earthly paradise. Aye, and let the name bear the same remembrance: Highbury, to bury those that are mounted never so high in this world.

22. Is't true, indeed, to me and mine
That many blessings richly shine
On the frail stock[670] of flesh and blood?
'Tis more than can be understood.
We exalted and made high;   [5]
Others in their anguish lie.
We accessions[671] of this world;
They in penury are hurled.
Beyond my apprehension comes
Our favors in the largest sums.   [10]

668. "A subdivision of a county or shire, having its own court" (*OED*).

669. This paragraph is located at the bottom of Austen's original page 148. Her cross-reference at the end of the poem she numbers her eighteenth, "On My Fall off the Tree," is to this account of a boy's fall from a tree. See note 648 above.

670. "Trunk or stem" (*OED*).

671. "Something which is added or joined to another thing; an augmentation" (*OED*).

Yet, one thing we must sure to know:
By engagements,[672] more do owe
Unto heaven and one another,
To our God and our poor brother.

23. On the Situation of Highbury

So fairly mounted in a fertile soil,
Affords the dweller pleasure, without toil.
Th'adjacent prospects gives so rare[673] a sight
That Nature did resolve to frame delight
On this fair hill, and with a bounteous load,   [5]
Produce rich burdens,[674] making the abode
As full of joy, as where fat valleys smile,
And greater far, here sickness doth exile.
'Tis an unhappy fate to paint that place
By my unpolished lines, with so bad grace   [10]
Amidst its beauty; if a stream did rise
To clear my muddy brain and misty eyes
And find a Helicon[675] t'enlarge my Muse,
Then I no better place than this would choose:
In such a laver[676] and on this bright hill,   [15]
I wish Parnassus[677] to adorn my quill.

672. "Moral or legal obligation; a tie of duty or gratitude" (*OED*).

673. Austen first wrote "sweet" but inserted "rare" without marking out either one.

674. "What is borne by the soil; produce, crop" (*OED*).

675. "Name of a mountain in Boeotia, sacred to the Muses, in which rose the fountains of Aganippe and Hippocrene; by 16th and 17th c. writers often confused with these. Hence used allusively in reference to poetic inspiration" (*OED*).

676. "The basin of a fountain" (*OED*).

677. "Mount Parnassus, regarded as the source of literary, esp. poetic, inspiration" (*OED*).

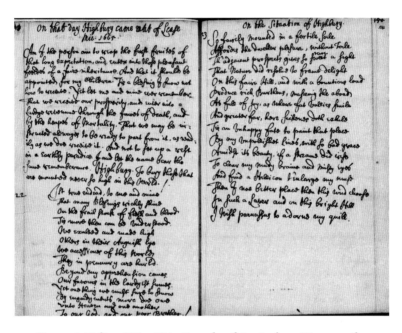

Figure 8. Folios 103v-104r. Sample of Austen's writings on the
Highbury estate, including the country house poem, "On the
Situation of Highbury." © The British Library Board. Add. MS 4454.

When I deduct the legacy my dear mother left me (at her decease) and sever it from my husband's estate, I have added to our estate—by God's great blessing upon me these seven years of my widowhood—such another estate as was left to me and my children.

And if we inherit Highbury, is as much as any one of those two parts.

I do reckon our estate in 3 parts:

First, what my husband left;

2nd, what by God's extraordinary blessing added;

3rd, that long expectation, the discourse of many, the interruption of more.

And that so much should come in my possession! O, my God, what am I to receive so much? And that by such plentiful acquisitions, our God should please to free me and mine from a great many of those huge miseries of want which do afflict the most of Mankind. Yet, our God pleases to mingle some bitternesses in my comforts. Grant, Lord, they may be advantages to me of wisdom and piety to draw me from the love and desire of this world to the pursuit of the divine and spiritual felicities will last forever.

O, that Heaven would direct me what I should do: whether I shall glorify his name by a contemplative private life or by an active public life? Direct thy servant in what may be conducing to thy praise, and not to me, O Lord, but to thy name be the glory of my whole life.[678]

It is the infinite desire of my soul to glorify thy name that I may become an instrument to serve my God. Take not thy assistance away from me. Give thy blessing to my endeavors, and give me understanding what to do and wisdom to act thy blessed commands and continually guided to discharge those things put in my hand to act, O God, that art worthy to be praised with all pure and holy praise. Therefore, thy saints praise thee with all thy creatures. Thou art to be praised, for thou hast made me joyful.

We are not to disclose the secrets of a king, but it is honorable to reveal the works of God.

678. Cf. Psalm 115:1.

Meditation

Bless thy servant with wisdom and industry to the performance of my duty in this world that the generation to come may find my help and assistance, as I have found and been greatly blessed by the industry and employment of my predecessors.

February 1665/6

Surely I ought to sit down and call my own ways to remembrance. Nay, and let me call the works of my God into memory with me, whose favors and the outgoings of my God hath so many[679] eminent ways appeared to me, never to be forgotten one moment of my life. O God Almighty, be with me still in the many trials that attend my life. Thy grace was sufficient for St. Paul; I know thou wilt afford it so for me.[680]

And now I am detained with suspension between hope and fear what my adversaries will do shortly, I can have that retreat to David's confident argument: that had overcome the lion and the bear might also vanquish stout Goliath.[681]

24. O, spare me that I may recover
Strength to pass my troubles over;
Then, in thy aid and not to me,
I may exalt thy Majesty.
Thou'rt greater than my potent foes,   [5]
When they invent me many woes.
O, thou art higher to subdue,

679. Austen used a caret to insert "many" between "so" and "eminent."

680. Cf. 2 Cor. 12:9.

681. For the story of David slaying the giant, Goliath, see 1 Sam. 17; Austen refers especially to David's comments before the fight in 1 Sam. 17:37: "David said moreover, The LORD that delivered me out of the paw of the lion, and out of the paw of the bear, he will deliver me out of the hand of this Philistine [i.e., Goliath]. And Saul said unto David, Go and the LORD be with thee." On David, also see note 61 above.

Though they convent[682] with all their crew.
In my destitute condition,
Thou'rt my Sovereign I petition;   [10]
'Tis thou, who dost low orphans right
And to depressed widows fight.
Mercy that has been often found,
Thy mercy that is often crown'd
Upon my weakness, let me find,   [15]
When men's justice may be blind;
Unveil, O God, their dire deceit.
No more their furrows[683] may repeat
Upon our shoulders, nor their rod
Still interrupt our peaceful bode.[684]   [20]
Give us quiet, and then we
Will give ourselves up unto thee.
Or if a mighty knot conspire
Our overthrow, then be thou nigher.
I know canst make a gain to loss   [25]
And sublunaries[685] be no cross.
To thy great pleasure lowly yield,
Or lose or win, in thee I'll build.

---

682. "To come together, assemble, meet" (*OED*). Austen first wrote "Although they band," instead of "Though they convent." However, since she spelled "although" as "all tho," she put "all" in parentheses, thereby leaving only "tho." She inserted something above "all" but marked it out. She inserted "convent" above "band" and put the entire first half of the line (including her revisions) in parentheses.

683. "A rut or track, a groove, indentation, or depression narrow in proportion to its length" (*OED*); cf. Psalm 129:3.

684. Although "bode" can, in some obscure cases, mean "prayer," "petition," or even "perch" (*OED*)—any of which could make sense in this context—Austen might have meant "abode." She clearly wrote "boade"; perhaps she wrote the letters out of order by accident or deliberately truncated the word for poetic purposes.

685. "Characteristic of this world and its concerns; mundane; material; temporal, ephemeral (*OED*).

King David was the great example of trouble and confidence in that trouble; to his meditations I resort to, and he that was his retreat shall be mine.

As now I can say with him,[686] "many are the troubles of the righteous," I trust that second part shall also declare, "the Lord delivers them out of all."[687]

This conflict and stratagem of my enemies' devices against us—by the former gracious experience[688] of my heavenly Father's deliverances to me—gives me encouragement I shall be victorious over them. My God, if that blessing I obtain in behalf for a helpless family I am guardian and if the wings of prosperity and peace pitch[689] upon our dwelling, make me, O God, to be as humble as I now am often dejected, often disturbed. Yet, howsoever thy disposal shall command, I trust shall be fitted by those suffering graces to attend thy will because I know my enemies can go no further, nor do no more than by thy permission.

My Nancy[690] is busy and inquisitive into all things of housewifery—to be informed and to learn—and every country affair delights in, which I am very well pleased to see. And if be the will of God, may she never come to such a task as I have. Yet, why should I say so? Is not that all-sufficient Father of mercies able to help her as to me, that she, as well as I, may see every day assisted, relieved through what heap of troubles God shall cast?[691]

---

686. Austen used a caret to insert something unintelligible and "him" between "say" and "many." The unclear marks probably abbreviate "with."

687. Austen quotes Psalm 34:19 almost verbatim: "Many are the afflictions of the righteous: but the LORD delivereth him out of them all."

688. Austen first wrote "encouragements" but marked it out and inserted "experience."

689. "To settle, alight, land" (*OED*).

690. Her daughter, Anne.

691. Austen marked out a word—probably "upon"—after "cast."

On February 12, 1665/6: On Sister Austen's Renewing Again Her Pretension[692] for the Red Lion

What will envy, hatred, and covetousness do? No bounds these enormities hath; it cancels all obligations, respects, and gratitude and comes now to triumph and to perfect the ruin to an orphan by its endeavor.

All along I have been persecuted for Highbury; I must have an addition from them. It is not sufficient to enjoy £350 for life.[693] He will deny her the blessing of her posterity to keep away and beguile as much more. This is not all insatiable thirst drives at, will compass unjustly the rest forever.

Lord, let those[694] dragging away of our estate from men by the cords of covetousness and oppression be so many chains, so many lines to pull us unto that place of the blessed, where no enemy can assault us.

On Valentine's Day, This 14 February 1665/6: My Jewel

Welcome, thou best of Valentines,
Firmer to me than lover's twines.
Alas, they vanish, but this tie,[695]
A pledge, a surety annually,
Grand omen of a bles't presage   [5]
To wade me through a stormy age,
Throughout my desert solitude,
A reflex[696] brings beyond my food.[697]

692. "The assertion of a claim as a right; a claim made; a demand" (*OED*).

693. Ross notes that Austen's husband, Thomas Austen, left £350 to his brother, John. *Katherine Austen's Book M*, 162n527.

694. Ross reads this word as "these." *Katherine Austen's Book M*, 162.

695. Ross misreads "tie" as "lye." *Katherine Austen's Book M*, 163.

696. Probably in a primary sense of "return, rebound" but possibly resonating with "reflection of light, heat, etc." (*OED*).

697. Possibly in the expansive sense of "livelihood," in addition to the common meaning (*OED*).

When I am poor, by vast expense
Supplied have been beyond my sense.   [10]
In this scarce year, dire want was seen
To many thousands in extreme.
In my obliged enterprise,
Where many failances[698] did rise,
Successive burdens came apace,   [15]
And poised even in that chase,
My dear propitious Valentine
Seven annual circuits didst confine.
(This day assaultments makes me sad;
This day reboundments makes me glad.)   [20]
Why should I speak thus to a stone?
Unto a thing, that life has none?
We know that heretofore was told
By outward things did secrets hold.
Why may not I this jewel prize,   [25]
Wherein mysterious record lies?
Nor is it that I do adore,
As it's a key or is the door,
Similitude of providence
Declaring stories out from thence.   [30]
Heaven is my great resorting rock:
There am I harbor'd in my shock.
From thence, his hand will place a crown
Of ample joys, sink sorrows down.

Most welcome day, wherein I found a ray,
For 15 years has been a chanting lay.[699]

---

698. Austen appears to have written "fallances." She could mean "fallaces" ("deception, trickery, falsehood") instead of—or perhaps in addition to—"failances" ("the quality or fact of failing; failure, neglect, falling off") (*OED*). Ross reads this word as "Fallauces." *Katherine Austen's Book M*, 163.

699. "A short lyric or narrative poem intended to be sung" (*OED*).

March 20, 1665/6

Our estate is sunk now almost to half it was, which seems to be a paradox at this time that it appears to the eye of the world to be quite as much again, if not twice more. Now let me do as the merchant to save his credit and to promote his adventure. Let me borrow, too, and keep up my repute, and freely pay the incumbents[700] and taxes and debts I am engaged. And there may come a prize in the benefit of Highbury's farmery, and my buildings' fines may wade me over those present blocks and failances, which are not a few.

The rents of Essex for about a year and half is owing £70 more a year and quarter's rent nigh me.

£200 per annum is in my hands that was rented of houses and land. My building continues a dead drug;[701] £700 I received interest for is at an end. £200 Cousin W.[702] can receive none of this year and quarter. Highbury is a hazard in two respects: in the opposition and in the ill management. And still I am attended with lawsuits—Sister Austen again and another troublesome man sues in form of paupery.[703] These make up to me a triple tax: now that the taxes by appointment are doubled, by molestations are trebled, too. How I shall come off of all? Time must tell the narration, whether good or bad. (And now do borrow good sums.)[704]

And now must I reckon up my error that I have been mistaken in my account and calculated wrong by measuring that Highbury and the Swan would arrive both together in their profits at Michaelmas last. It is true then my buildings were most of them finished and the other out of lease. Yet, accidents and general troubles and the unseasonable former year of drought and mortality hath gave an interruption, so

---

700. Austen probably means "incumbent charges." She spells this word "encombents"; Ross interprets it as "encumbrance." *Katherine Austen's Book M*, 164n536.

701. "A commodity which is no longer in demand, and so has lost its commercial value or has become unsaleable" (*OED*).

702. Cousin William.

703. Austen refers to a legal opponent claiming to be a "pauper," that is, "a person allowed, because of poverty, to sue or defend *in forma pauperis* (i.e., without paying costs) in a court of law" (*OED*).

704. This parenthetical comment is squeezed into a blank space between paragraphs.

that at this time, instead of profit, they are a hydra;[705] a cormorant of a double head devours all I can procure (and makes me feel the charge of Oxford and necessary things more pinching). £40 in a [?][706] is pay taxes for Highbury, £33 fee farm and to fit it up by gates and fences, etc. (There is nothing but has interruptions, and these little things may blow away.)[707]

O my God, thou hast helped thy servant through infinite many plunges and obstacles formerly, and still there does grow more, and more will arise while this world is strewed with thorns and thistles, with ruggedness and trouble. Lord, let me never determine when my tumults, when my crosses, when my disappointments shall cease but inform myself to wait thy leisure to learn what my duty is, my part of the covenant that is the condition for me to perform, of resignation and obedience, not to place my expectation on the promised part. For I know not thy pleasure, whether the full performance of it may not be respited[708] until that time when I may be sure, by the merits of my Savior, no interruption shall ever come, no inheritance in danger of wresting away, no impositions there which sin and (the) misery to destroy Mankind enforces by the law of that deplorable necessity.

One Persuading Me to Pull Down That Old Building on the East Side of Our House to Build It New

I don't love to blot out originals. No, that was their old grandfather's habitation, Richard Austen's.[709] It shall remain as ancient evidences to oblige our thankfulness to God Almighty's goodness. And that low un-uniform building, we will leave it for Fancy to model, and it is supposed, if she well contrive, it may make[710] many fair rooms, and

---

705. "The fabulous many-headed snake of the marshes of Lerna, whose heads grew again as fast as they were cut off; said to have been at length killed by Hercules" (*OED*).

706. Austen used a caret to insert "in a [?]"; the last word is illegible.

707. This parenthetical statement appears to have been squeezed between lines.

708. "To delay, postpone, put off" (*OED*).

709. Todd notes that this passage describes Hoxton, the family seat. "Property and a Woman's Place," 185.

710. Austen appears to have marked out a word—probably "a"—before "many."

though the front be[711] plain, the adjacent dimensions and galleries it conveys you to may not make you unwilling to salute the threshold. Yet, I do not by this discourse put a bar but that other reasons may take place.

Advising to Marry and to Keep What I Could

It shall never be said I lived a widow (if I do)[712] under the veil of hypocrisy, pretending to honor the memory of my deceased friend and make it the foundation of my particular fortune and raise a second bed. It is true I will allow a proportion to myself, and my two younger children shall have their part to do them good in the world, as well as myself. For my eldest, I never intended him but with a proviso— which I hope by God's Almighty's blessing—he will not need our three interests.

1666[713]

Though I may be mistaken in many conceits of things, yet let me endeavor to trace the love and favor of God to me in his many kind dispensations to me, though they appear at first sight displeasant.

The accidents and crosses and unkindnesses we meet with in this world is like a pair of stairs, one part of which goes down into a deep dungeon; the upper part conveys you to large and beautiful rooms. For when we murmur and repine,[714] our discontents are apt to end in a cloudy melancholy or produce passionate designs of revenge and retributions towards our enemies.

But when we improve our afflictions and turn and look upon the right side of them, when we cast away the malice of men, when we

711. Austen first wrote "is" but inserted a word that is probably "be" above it without crossing out either option. Ross reads "be" as "it." *Katherine Austen's Book M*, 165.

712. Austen wrote "(now almost 8 years)" but inserted "(if I do)" without marking out either option.

713. This date was squeezed into a small blank space at the very top of a page.

714. "To feel or express discontent or dissatisfaction; to grumble, complain" (*OED*).

will not look on interests and fortunes are supplanted of, when we are patient at our charge to defend our title another reaps the benefit of, by[715] all this is to look upon him that sees it best to be so, that intends my future happiness by a medicinal draught. Let them prove supplanters and lessen my own estate and give me expenses, yet this will be for good. And it is not from my enemies; it is appointed from my best friend to do me good by them. Therefore, will I look still upwards what the meaning of my God is, who can best dispose of accidents. And how should I see the grace of my God then?[716] Through these dark shadows, I may behold his bright protection to me and mine.

To him I repose and fly to.

My God, I do acknowledge thy providence in preferring me and bringing me into this condition and giving me just confidence and hope of prosperous expectation. O God, preserve me in it, and suffer not these hopes that have honest grounds of establishment, let not the envy and injustices of men circumvent me of. And for as much my oppositions are powerful, my enterprise hard, and how can I go in and out before so many contests and burdens as lie before me? O God, do I not read David's story, how weak he was, brought up to tend on ewes and cattle not to govern men and territories? Thou didst give to him a generous, noble, wise spirit to qualify him before he was possessor of what was promised him. O God, endue thy servant with fitness for my condition; give me a supply of prudence, of judgment, of consideration and activeness to perform what I am steward of to thy glory and not unto my own.

But if our God deny us the accessions of this world, which is our right from the law of men, and cast upon this family all the intendments of our adversaries, deprive us of that lovely seat of Highbury, if we lose Fleet Street estate, and though we shall never possess that gift of Durhams,[717] if 15 hundred pound a year is gone (which now ap-

---

715. Austen used a caret to insert "by" between "of" and "all."

716. Austen wrote "surely," marked it out, and used a caret to insert "then."

717. As Todd explains, "Durhams in South Mimms, on the northern outskirts of the westward-expanding city, was originally inherited by Katherine's brother-in-law John, but in consequence of his early death, and then almost immediately the death of John's only child, it and the Fleet Street properties came, controversially, into Katherine's control." "Property

pears upon the sale and flight to[718] my son), and not one remaining to him, the page behind tells me if Heaven permits it, Heaven will dispose it for the best.

And now I have propounded the preparations of hope and fear, of gain and loss before me, and in the way of my life find disgusts and unpleasantnesses, insomuch as these little occurrences[719] makes me long for rest and peace and freedom, for Solomon's [designation?][720] of mediocrity; for one handful of quiet rather than two handfuls with trouble.[721]

I shall conclude my meditations with my Savior's resignation (when the sin of all mankind depressed him). And though I dare not make a parallel between momentary earthly troubles and my Savior's for worlds of sinners, yet I am incited from him, our Captain, and in my soul shall say his words of releasement, which refreshes me. For there, O my Savior, in thy bitter agony, though it was not long ere it[722] was over, yet thou wast strengthened by an angel to sustain that stroke of wrath.[723] Thou art the Angel of the Covenant; I appeal and shelter myself until all these calamities are over in thy time.

---

and a Woman's Place," 185–86. Also see Ross, introduction to *Katherine Austen's Book M*, 12–13.

718. Austen wrote "from" but inserted "to" without marking out either one.

719. The phrase "as these little occurrences" starts a new recto folio, at the top of which Austen squeezed in "1666."

720. Austen's spelling of this word is unclear. "Designation" (spelled "desseination") is a reasonable possibility, given the context. Ross suggests "dessemation" (i.e., for the modern term, "dissemination," meaning "promulgation"). *Katherine Austen's Book M*, 167. A less likely possibility is "definition" (spelled "deffeination").

721. Austen alludes to Eccles. 4:6: "Better is an handful with quietness, than both the hands full with travail and vexation of spirit."

722. Austen used a caret to insert "it" between "ere" and "was."

723. Austen alludes to the account in the gospels of Jesus praying in the Garden of Gethsemane before his arrest and crucifixion; see, for example, Luke 22:42–44: "Saying, Father, if thou be willing, remove this cup from me: nevertheless not my will, but thine, be done. And there appeared an angel unto him from heaven, strengthening him. And being in agony he prayed more earnestly: and his sweat was as it were great drops of blood falling down to the ground."

I see seldom anything must happen to me but must look big—not one lawsuit but diverse together.

Now not one house or ground to let but almost all. Accidents[724] by sickness brought some into my hand. But two great estates to us lie in my hand: my buildings and Highbury.

Sir Geoffrey Palmer's[725] Telling Me Our Business Was Ordered to Be Brought before the Privy Council

Did I think I was come to the haven, and am I sitting still in the storm? Have I entertained myself with pleasing expectation that if I lived to this day, my molestations and reencounters with my adversaries should be ended? Still I am attacked, am pursued by them.

When I view over the assurances and hopes I have had in this book of my meditations, as sometimes I am putting on wreathes of victory I have overcome my enemies and my fears, but such is the unsureness of every ground in this world to anchor on as I soon come to wade in deep places again.

The moon hath not more variations than the affairs of this life, than the ebbs and flows of Fortune. Alas, with how many various accidents are we assaulted in this life, as sometimes in hope, sometimes in fear, sometime have the apprehension of peace and deliverance and freedom from environments?[726] My error hath been I have anticipated these desires too soon, have created imaginary[727] halcyon days.

Well, though I am assaulted still by adversaries and cannot tell when a dismission will come, yet if I consider in all that hath befallen me to this day, I have found a supportation, a shelter, a hope, and surely this is deliverance to me all along. Neither have I been really molested this last year and 1/2, never since February 1664 by law or Parliament. Yet, on every occasion of the Parliament sitting puts me to be on my watch, as when it was in April 1665, then in October 1665 at

---

724. Austen seems to have marked out a partial word before "Accidents."

725. Sir Geoffrey Palmer, first baronet (1598–1670), lawyer and politician (*ODNB*).

726. "The state of being encompassed or surrounded" (*OED*).

727. Austen first wrote "halcyon" before "imaginary" but marked it out and inserted it after "imaginary" instead.

Oxford, then again at Westminster—all which times no opportunity was gave to molest me. Now it is September 1666, and it may please God to prevent their doing us danger, as his preventive favor in our aid hath hitherto[728] disappointed them.[X729]

These two whole years have been general grievances to be afflicted with.

February 1665/6: a lawsuit did begin again that was ended, not as yet grown[730] to a disturbing proceed.

[X731] Aye, and now hath disappointed them also. And so far is the ground of our hope as there is little fear.

Great God, thy mercies how can I unfold?[732]
They are so numerous not to be told.
Deep are th'impressions of th'Almighty's love,
To wonder and astonishment do move,
Impossible to think, to speak, to write,   [5]
And what's innumerable[733] to indite.
Lord, in the mass and of[734] their volumes, I
Can only speak, and they transcend the sky.
But the particulars that my God hath wrought
For soul and body is beyond all thought.   [10]
My wonder rises still to such a height
Can only gaze upon that mountain's sight.
'Tis my high joy, when in Heaven's orb refin'd,

---

728. Austen wrote "either to" for "hitherto."

729. Austen marked with an "X" the passage to which the sentences below—also marked with an "X"—refer; see note 731.

730. Austen used a caret to insert "grown" between "yet" and "to."

731. These are the sentences that refer to the material similarly marked with an "X" above, see note 729.

732. Austen numbered this poem "26" but crossed it out.

733. Austen wrote "immeasurable" but inserted "innumerable" above it without marking out either one.

734. Austen wrote "by," marked it out, and replaced it with "of."

Shall understand that love with a new mind,
With new capacities, and with a beam   [15]
Drawn from his glory, clarify my dim,
My purblind[735] soul. Fit me for that abode
To enter in the temple of my God;
Celestial soliloquies inspired shall learn
And to eternity sing notes serene.   [20]

"My strength will I ascribe unto" my God.[736]

Dear Sister, I hope—now this calamity is almost gone—to have an opportunity to see you. The absence of friends in a time of so many fears was with more impatience than when safety and health gave more confidence of the welfare one of another. By my danger I passed, I see it is not the going away from (danger) can free one from peril. But it pleased God when so great a calamity was in the kingdom to give me a particular hazard, though not in the same (degree and) manner.

Still when more troubles do abound,
By thy supportance I am crown'd.

Book M[737]

12 of May 16[?]0 but now [?] made a dust and a powder, now [?] dance [?] it.[738]

The 12 of March 1664: my Aunt Marget was 68 years old.

---

735. "Having imperfect perception or discernment; lacking in or incapable of understanding or foresight; dim-witted; stupid" (*OED*).

736. These letters are several times larger than most of Austen's writing; they are centered prominently on a recto page and occupy almost its entire top half. She borrows from Psalm 59:9: "My strength will I ascribe unto thee: for thou art the God of my refuge" (*BCP*). Also cf. Psalm 68:34 in the King James Bible.

737. This title appears at the top corner of the last page of Austen's book.

738. There are several illegible marks—possibly shorthand—in this phrase.

"But were I to begin my youth again,
I could redeem the time I spent in vain.

Fame, whereof the world seems to make such choice,
Is but an echo and an idle voice."[739]

To Willy Wilson, When Nancy[740] Was with Him, 1665

Dear Nephew, your pretty letter was very acceptable and am well pleased your Cousin Nancy and you are loving comrades. Yet, if there should be a quarrel between you, I know it will create more kindness when loving play follows a little fall-out. Therefore, I assure myself you will be ready to pardon any mistake from your Cousin Nancy, and I do persuade myself that each of you will strive to love one another best. I must have you remember me to your Brother Jonny, who I know makes up a consort of joy and prettiness among you. I leave you to your playing society. Am your loving aunt, Katherine.

22nd November [?][741] Anne[742] 1664
22 February, Robin[743] went to school.
Tom[744] went to Oxford.

"'Charity begins at home' is the voice of the world."[745]

---

739. Austen takes these couplets from Samuel Daniel's *Complaint of Rosamond*; see Ross, introduction to *Katherine Austen's Book M*, 32.

740. Austen's daughter, Anne

741. This illegible word appears to begin with "H."

742. Austen wrote "anne"; this could be an abbreviation but probably refers to her daughter.

743. Her son Robert.

744. Her son Thomas.

745. Austen borrows from Sir Thomas Browne's *Religio Medici* (London: Printed by Andrew Crooke, 1642).

Amussen, Susan Dwyer. *An Ordered Society: Gender and Class in Early Modern England.* New York: Blackwell, 1988.

Anselment, Raymond A. "Katherine Austen and the Widow's Might." *Journal for Early Modern Cultural Studies* 5.1 (2005): 5–25.

Austen, Katherine. *Book M.* British Library, Additional Manuscript 4454.

_____. *Book M.* Edited by Sarah C. E. Ross. *Perdita Manuscripts.* http://www.perditamanuscripts.amdigital.co.uk/ (accessed August 12, 2009).

_____. *Katherine Austen's Book M.* Edited by Sarah C. E. Ross. Medieval and Renaissance Texts and Studies, vol. 409. Tempe, AZ: Arizona Center for Medieval and Renaissance Studies, 2011.

"Bellarmine, Robert, St." In *The Concise Oxford Dictionary of World Religions*, edited by John Bowker. *Oxford Reference Online.* Oxford University Press. http://www.oxfordreference.com/ (accessed June 2012).

The Book of Common Prayer. New York: Oxford University Press, 1969.

Brome, Richard. *A Jovial Crew; or, The Merry Beggars.* London, 1652.

Browne, Thomas. *Religio Medici.* London: Printed by Andrew Crooke, 1642.

Campbell, Mary Baine. "Dreaming, Motion, Meaning: Oneiric Transport in Seventeenth-Century Europe." In *Reading the Early Modern Dream: The Terrors of the Night*, edited by Katherine Hodgkin, Michelle O'Callaghan, and S. J. Wiseman, 15–30. New York: Routledge, 2008.

Capp, B. S. *The Fifth Monarchy Men: A Study in Seventeenth-Century Millenarianism.* London: Faber and Faber, 1972.

"The Church of St. Leonard, Shoreditch." In *Survey of London: Volume 8: Shoreditch*, edited by James Bird. *British History Online.* http://www.british-history.ac.uk/report.aspx?compid=98229/ (accessed May 2013).

"Clement V." In *The Oxford Dictionary of Popes* by J. N. D. Kelly. *Oxford Reference Online.* Oxford University Press. http://www.oxfordreference.com/ (accessed June 2011).

Cope, Esther. *Handmaid of the Holy Spirit: Dame Eleanor Douglas, Never Soe Mad a Ladie.* Ann Arbor, MI: University of Michigan Press, 1992.

Crawford, Patricia. "Women's Dreams in Early Modern England." In *Dreams and History: The Interpretation of Dreams from Ancient Greece to Modern Psychoanalysis*, edited by Daniel Pick and Lyndal Roper, 91–103. New York: Routledge, 2004.

Crawford, Patricia, and Laura Gowing, eds. *Women's Worlds in Seventeenth-Century England.* New York: Routledge, 2000.

Cressy, David. *Travesties and Transgressions in Tudor and Stuart England: Tales of Discord and Dissension.* New York: Oxford University Press, 2000.

Donne, John. *John Donne: The Complete English Poems.* Edited by A. J. Smith. New York: Penguin, 1986.

Eisenstein, Elizabeth. *The Printing Press as an Agent of Change: Communications and Cultural Transformations in Early-Modern Europe.* Cambridge, UK: Cambridge University Press, 1979.

Erickson, Amy Louise. *Women and Property in Early Modern England.* New York: Routledge, 2002.

Ezell, Margaret J.M. *Social Authorship and the Advent of Print.* Baltimore, MD: The Johns Hopkins University Press, 1999.

_____. *Writing Women's Literary History.* Baltimore, MD: The Johns Hopkins University Press, 1993.

Featley, Daniel. *Clavis Mystica; A Key Opening Divers Texts of Scripture.* London, 1636.

Fell, John. *The Life of The most Learned, Reverend and Pious Dr H. Hammond.* London, 1661.

Fuller, Thomas. *The Holy State and the Profane State.* London, 1663.

Gowing, Laura. *Domestic Dangers: Women, Words, and Sex in Early Modern London.* New York: Oxford University Press, 1996.

Greenberg, Lynne A. Introductory Note. *Legal Treatises*, vol. 1. *The Early Modern Englishwoman: A Facsimile Library of Essential Works. Series III. Essential Works for the Study of Early Modern*

Women: Part I, edited by Betty S. Travitsky and Anne Lake Prescott. Aldershot, UK: Ashgate, 2005. ix–lxiii.

Hall, Joseph. *Characters of Vertues and Vices.* London: Printed by Melch. Bradwood for Eleazar Edgar and Samuel Macham, 1608.

Hammons, Pamela. "Despised Creatures: The Illusion of Maternal Self-Effacement in Seventeenth-Century Child Loss Poetry." *ELH: English Literary History* 66 (1999): 25–49.

_____. *Gender, Sexuality, and Material Objects in English Renaissance Verse.* Farnham, UK: Ashgate, 2010.

_____. "Katherine Austen's Country House Innovations." *SEL: Studies in English Literature* 40.1 (Winter 2000): 123–37.

_____. *Poetic Resistance: English Women Writers and the Early Modern Lyric.* Aldershot, UK: Ashgate, 2002.

_____. "Widow, Prophet, and Poet: Lyrical Self-Figurations in Katherine Austen's 'Book M' (1664)." In *Write or Be Written: Early Modern Women Poets and Cultural Constraints*, edited by Ursula Appelt and Barbara Smith, 3–27. Aldershot, UK: Ashgate, 2001.

Harris, Barbara J. *English Aristocratic Women, 1450–1550: Marriage and Family, Property and Careers.* New York: Oxford University Press, 2002.

Heal, Felicity, and Clive Holmes. *The Gentry in England and Wales, 1500–1700.* Stanford, CA: Stanford University Press, 1994.

Hill, Christopher. *The Century of Revolution, 1603–1714.* New York: Norton, 1980.

_____. *The English Bible and the Seventeenth-Century Revolution.* New York: The Penguin Press, 1993.

_____. *The World Turned Upside Down: Radical Ideas during the English Revolution.* New York: Viking Press, 1972.

Hobby, Elaine. *Virtue of Necessity: English Women's Writing, 1649–88.* Ann Arbor, MI: University of Michigan Press, 1989.

The Holy Bible: King James Version. New York: Ballantine, 1991.

Houlbrooke, Ralph, ed. *English Family Life, 1576–1716: An Anthology from Diaries.* New York: Basil Blackwell, 1989.

Krontiris, Tina. *Oppositional Voices: Women as Writers and Translators of Literature in the English Renaissance*. New York: Routledge, 1992.

Laurence, Anne. "A Priesthood of She-Believers: Women and Congregations in Mid-Seventeenth-Century England." In *Women in the Church*, edited by W. J. Sheils and Diana Wood, 345–63. Cambridge, MA: Basil Blackwell, 1990.

Lewalski, Barbara Kiefer. *Protestant Poetics and the Seventeenth-Century Religious Lyric*. Princeton, NJ: Princeton University Press, 1979.

Longfellow, Erica. *Women and Religious Writing in Early Modern England*. New York: Cambridge University Press, 2004.

Love, Harold. *Scribal Publication in Seventeenth-Century England*. Oxford: Clarendon Press, 1993.

Mack, Phyllis. *Visionary Women: Ecstatic Prophecy in Seventeenth-Century England*. Berkeley, CA: University of California Press, 1992.

Marotti, Arthur. *Manuscript, Print, and the English Renaissance Lyric*. Ithaca, NY: Cornell University Press, 1995.

Mendelson, Sara Heller. "Stuart Women's Diaries and Occasional Memoirs." In *Women in English Society, 1500–1800*, edited by Mary Prior, 181–210. New York: Methuen, 1985.

Mendelson, Sara, and Patricia Crawford. *Women in Early Modern England, 1550–1720*. Oxford: Clarendon Press, 1998.

Nuttall, Geoffrey. *The Holy Spirit in Puritan Faith and Experience*. Oxford: Basil Blackwell, 1947.

The Oxford Dictionary of National Biography Online. Oxford University Press, 2004; online edition, January 2008. http://www.oxforddnb.com/ (accessed July and August 2011).

The Oxford English Dictionary Online. Second edition, 1989; online version June 2012. http://www.oed.com/ (accessed June 2012).

Purkiss, Diane. "Producing the Voice, Consuming the Body: Women Prophets of the Seventeenth-Century." In *Women, Writing, History, 1640–1740*, edited by Isobel Grundy and Susan Wiseman, 139–58. Athens, GA: University of Georgia Press, 1992.

Richey, Esther Gilman. *The Politics of Revolution in the English Renaissance*. Columbia, MO: University of Missouri Press, 1998.

Ross, Sarah C. E. "'And Trophes of His Praises Make': Providence and Poetry in Katherine Austen's Book M, 1664–1668." In *Early Modern Women's Manuscript Writing: Selected Papers from the Trinity/Trent Colloquium*, edited by Victoria E. Burke and Jonathan Gibson, 181 204. Burlington, VT: Ashgate, 2004.

_____. Introduction to *Katherine Austen's Book M*. Medieval and Renaissance Texts and Studies, vol. 409. Tempe, AZ: Arizona Center for Medieval and Renaissance Studies, 2011. 1–39.

_____. "Katherine Austen." *Perdita Manuscripts*. http://www.perdita manuscripts.amdigital.co.uk/ (accessed August 12, 2009).

_____. "'Like Penelope, Always Employed': Reading, Life-Writing, and the Early Modern Female Self in Katherine Austen's *Book M*." *Literature Compass* 9, 4 (2012): 306–16. 10.1111/j.1741-4113.2012.00878.x.

_____. Textual introduction to *Katherine Austen's Book M*. Medieval and Renaissance Texts and Studies, vol. 409. Tempe, AZ: Arizona Center for Medieval and Renaissance Studies, 2011. 41–47.

Shakespeare, William. *2 Henry IV*. In *The Norton Shakespeare: Based on the Oxford Edition*, edited by Stephen Greenblatt, Walter Cohen, Jean E. Howard, Katharine Eisaman Maus, 1321–405. New York: W. W. Norton & Company, 2008.

Snook, Edith. *Women, Beauty and Power in Early Modern England: A Feminist Literary History*. New York: Palgrave, 2011.

Spencer, Thomas. "The History of an Unfortunate Lady." *Harvard Studies and Notes in Philology and Literature* 20 (1938): 43–59.

Stevenson, Jane, and Peter Davidson, eds. *Early Modern Women Poets: An Anthology*. New York: Oxford University Press, 2001.

Stretton Tim. *Women Waging Law in Elizabethan England*. New York: Cambridge University Press, 1998.

Thomas, Keith. *Religion and the Decline of Magic*. New York: Scribner's, 1971.

Todd, Barbara J. "'I Do No Injury by Not Loving': Katherine Austen, a Young Widow of London." In *Women and History: Voices of Early Modern England*, edited by Valerie Firth, 207–37. Toronto: Coach House Press, 1995.

———. "Property and a Woman's Place in Restoration London." *Women's History Review* 19.2 (2010): 181–200.

———. "The Remarrying Widow: A Stereotype Reconsidered." In *Women in English Society, 1500–1800*, edited by Mary Prior, 54–92. New York: Methuen, 1985.

———. "The Virtuous Widow in Protestant England." In *Widowhood in Medieval and Early Modern Europe*, edited by Sandra Cavallo and Lyndan Warner, 66–83. New York: Pearson Education, 1999.

Trapnel, Anna. *The Cry of a Stone*. London, 1654.

Walton, Izaak. *The Life of Sir Henry Wotton*. In *Reliquiae Wottonianae* by Sir Henry Wotton. London, 1651.

———. *The Lives of Dr John Donne, Sir Henry Wotton, Mr Richard Hooker, Mr George Herbert*. London, 1675.

Wiseman, Sue. "Unsilent Instruments and the Devil's Cushions: Authority in Seventeenth-Century Women's Prophetic Discourse." In *New Feminist Discourses: Critical Essays on Theories and Texts*, edited by Isobel Armstrong, 176–96. New York: Routledge, 1992.

Woodbridge, Linda. *Women and the English Renaissance: Literature and the Nature of Women, 1540–1620*. Urbana, IL: University of Illinois Press, 1984.

Wynne-Davis, Marion. *Women Writers and Familial Discourse in the English Renaissance: Relative Values*. New York: Palgrave Macmillan, 2007.

Index

Note: Page numbers in italics indicate figures.